Marion Urlenwlaw

Feb. 1938

Cleopatra

THE STORY OF A QUEEN

Cleopatra

CLEOPATRA

THE STORY OF A QUEEN

Emil Ludwig

Exceptional people exist beyond the confines of morality;
in the final analysis their impact is that of a physical cause,
of fire or water.
—GOETHE

TRANSLATED BY BERNARD MIALL

NEW YORK: THE VIKING PRESS

1937

Published in December 1937

Preface

THE last time I met her was on the Nile; yet her mind was fixed upon the North; to her, Egypt was almost a foreign country. Her home was the Mediterranean, and the sea-breeze sighs through her story.

Of all the biographies that I have written, this is distinguished by an all but total absence of quotations. The personal documents—letters, speeches, memoirs—which I have accumulated in other cases in order to elucidate the character of my subject by his own words, or those of his friends and foes, are here completely lacking. Such documents as the love-letters of Cleopatra, and most of the private papers of Antony and Cæsar, are lost to us; there survive only three sentences of a single letter of Antony's. But the public life of the queen, apart from one brief unknown period, has been reliably recorded for posterity, though only because the three Romans with whose lives her own was intertwined have their places in the history of the world.

Yet such characteristics of hers as are recorded by the half-dozen authors of antiquity who wrote in the years following closely upon her reign present us with a living portrait, and this is confirmed by at least one authentic bust. Plutarch, my master, above all, I am able to follow closely, and for the first time; for although by virtue of my race, my life, and my education I belong to the Mediterranean, I have hitherto described Greek characters only as dramatis personæ, never historically.

In view of the naïvely subtle records of the ancients all the modern historians have seemed to me superfluous; but I have read and profited by Ferrero's great history of Rome, and also Stahr's and Weigall's fine studies of Cleopatra (1864 and 1927). For even if Plutarch were not more modern than all the analytical writers of our time, he would still be closer to his subjects; and when he writes that his grandfather learned the secret of his roast meats from Antony's head cook in Alexandria, this statement has for me more actuality than any discussion between two scholars of today, of whom one accuses the other of giving too much credit to Suetonius and too little to Appian.

The absence of psychological documents leaves me free to dwell more insistently on states of mind and soliloquies than would have been possible had my sources been more abundant. When in 1919, with my *Goethe*, I began to write a new kind of biography, I permitted myself an occasional soliloquy, and also in my *Napoleon*, but I did not follow this practice in my later books. Here, however, in the complete absence of psychological sources, the monologue was compulsory. For the action there is everywhere sufficient warrant, but even Plutarch could only deduce the actors' feelings. Yet no battle of those days, no clash of parties, no Roman province has any significance for us; only the feelings are eternal, they are of the same nature as our own, and only by their light are we able to perceive a human being like ourselves in this or that historical personage.

Though here the limit of the historical novel is reached, it has nowhere been overstepped; here, as elsewhere, I have dispensed entirely with the hundreds of dialogues which historical figures are wont to exchange in the hearing of the attentive observer; and even in the setting of the scene I have faithfully followed the ancient writers, as far as they go. The few sentences which are actually spoken may be found in my sources.

Thus this unquiet history is dedicated almost entirely to the psychological life of the heroine and her three Romans. Not here will the reader find the soul of the *grande amoureuse* which the legendary Cleopatra has become, in defiance of all the sources, but a lover, mother, warrior, and queen. All problems of form apart, I hope my readers will accept this representation as a contribution to the history of the human heart on which I have been working these thirty years.

—EMIL LUDWIG

Moscia, January 1937

Contents

Illustrations

The busts of Cleopatra and Cæsar herein reproduced are from photographs copyrighted by the British Museum; the head of Augustus is from an Alinari photograph of a statue in Rome. The relief portraits of Cleopatra and Antony represent coins of the period.

CLEOPATRA
Frontispiece

CLEOPATRA
Preceding page 15

CAESAR
Preceding page 81

ANTONY
Preceding page 153

AUGUSTUS
Preceding page 207

CLEOPATRA
Preceding page 267

Aphrodite

When a woman takes on some of man's attributes, she must triumph; for if she intensifies her other advantages by an access of energy, the result is a woman as perfect as can be imagined.

—Goethe

Cleopatra

CHAPTER I

Aphrodite

I

PERCHED in the open window-niche, in the shadow cast by the pillars, a little princess is gazing out to sea. She is eleven years old. Her hands are half folded between the brown curly head and the marble wall; her feet are drawn up in childish fashion, so that she is sitting on her sandals. There she crouches, in her yellow silk shift—for she wears little more —and the light wind puffs it out a little around the small pointed breasts. She is already a woman. In the North she would pass for fifteen, but here we are on the Mediterranean, and the palace is in Alexandria, on the African coast.

She is not tall, but incredibly light on her feet, and now, if she were to leap from her post, the eunuch squatting on the ground would be too late to help her; she would be already at the door, so swift and supple is the little princess. From his shadowy corner he can watch her, imagining that she does not notice him. But she is aware of everything that goes on around her, and while her golden-brown glance follows the great sail that is just passing the lighthouse, she is conscious of the humid eyes of the cowering slave in the corner, and the rustling of the silken smock as he softly rubs his brown back against it. As for what he may be feeling, that is nothing to her; he is only a slave, an animal; he is not even a man. And at the same time she is aware of a tarry smell, from which she concludes that the wet hawsers with which her little yacht was yesterday hauled up the slipway have been hung in the arcade under her window to dry.

Like a silent complaint, the humid gaze of the unmanned slave rests on the princess. She is white, he thinks; Berenice, her sister, is yellow-skinned, and her father, the king, is really almost brown. But she will not always be so white; a little while now and she will be flushed with love and wine. Why are her nostrils fluttering? No doubt she is still considering how her sister can most readily be poisoned. If she would trust me with the business I would do it without delay; her voice alone is enough to drive one crazy. It was my father who killed her great-uncle. In the end he was beheaded for it. But we all have to die some day. And he stares at the princess.

She sits there motionless, gazing across the sea, her hands half folded behind her curly head, her little feet drawn up. When she sees the sail of her father's ship, her imprisonment will be at an end! But perhaps they have killed him long ago, in Rome, or else at sea. And tomorrow, it may be, a lateen-rigged ship will bring a Roman into port, with his short jerkin and his short sword, and his keen, austere features, to depose that devil of a sister and free her in her father's name.

From Rome, she muses, comes all good fortune, and all calamity. Why from Rome? Does not half the harvest leave the port every spring, in the long ships bound for Italian harbours? The finest fabrics, the splendid amethysts that hold the secret of Dionysos, golden-yellow amber and musk and incense, all that enters the port here, and is dearly bought, is brought ashore almost as soon as it arrives, only to be sent in the long ships to Rome. What do they pay for it? Every few years her father has to bring up the great bars of gold from the vaults and send them on board the ships, and again a thousand talents cross the sea to Rome. The more they buy of us, the more we have to pay them. Why?

For two years now her father has been in Italy, in Pompey's country villa, haggling as to how much he must pay them if he is to keep his crown. Who are they, after all, these Romans, always demanding, always threatening? He looks plebeian enough on the coins, the "great" Pompey! They say the other one, Cæsar, is better to look at, but there are no coins as yet with his head upon them. They are all a lot of self-made tradesmen and warriors! And we, who are descended from Alexander, who for three hundred years have been of kingly blood, we, the offspring of the gods, and their representatives on earth, must we go begging to Rome before they condescend to leave us in our palaces? There, even now, another grain-ship is sailing past the mole—and again they won't pay for it.

Suddenly the princess is aware of the reason. She recalls her father's puffy face; his unkingly behaviour in his own capital; how he used to join the musicians and play the flute in the streets, and make his slaves dance to his piping. Is there a child in the great city who does not call his king Auletes, the Fluteplayer? Is there a nobleman who has not seen his king reeling drunken through the streets? How many women have

struck his fingers as he fumbled at their breasts? No wonder
they suddenly deposed him and proclaimed Berenice queen—
Berenice, the eldest of his children, whom he, himself a bastard, had begotten upon some dark-skinned slave!

To poison her! thinks the princess. As another Ptolemy poisoned his mother! As the fourth Ptolemy strangled his brother
and sister! Always, when her tutor speaks of the sudden death
of some member of her house, history should record a conspiracy. She knows—she has other sources of information.

To have a juggler for a father, for a king! she thinks. A
mother who vanished; no one knows who she was! A harlot
for sister and queen! Could the slaves, could the people still
believe that the king was the living image of the god Amon,
the chosen of Ptah, when he drove in purple to the temple,
the royal asp upon his brow? Could the scholars still do homage to him in their writings, after he had threatened the famous sage Demetrius with death if he would not get drunk
in the public street?

There comes Demetrius. How deep he bows his handsome
head, almost to the ground! He speaks the most beautiful
Greek to be heard in the city; he knows so much about the
gods and the elements; and when he lectures his pupil in his
gentle voice she asks herself whether—as the Jewish philosopher taught her—the intellect may not really be more precious
than the crown; but then she smiles to herself, and does not
believe him.

Yet one must learn; one must learn all that the Greeks
know, so that one day one may be able to deal with the
Romans, who know nothing, and can only fight! All wisdom
and all beauty come from Athens; they will tell her that again

today, the three scholars who come to the palace, for she is insatiable in her thirst for knowledge; she is learning more than her father ever learnt, and far more than her elder sister and the three younger children are learning. The whole Museion knows that now, after a hundred years, there is once more a princess in the palace who wants to know everything, who instantly grasps and retains all that the drawings and apparatus in the great hall teach her: mechanical diagrams, the plans of the shipbuilders, skeletons and the human body, and coins, many coins, from which she learns to read faces, as well as half a dozen Mediterranean languages. Best of all, she likes to stand in front of the great maps, and when her firm hand, which never trembles, draws with a fingernail a line from the Nile Delta eastward (and this she does often, compressing her lips the while), it journeys through Syria, Cappadocia, Epirus, even Brundusium; but then the nail scratches its slanting way across Italy and hastens southward, making straight for home, as though she would annex the whole of the eastern Mediterranean; as though all the coasts were to be subjected to Egypt. But the line drawn by her finger never encloses Rome.

And yet for her Egypt is only a name. She knows as little as her fathers knew of the country up-Nile. Its faith is not hers, its gods are not her gods. The Nile is a foreign river, no longer to be seen from the lagoon here, beyond the wide expanse of Lake Moeris. For Alexandria does not lie on the banks of the Nile, like Memphis, but on the Grecian Sea. All that she feels, the language of her dreams, all that she learns, and all that she makes of her learning—her ancestors, the houses of Alexandria, the hubbub of the port with its hun-

[19]

dred tongues and races—all has a Greek colouring, and when she runs through the echoing halls of the palace with her light, pattering steps, the busts of the Ptolemies look down upon her. True, they no longer have the classic nose, but they are still Athenian in form, aping in style and bearing the great Alexander, who one day landed on the desert shore, gazed about him, and resolved to found on this spot the capital of the world. And is it not still the capital of the world?

In the evening the princess goes up to the flat roof of the palace. There one can see almost as far as from the lighthouse; perhaps as far as Cyprus, as far as Greece, even as far as Rome! Now the ships lie dreaming at anchor. They are dreaming of their cargoes—papyrus and glass, perhaps—of their voyage across the blue sea, of the next harbour, and the rough hands that will seize their hawsers and unload them amidst the din and bustle of the wharves, of their hazardous future, and the great problem of the storms that are lying in wait to destroy them. Messengers from race to race, bearers of commerce, and war, and power, they are always heading for danger, since if they lie long in harbour they are doomed to rot and perish.

From the roof of the palace the princess follows their watery track, but her dreams are not theirs. One day—so says her passionate heart—one day—so her keen understanding tells her—I will set out on one of these swift-sailing ships for the shores of Syria and Cappadocia, followed by six hundred triremes, for Ephesus, Corinth, and Athens! All the isles in the great gulf shall be mine! Berenice will be among the shades, and I shall wear the crown with the royal asp, Aphrodite and Isis, and the seal on my ring will say: Cleopatra the Seventh,

Queen of Egypt. Then there will be only Rome and myself in the world—and then we shall see whether Egypt's grain will still go to these Italians, and if it does go to them, whether they will not send gold to Alexandria in payment, instead of taking it from us! Gold and homage from inland Rome to the brimming capital of the world!

II

At night such visions of the future of the East sank with the sun into the western sea.

What she heard of Rome—now from the philosophers, now from a captain, now from a eunuch—was dark and confused; and so was what she heard of the past life of her father, and the present state of the Roman Republic, which was on the point of foundering.

She knew what had happened during the eleven years of her young life; twenty-seven years before her birth a Ptolemy had bequeathed Egypt to the Roman people, but the Senate had been unwilling to enter upon its inheritance, so great was the jealousy of those who might be called upon to administer this wealthiest of countries. Was not a feeble kingdom on the Nile Delta less dangerous than a powerful Roman proconsul? It had preferred to give Egypt and Cyprus to two illegitimate sons of the royal testator, confident that they would prove to be drunken and dissolute rulers. The more one squeezed out of them, the weaker would they become. Each of the three or four potentates of Rome waited secretly for the day which would find him powerful enough to seize and hold the wonderful country, concerning which Rome had more appetite for fables than for sober reports.

Every few years the great Roman lords had got hold of the flute-playing king, and then, as a cat plays with a mouse, had let him go again, to bring more gold from the legendary, inexhaustible treasury of the Ptolemies, making him pay again and again, until at last, in return, the Roman people and the Roman Senate recognized him as King of Egypt.

In the year 59 B.C.—but the Roman year was reckoned from the foundation of the city—Gaius Julius Cæsar was Consul. But he was far from being powerful enough to prevent another potentate, his enemy and rival, Clodius, who was discontented with the bribe he had received, from deposing the King of Cyprus, the brother and vassal of the King of Egypt. His treasury was confiscated, and Cyprus became a Roman province; but the flute-playing king behaved as though Cyprus had meant nothing to him. What was more, he even attempted to wring such an enormous sum of money from the country that he could pay Cæsar's party in Rome without breaking into the private treasury of his house.

But at this rebellion broke out in Alexandria. Now the dignitaries of the palace and the city, the priests and nobles, the landowners and court officials, found it easy to convince the unstable, faithless population of the capital, ever eager for change, that their king was beneath contempt. He fled to Rome; Berenice, his eldest daughter, was declared queen by her party. But his brother, the King of Cyprus, drank poison and died.

Eleven-year-old Cleopatra had heard the news with amazement. There were many bloodstained pages in the history of her house. In the course of two hundred and fifty years, thirteen Ptolemies had succeeded one another, governed or persecuted by their wives and children, like the Pharaohs, their predecessors on the Nile. She had seen how poison and the dagger had worked havoc in the lives of her forebears; how brothers had slain sisters, princes their fathers, and queens their consorts, who were also their brothers. All these things had been done for the sake of power, for the sake of an intenser life; often merely because he who did not strike quickly would himself be struck down. But hitherto none had fallen by his own hand. Yet now a late heir of this race that was sinking into dishonour had for once raised the standard of pride. There had emerged from this decaying dynasty a virile successor of those Greeks whom legend had glorified and whose verse the island king had echoed as he lifted the poisoned cup. The princess was deeply moved. If she had learned to despise her father, haggling for power in Rome as the years went by, she must now revere his brother. So it was true, what the philosophers of the Museion had taught her: even today there was something that stood higher than the crown, and gold. The ten-year-old Cleopatra realized that the pride of a king may be a finer thing than power; and the knowledge that such bondage as her father's was unworthy, and poison a swift release, impressed itself deeply upon her youthful mind, never to be effaced.

But she, in her young vitality, was resolved to overcome the bondage in which her sister was keeping her. Was Berenice happy? The first husband who had slept with her—a cousin of sorts, chosen so that he could be called a king and beget her children—was so degenerate that the officers of the palace had soon put him to death. The second husband they had forced upon her was better. But was it not possible that this reputed son of the Persian king was a mere adventurer? And, after all, who were these Persians, who always went about in tight-fitting trousers, and who certainly knew how to ride, but had no understanding of the Greek spirit, of the subtleties and refinements of life? Was he a free man, independent of the eunuchs who ruled the palace? Did he love or despise his wife? Were they ever for a day free of the dread of Rome? Exacting or insolent, Rome lay invisible in the North, and any day it might come and kill, stealing everything, destroying everything.

Her father was treading the path of shame; yet since it was impossible to rule against the will of Rome, one must come to an understanding with the Romans; the princess knew that. So did the people of Alexandria; so did the royal pair. This was why they had sent after the deposed king a hundred noble citizens, who would seek to persuade Rome to form an alliance with their party. Month after month went by; nothing was heard of the embassy; but the lonely princess was almost the only person in Alexandria who hoped that the envoys would be turned away. For only if her despised father was victorious in Rome could she herself hope for the crown.

But when the winter was over and the first ships again came gliding past the Pharos, she learned, with the whole city, that Auletes had had the envoys killed one by one. But the impatient princess had, of course, her own spies, so that she heard many things that were unknown to others; knew that her father had offered six thousand talents from his treasury if the Romans would restore him to power; that Rome was now impoverished as the result of the unsuccessful Persian wars; that Cæsar and Crassus, Crassus and Pompey, were conspiring against one another, to determine which of them should take Egypt and the treasure of the Ptolemies, in order to win the mastery over his rivals. Everything depended on her father's ability to pay such a price that he would leave Rome not as a subject, but as an ally.

And already there was news from oversea. Now, it was reported, the struggle was nearing its political culmination; Cæsar, back from Gaul, had proclaimed the Fluteplayer, by his "Julian law," the "ally and friend of the Roman people." At the same time, the crafty rulers had involved their new friend and ally in millions of debt to the Roman usurers; a debt that he could never pay, so that in the end he would have to knuckle down to them.

Already a circle of men with grievances, eager for a new revolution, was forming about the little discarded princess. Auletes had issued secret instructions: they must give their support to the little Cleopatra; and while in Rome the cunning and cowardly Ptolemy was a mendicant for his throne, here in the palace the silent sister was laying her plans, considering how she could best make use of the Romans, how rise to power by their aid.

And then, one day, they really came. A Roman general in Syria, already head-over-ears in debt, and unable any longer to pay his cohorts, set forth to get hold of twelve thousand talents, the very price which the Fluteplayer was asked to pay for his throne. Pushing through the desert with a few thousand men, from Gaza to Pelusium, in the Eastern Delta, he marched upon the Nile by the route which had been followed by Alexander, three centuries earlier, and thousands of years ago by many a Persian, Hebrew, and Assyrian commander.

At last liberation was at hand, even though it came through the detested Romans. Cleopatra's heart beat high; now she hid from her powerful sister, now showed herself, claiming her rights, in the ranks of the new party. Now Alexandria heard the din of battle as the foreign horsemen pushed onward to the city; heard how they thundered at the gates, and how the gates burst open; saw how the fugitives went to ground or surrendered. And now Cleopatra saw once again the ravaged face of her father, returning to his house and his throne, guarded by the foreign legions; saw the disfigured corpse of the young king, watched the submission of the priests and nobles, noted the defenceless attitude of the ever-inquisitive Alexandrians—and observed how they promptly swore loyalty to their old king, whom they had once driven from the throne. And at last she saw the head of her hated sister, condemned by her father, roll in the sand; the condition of her future power! Now no one stood between her and power but an elderly, effeminate criminal, whom she must call her father. It was a day of speechless triumph when her sister died.

Higher yet beat the proud heart of the young princess when she saw the foreign soldiers face to face. Were these the Romans? Was this the Roman army? Here were fair-haired men with wild Germanic faces; men who could not answer her in any common tongue; little, wild-looking Asiatics, large-eyed Jews, low-browed Byzantines: the Roman army, it seemed, had been shattered in Africa. She, who so distrusted Rome, saw the worst Romans, not the best—and her old fear of them began to abate.

At the same time, her amazement grew. A captain of horse —the captain who had taken Pelusium and led the assault on the capital—sat feasting with her father in the palace. He was honoured equally with the general, but he seemed to outshine the latter in every way. If this was a Roman—well, he was a man! With his loose tunic girt very low, and his great sword still at his side, he was half sitting, half reclining, at the table. He had the head of a Hercules, a short beard, and a great aquiline nose. The princess, gazing, silently revised her prejudice against the Romans.

The captain of horse did not notice the pretty, nervous child. Cleopatra was fourteen and he twenty-eight when they first met at this solemn royal banquet. Mountains and rivers, seas and cities, would hear the din of battle, and the destiny of a hero would move to its fulfilment, before these two would meet again after thirteen years. Perhaps that meeting would never have taken place had they now exchanged more than a word and a glance; perhaps the desire to blossom and bear fruit in that later period of her summer might never have drawn them together, if now, during this brief sojourn, the spring breezes had wafted them nearer. There they sat at table, an Aphrodite bright as the crescent moon, a merry Hercules with youthful features, both far enough from the mature divinities whom they would one day mime and represent; a tender Greek virgin, a Roman officer, Antony and Cleopatra.

III

Three years later she was queen.

Cleopatra came to the throne of an Egypt in a state of dissolution. The royal Fluteplayer had passed these last years of his reign in a series of shifts and manœuvres. A Roman minister of finance had *de facto* distrained upon all that he possessed, and when the king was forced to drive him away Rome came to the conclusion that now at last the realm of Egypt, like the greater part of the Mediterranean littoral, must be annexed. Then and there it would have become a Roman province but for the fact that in that same year Crassus, in the midst of his Persian campaign, had perished with all his army. This chance it was that saved the country from subjection, but it was shaken in every respect when the inglorious king died.

In a solemn invocation he had appointed the Roman people the executors of his last will and testament, for on placing the seventeen-year-old Cleopatra and the ten-year-old Ptolemy together on the throne of Egypt—stipulating, in accordance with the ancient custom of the Pharaohs, that the brother and sister should marry—he, knowing the ways of the palace, could but dread the intrigues which would centre round the two younger children: Arsinoë, then thirteen, and a second little Ptolemy. Which of these four would suppress, banish, or murder the others? Which party would pave the way for such deeds? As though he were addressing a god, even so this Greek Egyptian conjured the Roman Senate to preserve peace and order. Even from the grave his voice called upon Rome for help—Rome, the dispenser of destiny; Rome, which sooner or later must either conquer Egypt or surrender world-power to that country.

Cleopatra never consummated her marriage with her younger brother. What she did between the ages of seventeen and twenty-one is unknown; it is the only lacuna in the story of her life. Yet in these years something of importance happened, no less than this: that she was driven from the throne; and, being dethroned, she withdrew herself, only to retrieve her position. From a single order which an ancient writer has preserved for us we know something of her feelings as a sovereign.

At the very beginning of her reign a Roman proconsul of Syria sent his son to Alexandria in order to fetch the troops which had remained, from the time of Antony's visit, as a sort of Roman garrison. In the place of disciplined bodies of troops he found demoralized hordes, mainly Celts and Germans, who preferred to be left there with their Egyptian wives, and had no inclination to get killed in the next Persian war. On the contrary, they slew the officer and drove off his escort. What did the queen do? Did she not rejoice in her pride to see the arrogant command of the distant Roman thwarted by these half-subjects of hers?—Cleopatra was not one of those rulers who give way to their emotions. She had the murderers taken prisoner, and sent them in chains to Syria, to the Roman proconsul, the father of the murdered man.

But she was yet to learn! The Roman potentate also was above giving way to his emotions. Instead of avenging himself cruelly upon the murderers of his son, he sent the prisoners back, with a message for the queen: Only the Roman Senate or its officers had the right to arrest Romans! A significant lesson for the proud Cleopatra. What would she learn from it?

It was not long before a Roman ship again put into Alexandria. Gnæus Pompeius stepped ashore, the son of the great Pompey, commissioned by his father to fetch these very troops. Now the barbarian hordes were ready to go; this time they were to fight under the greatest general of the age, and against Cæsar himself! In this great, final battle for power one must hasten to side with Pompey! Cleopatra heard of the matter; she not only released the troops, but she gave the Romans fifty ships to use as transports. True, Pompey had sent a son of his as messenger, younger and far more elegant than Antony! If his father was victorious she would have rendered a service to an old friend of her house.

Of Pompey's rival, of Cæsar, the Fluteplayer had spoken only in ambiguous terms. Such tales of Cæsar as had crossed the seas were more fascinating than anything related of Pompey. But as yet Cleopatra had seen no coin bearing his effigy, while the other had sent her the finest of portraits, a rejuvenated Pompey. This, if it was not clever calculation, was a lucky chance, for at first, as a spectator of the great contest, she had thought of the two generals merely as two elderly gentlemen.

For the inmates of the palace, the strange errand of this young Roman was a welcome pretext for blackening the young queen. She was in league with the Romans, then, and she had surrendered the Egyptian fleet to them! A handsome pair of legs, the property of an elegant young officer, had been enough to bewitch her! What might not such a sovereign do?

[30]

The young woman's camarilla was too powerful, too intelligent, and much too independent, but the boy, who ruled jointly with her—one could influence him; he was rather backward for his twelve years. What could be easier than to show him how his sister despised him? Did she not obstinately refuse to consummate their marriage? Did she not let her angry young husband wait in vain at the bolted door of her bedroom? The inmates of the palace knew everything. Before long his three mentors—a eunuch, a philosopher, and a general—had successfully incited the palace and the army, the nobles and the people, to rebel against a queen who had sold her country to the Romans.

Just how it happened no one can say, but one day the twenty-year-old queen had to flee the city. Should she go to Rome? The Senate and the people of Rome had been invoked as trustees of the will that had made her joint sovereign. But the young Cleopatra, who was not led by her emotions when her interests were at stake, was not the person to consider her interests when she felt that she had been insulted. Appeal to the Romans to bring her home, as they had brought her father, whom she despised for that very reason? Rather die by poison, like his brother, if all was lost!

Cleopatra, with a few troops, fled to the Red Sea. There were Arabs there, and other tribes, whose language and sympathies and idiosyncrasies she had studied. There she recruited an army by her own efforts, having resolved to match herself against the forces of her brother and his prompters. Did she not know the weakness of his troops? Achillas, the general who was now supreme in the capital, she knew to be irresolute. So, a new Amazon, she advanced upon Pelusium with her own forces, partly along the hills, partly through the desert. From the west Achillas came to meet her. There, at the eastward edge of Egypt, a battle would be fought for the throne of the oldest realm on earth.

Yet at this moment the eyes of the world were not turned toward the Nile. They were fixed upon Greece, where for some weeks two far mightier armies were facing each other; like hers, prepared for battle, but for a far greater prize! No Amazon was there, with her rabble of adventurers, but the two greatest generals of their age, and the stake for which they would fight was the empire of the world; for as yet no third power was at hand, or, at least, was not visible. While the Ptolemies, brother and sister, armed themselves in the Delta and spied upon each other's doings, Cæsar, at Pharsalus, defeated Pompey. The defeat was absolute, and the news flew along the shores of the Mediterranean, and all men trembled, for until yesterday Pompey had been thought unconquerable. The news reached the Nile. The two royal enemies were startled; they listened, and waited. Close on the first report followed another, even more astonishing. It reached the legitimate government first. The mighty Roman, who a few years ago had the power to make or unmake a king of Egypt, was now a fugitive. Approaching Alexandria with two thousand men, the poor remnant of his splendid army, he was about to seek asylum there and to ask help of the Fluteplayer's son! A month after the decisive battle Pompey put in at Pelusium.

He had intended to go ashore, but in the war-council of gods and men it was otherwise decided. Pothinus, the eunuch, the virtual head of the government which was opposing Cleopatra, promptly made up his mind to murder the defeated Roman. They would thus be obliging Cæsar, the new master of the world, and they would not have to look on while two foreign armies fought upon Egyptian soil. When Pompey was close inshore the Egyptian general went to meet him in a swift rowing-boat, and with him were the hireling murderers.

The sea was shallow there, they said; the galley could not come closer inshore. Cornelia, in a premonition of evil, took fright and warned her husband. But Pompey, seeing the shore thronged with Roman soldiers, got into the boat; with some difficulty, for the sea was running high, the boat was small, and he was a man of sixty. In the act of disembarking he was stabbed in the back. His wife saw the blow from the deck of the galley; saw, too, how his head was struck off; whereupon she shrieked aloud and fled. The head and the dead man's ring were kept; the body was thrown into the sea.

Three days later Cæsar, Pompey's enemy and conqueror, landed in Alexandria. He immediately sent out messengers, requiring the royal pair to retire to their hostile camps: he had come to restore order in Egypt.

IV

Order? thought Cleopatra, in her tent. She threw herself on the few remaining cushions, which lay on the ground in warlike confusion, unadorned, and not even soft. As her habit was when she had to come to a decision, she lay for a long while motionless, flat upon her stomach, propping her breast and head on her hands, so that she might breathe freely, and think. It was only a temporary camp; for weeks her scanty force had had to follow the movements of her brother's army, always on the edge of the desert; but the soldier's life had only steeled the Amazon within her.

Did a lover enter her tent in the nights that followed those hot, perilous days? We do not know; the ancient historians and authors, almost all of her adversaries' party, and therefore full of malice, do not record a single love-affair up to the time of these hostilities. Yet here they can hardly be doing her justice; what with her lonely position, the climate, the adventurous life, her ripeness, and her mouth, it seems improbable that this Aphrodite was a virgin at the age of twenty-one. But in her youth the young warrior that was one side of her nature thrust all voluptuousness aside; swiftly she grasped at what her blood craved for, only to shake it off again; her heart and her head were cool.

There she lay in her tent, resolute to fathom the great event: her capital was besieged by a Roman, whose first movements her spies had reported a few days ago; her fellow-sovereign, brother and husband, lay only a few thousand paces away, in his fortified camp on the hill, with water and a fertile countryside behind him, and greatly her superior in strength. She herself was surrounded by a few thousand savages, whose spears and arrows would protect her only so long as no wealthier general offered them money to slay or surrender the fugitive queen in their midst. Her brother would obey the Roman's summons, for how could his counsellors dare to confront the greatest of generals, now without a rival, the representative of a world-wide empire, with a host of adventurers of whom half were Roman soldiers! He would hurry off to the capital, do homage as his father had done, and pay tribute; and his troops, under the Roman's command, would capture the disobedient queen by a sudden onslaught.

But what if the excitable Alexandrians were to rebel against the foreigner? They say he came here with thirty-four ships; that means that he cannot have four thousand men with him, and my brother has twenty thousand! If one could hold the Roman in check for a time one could delay the reinforcements from Roman Syria. If they had only prevented him from landing, these scoundrels whom their king had left behind him as a guard! But he had landed—so ran the report—and with true Roman arrogance had paraded his lictors, with axe and fasces, and had entered through the main streets of the capital; all marching, with surly faces, to the sound of a harsh music, just behind the hurrying general with his golden helmet. And then—tumult.

How did the rioting begin? thought Cleopatra; and she remembered what she had seen long ago in Alexandria. Some Roman emigrant would whistle; two or three others would shout a term of abuse; then twenty or thirty would cut off a handful of the invaders, and one of these insolent Romans would be slain. Then, of course, the arrows began to fly; the mob replied with stones; the tumult increased, and the mighty Roman was thankful to reach the palace. Once there, it would not be too difficult to crush the townsfolk with regular troops, and at the same time to conciliate them—Peace be with you! We are the allies of great Egypt! Oh, she knew all the tricks of a conqueror taken by surprise! After all, it was a sore disgrace to the great man that only three days after his grim entry he should be forced to humiliate himself!

[35]

Were she in the palace now, reigning alone, how long could she hold Egypt? Why, even if she could assassinate the general and drive his fleet out to sea, would not Rome sail eastward with all her forces and degrade the land of her fathers to the status of a province, as the Senate had already twice resolved?

Then, as though to tempt her further, her imagination pictures the arrival of another messenger. He enters her tent; she springs to her feet, dragging the news from his unwilling lips. The little king has hastened to obey the summons of the Roman; with him are his general, his eunuch, his philosophers— the pitiful triumvirate; with much bending of the back they have greeted the invader, who plays the host, and courteously invites them to live in their own palace, so far as he himself is not occupying the apartments. Order! The great man is always preaching order! The testament of the deceased king must be fulfilled. The armies, of course, will be disbanded; on the other hand, he must remind them of the debts of the late monarch, which were to be paid to the Dictator of Rome in ready money. When all this has been done peace shall reign between the two peoples, for no one has any thought of infringing upon Egypt's liberty.

Kill him! Poison him! thinks the fugitive queen. She waves the messenger away, and begins to pace to and fro in the narrow circle of her tent, her hands clasped behind her back, her head now drooping, now tossed upwards, as befits her train of thought. Is there no way out? Oh, if only she had the twenty thousand who now stand under the orders of those rascals yonder! Pothinus? That criminal? And cannot he contrive the murder of this Roman too? Has he not just had

Pompey slain? Then why not Cæsar? Surely he bows so deeply only to hide his cunning gaze from the foreigner! Surely they are plotting together to deceive him! A first battle; for a few weeks, at least, Achillas could easily keep the upper hand; the Romans are too few in number, and one could cut off their water.

But then she herself would be lost. Then all Alexandria would rise and help the valiant conqueror to drag the cowardly queen from her hiding-place; then all would be over. She knows that there is only one means of salvation: to side with the Roman! Who is this Roman? Who is this Cæsar?

She steps out of the tent as though seeking light and air; but outside it has suddenly grown dark, and the north-west wind that blows oversea in autumn is cold. She shivers; she is almost afraid of this wind. Growling softly like watchdogs before their master's house, the guards lie resting in a circle about the fire. What a dog's life, she thinks, have they had to lead all these months! There, in the west of the Delta, is her palace, and the northern barbarians are tumbling the delicately coloured silken beds. But she, the queen, feels the grit of the desert in her sandals, and for all she knows some conspirator may be lying by the fire yonder, to win a few pieces of gold by plunging his knife into her throat. She cannot see the beacon of the Pharos; the palms and the dunes limit her view, and the capital, of course, is too far away. She shivers, and returns to her tent. There she lies, her head supported on her left arm, her knees drawn up in childish wise, considering what she shall do on the morrow.

If she did as the Roman requires—if she returned with her troops to the capital—what a pitiful figure she would cut!

[37]

What a rain of epigrams there would be among the cynical Alexandrians, if her mythical Red Sea army were considered in the light of modern walls and catapults! The Roman would laugh. Cæsar? They say he only smiles.

Once more her thoughts begin to centre upon the stranger. A few months ago he was still regarded as an adventurer, but today he seems the master of the world, before whom Egypt trembles, though she has not yet seen his face. From what her father told her in his sober moments, and the reports of her agents, she has long ago created an image for herself, but she still lacks the key to it; the portrait, were it only stamped on a poor drachma, which would serve as a guide to her woman's instincts. For all her musings this night are concerned with the degree, the form, the nature, and suggestive power of a virility which she must understand and play upon if she is to save her life.

But what friends and women, what legend and faction and calumny, report of Cæsar yields nothing but contradictions. A great connoisseur of women, yet half-way through the fifties; three or four times married, yet still without a son; his love-affairs have always been carefully veiled, yet he was the first Roman to deliver a public funeral oration on the death of his wife; wholly masculine, yet an old scandal is always recurring in new epigrams, to the effect that in his youth he slept with King Nicomedes. Once, it was said, he himself was betrayed; at the feast of Dionysos his wife had prostituted herself to an impudent youth in women's garments, who had concealed himself among the priestesses. When she was accused of this offence, Cæsar had solemnly declared that he did not believe in the truth of the accusation; nevertheless, he divorced her, for Cæsar's wife must be above suspicion.

What an enigma the man is! thought Cleopatra. He is tall, that is certain, and they say his skin is quite white, like mine, and that he washes often, even when he is fighting, he is always loosely girt, just above the purple stripe, yet he is definitely elegant; on his campaigns he is said to take marble flags and mosaic floors along with him; he must always live like an aristocrat, yet the common people love him. While the last Roman matrons of the old school warn their daughters against this seducer, he surrounds himself with handsome youths, and they say he pays such a price for graceful slaves that he will not allow the transaction to appear in the ledger.

So what sort of a man is this Cæsar? Who loves him? Strange: the rabble love him, the freemen and the artisans, the little people, for he gives them corn and gladiatorial shows. Once, before a festival, he had every plebeian shaved free of charge, which earned him a few thousand votes. In the field he sits down among the soldiers and eats their groats and calls them comrade. How does he speak? In a deep, full tone; not wittily, like the tribunes, not showily, like Cicero, but plainly and naturally. But what all commend, though none can understand, is the speed with which he appears wherever he wishes to be, the rapidity with which he obtains information —everywhere in the Mediterranean he has posted his slaves and his runners—and the laconic speech which he seems to waft through the air, so quickly does it reach its destination and become an order. Cæsar, they say, is the quickest man alive.

What does this cost him? He does not count the cost. Does not fame declare him to be as generous as he is fleet, as rich as he is magnanimous? What a singular Consul!

As a young man, they say, he was so extravagant that his creditors would not let him set out for Spain until he found a wealthy surety. Again, he robbed the Gaulish temples in order to discharge his debts; and later, when he was already a Consul, he is said to have taken a great sum of gold from the State treasury in the capitol, leaving gilded bronze in its place. Then, of course, he was able to give his cohorts double pay, and free hundreds of his slaves, and make his daughter's funeral feast such a popular festival as Rome had never seen.

But why, thinks Cleopatra, is he so enamoured of children? As Consul he gave land to those citizens who had the greatest number of children, charging them no rent. Since his one child, Julia, whom he begat, of course, when he was only twenty, was sufficient guarantee of his fertility, perhaps he put his wives away because they had borne him no children. Did he not load Servilia with pearls and estates—perhaps merely because he thought Brutus, her son, was his own child? She is said to have held him longer than any other woman, until at last she was procuress to her own daughter.

This intrigue with Servilia, which for years had been one of the principal scandals in the great salons of the Mediterranean, but had now long been forgotten, recurred again and again in Cleopatra's perspicacious calculations. The woman who was years older than himself; then the beautiful boy slaves, extravagantly dressed; his youthful reputation as a pervert; his failure to beget a son—and yet he longed for a son; all this evoked, in her excited imagination, an elderly man who might perhaps be captivated by refinement. And was this beyond the achievement of the Queen of Egypt? Had she not such wonders of marble and silk, such golden beakers and shimmering fabrics, as his barbarian eyes had never beheld? What secret lusts of an ageing patrician could she not satisfy in a court which for three hundred years had cherished the erotic secrets of the East? Slaves of every complexion, slave-girls who were still children, dancers and courtesans, the very sight of whom was as stimulating as would be the fantastic bills of fare which she was already beginning to draw up.

But what if he wanted none of these things—what if he had heard only of Cleopatra? Perhaps this very night he was lying in her bed, holding in his hands a portrait which he must have had brought up from the cellars, for they would surely have hidden all her portraits long before this? Perhaps this Cæsar, the swift and generous, who pardoned his enemies and set them in high office—perhaps this Cæsar, a Roman, a dictator, and today the master of the world, had taken it into his head to seek out this young queen in the Delta of the Nile, the young queen of whose disdainful pride stories were told in Rome?

Already she felt sure that it was she, and not the hunted Pompey, whom Cæsar had come to seek on the shores of Egypt; and if it had not been so, yet it was so now; for why else should he send for her? The wealth he coveted was not here, on the edge of the desert; it lay in the treasury, in Alexandria, and in the form of grain, and woven fabrics, and taxes; where he was and she was not, there lay the gold—and yet he had sent for her, not once but twice! Now she saw it clearly: he was expecting her! All turned upon this: she must appear before this man, the most spoiled of mortals, in a novel fashion, as an incomparable surprise! And this called for prudence on her part, for the hostile party at home had surely more spies than the foreigner, and could easily contrive her disappearance, somewhere among the canals, or in the shadow of a grove of date-palms.

Cleopatra rose to her feet. Now she had laid her plans; now she knew how Cæsar must be taken unawares.

V

Two days later, at the same hour of the evening, Cæsar lay on one of the luxurious couches in the palace of Alexandria, holding in his hands a roll of papyrus which had been given him by one of the scholars, a technician who had constructed an automaton. Restless as he was, unable to concentrate on anything, driven to and fro by a certain nervous distress which of old he had often experienced in the field, where no women were available, though now it attacked him more rarely, he dropped the roll and picked up another. This contained passages from the scriptures of the Jews; it had been given him yesterday by one of their scholars; passages from the Greek translation on which a circle of philologists had long been engaged.

Twice already he had been to the Museion, and had admired the lofty, two-storied halls with their modern windows, whose light fell from above on the green floor. Here everything was arranged in open cabinets; and here were the hundreds of thousands of rolls of papyrus for which this greatest of libraries was famous throughout the world. How practical he had found everything! The titles were written on tickets that hung from the shelves, the different subjects were duly separated, and everything could be found promptly. The Pharos, too, the loftiest lighthouse in the world, with its huge speculum, which reflected and intensified the beacon-fire, the great Poseidon on the summit of the tower, and all these palaces, and the straight streets that crossed one another at right-angles—all this he had compared, in silent astonishment, with the confusion of his ancient Rome. He had learned much in the fortnight since he had landed here.

But the greatest thing he had seen was the dead Alexander. They had long ago stolen the golden sarcophagus, but when he entered the temple and they lifted the bronze lid for him, he saw, in a crystal coffin, only half decayed, but veiled by cloth and bandage, by the silvery-grey reflections of the ancient glass, in kindly unrecognizability, the form of Alexander, buried here in his own city, yet still mighty enough, after three hundred years, to serve as a shining example to an aspiring Roman. To have seen Alexander with his own eyes had made the voyage to Egypt worth while.

For some days he had been asking himself why he was not making ready to depart. The half-fearful, half-watchful eyes of the little king, the sly glances of his counsellors, the whispered words as he descended the stairs, and the very curiosity in the eyes of the slaves, had told him, what everyone knew, how weak he was, with all his fame, now and here on this alien shore. What if already, behind his back, the great Ptolemaic army was preparing to fall upon him? The port was in his hands, but who could assure him that the foreign fleet, which appeared to be so friendly to Rome, was not making ready at Pelusium, at a hint from the eunuch, to blockade him between the lighthouse and the palace? What safety was there here, with a handful of ships and his one legion? Why did he not sail away? What did he want in Egypt?

Gold—that was the answer! The dead king had owed millions to a consortium of wealthy Romans; mentally, he reduced this to a little more than half. But this sum he needed, for great as his victory over Pompey had been, he had found no gold in his camp; and gold he needed, in order to pay his troops, here and in Italy, for they would not be content with the mere honour of victory. Cæsar was inclined to justify the fact that he was still in Egypt—even to himself—by the expectation of obtaining the money.

Yet his subordinates were shaking their heads: he, with his keen glance, his sharp ears, had long realized that. What! Was it for this that Pompey's rotting head had been ceremoniously placed in his hands by the Egyptians? He had sent the signet-ring over the winter sea by the swiftest of his messengers, so that the witness of this dreadful end should be passed from hand to hand in the Senate, admonishing all to keep on good terms with the mighty conqueror. The head of his dead enemy—an older man than he, but once his son-in-law—Cæsar had deposited in a chapel which he had dedicated to Nemesis. He had followed the fugitive to Egypt, in Egypt he had sought him, to find that he had already been slain, so that now he need only take the money—and then, back to Rome!

Did anyone know, could he himself understand, why he lingered here from day to day? Of course, the succession of the dead monarch must be settled; peace must be made between the brother and sister. Would he have taken the matter so seriously if the second heir had been a brother of the first? Cæsar was restless this evening, as he had been for days; he felt the want of women, and those he had seen about the Court made him feel cold and scornful. In the field, now as always, he would probably have taken what offered—but what was there to be had here? He had known the whole gamut of indulgence. To stir this man of fifty something new, something out of the ordinary, would be necessary. Where would he find it?

He recalled his conversation with the Epicurean yesterday. To give oneself to the moment, to drain the cup that was offered, to multiply the hours of happiness, and yet to have no fear of death! He had never feared it. But life? Had it trickled through his fingers in all these years of war? Where was it to be found? Ten years among the barbarians, in Gaul and Germany; a few hundred tribes, some conquered, some pacified by negotiation; attack after attack beaten off; fortress after fortress planned and built; so many bridges, so many roads, so many proclamations and speeches—and always yet another battle! Was that the end of life? To win in the colonies the power that one seeks to wield in Rome? Always fresh popular festivals, and the never-ending bribery of ædiles and prætors, in order to win the common people and the Senate—until at last only one enemy was left. Then came the final struggle, and Pompey fell. The goal was reached.

The tragedy of fulfilment! He asked himself whether it really paid to renounce one's life; whether the scholar, the poet with whom he had spoken yesterday, had not drawn the

better lot. He asked himself what new, unimagined experience awaited him in Rome. The chorus of flatterers, the noise
and confusion of the triumph! *Tedium vitae*, cynical thoughts
concerning the venality of human beings, the suddenness of
fate—as witness the rotting head of great Pompey! And now
the victor was asking a senseless question: What now?

But yonder, at the edge of the desert, there was this young
woman, and she could not fail to reward him if he made her
queen again. He would not confess even to himself how curious he was concerning this lovely Amazon; but the experienced lover noted the familiar symptoms in his ageing limbs:
a sensation half weariness, half excitement; a tension in his
thighs, a twitching of the eyelids, a secret resentment because
he had so long been conscious of no stirring of sexual desire;
yet his passion was only waiting for the spark which would
ignite it. Cæsar, as he lay there, was in the very mood which
the instinct of the woman had divined: a mood of doubt and
unrest and ennui.

But now the door opened. A tall slave, perhaps a soldier,
was admitted. He lingered at the door. He was bearing a great
bundle on his shoulder. What did this mean? Here was a
messenger, the adjutant announced; he had brought a costly
carpet, the gift of King Ptolemy. The question in Cæsar's
glance—was there danger to be met?—received a silent answer.
Cæsar bade the man come forward and untie his carpet; he
looked on half expectantly. The carpet was unrolled before
him. And from the carpet rose Cleopatra.

This is no fairy-tale; it is the story that Plutarch has told
posterity. This is no fairy-tale, the Roman told himself, as he
sprang up to help the reclining vision to its feet. That he

recognized her at once was due to the uneasy dream on which Cleopatra had reckoned. That he asked her where she came from, and how, with the smiling curiosity of the man of the world, did not surprise her. She told him how this faithful servant—Apollodorus by name—had rowed her round the Delta, had smuggled her through the fleet, and had wrapped her in the carpet, finally carrying her on his powerful shoulders up the steps that led from the quay into the palace, past the sentry at the door, and now she was here. She smiled, and dismissed the obedient slave.

Cæsar did not hear all she said; he listened only to the sound of her voice. Nor did he at once reflect, as a soldier, how insecurely he was guarded against murderers. He beheld only the dream made flesh: charm and wit, a smile, and a voice that was music, daring and imagination, and, above all, the loveliest mouth he had ever seen. She is not a boy, he thought; there's her bosom under the silk; yet she might be, and that doubles her charm. For now, as she shook her curls and stretched herself a little to drive the weariness from her cramped limbs, it seemed to him that Aphrodite had come down to earth, in a late Alexandrian incarnation, a little goddess who was surely wise in all the secrets of earthly love.

It may be that so swift a conquest was hers because she forgot herself. For all her mysterious, innate knowledge of the arts of seduction deserted her when she saw the man before her. In the boat she had thought of the way she would stand, of the gestures she would make; but now she could not have acted her part. Indeed, she forgot, in that first moment, how dishevelled she must be as she emerged from the carpet, so great was her surprise. It was true, he had very little hair; she

saw that at once, but she overlooked the defect, so masterful
was the emotion of which those black eyes were eloquent, so
virile the thin, silently commanding mouth, so firm the sun-
burnt cheeks, while the neck seemed proud that it was bearing Cæsar's head. Everything about this man attracted her;
the challenging question of his glance, the subtle fragrance of
a well-groomed skin, and now, as they sat beside each other,
and after the first faltering glances became calm enough to
examine each other frankly, they both smiled; Cleopatra half
audaciously, half fearfully, but Cæsar as a conqueror. And
each noted the beauty of the other's teeth.

VI

Next morning, when Cæsar sent for the young king, the
little Ptolemy, who appeared with his diadem in his hair,
stamped with rage, vituperating the sister who smiled at him
disdainfully from the shadows of the lofty chamber, and
shrieked that he had been betrayed. All this Pothinus had
taught him, for by the time that long night was over the
whole palace knew, down to the humblest porter under the
colonnade, what had happened, and perhaps more than had
happened. The boy found it easy to feign rage; he was fourteen by now, and knew that he was capable of love, yet he
constantly felt repulsed as long as they were living together
in the palace. Now he saw his lawful wife in a dubious situation, beside a man who might have been his grandfather and
who was, moreover, a foreign conqueror. In the mood of sex-

ual fury that overcame him he had no need of the eunuch's advice: spontaneously enough, at the close of the brief interview he threw the diadem on the floor with a gesture of desperation and rushed out of the room.

They were still smiling in their high chamber, Cæsar and Cleopatra, when the cries of the everlasting spokesmen of the people were heard outside, swelling louder and louder, until the popular rage found vent in riot. Cæsar made a signal, and had himself armed; then standing in the lofty window, he invited the people to assemble on the following day in the Gymnasion. Cleopatra heard him from her own window; she listened to his voice, and wondered at its accent of unconcern. She did not ask him, when he returned, what he intended to do; this man, she felt, must not be questioned. Moreover, she saw him giving the most immediate orders; her apartments were to be guarded, her brother was to be brought back to the palace, and Pothinus must be sent for. What was in his mind? She asked herself the question when she was alone. The crown was in question, and he had summoned an assembly of the people for the morrow.

Meanwhile she drifted slowly about the halls which she had been forced for six long months to exchange for a chilly tent; brushing past silken cushions of whose warmth she was conscious, and alabaster benches of whose coolness she was aware; she inhaled the fragrance of the ebony doors, felt with her finger-tips the prominences of the encrusted emeralds, and passed the backs of her hands over the ivory door-knobs, all with a slow, feline sensuality. Now she took into her hands a statuette of Aphrodite which had long been a favourite of hers, stroking its bronze contours, and one hand went gliding sensuously over her own body. She was not ill-pleased with the comparison, for she smiled. This morning she was discovering many things in herself of which she had been only half conscious before the Roman had touched her. She had found him to be a man of great experience, but by no means old; firm and virile, as his voice had sounded as he spoke to the people without; tender but not amorous, masterful but not importunate, taciturn yet gallant, and in the end surprisingly grateful.

What an adventure! she thought a little later, stretching herself in her bath. Suddenly she began to laugh; to think how she had been carried into her father's palace rolled up in a carpet, how she had found the lonely master of the world in her own halls, and had awakened him—she remembered it all with fresh surprise, and she laughed, although she was alone; it was for such adventures that she was young, and eager for knowledge. But her laughter was only momentary; sober again, she asked herself what would happen on the morrow. What if the stranger boarded his ship again, what if he never returned? But if he remained in Egypt who would be the actual ruler? Why did he not have her inconvenient brother put away? It was power that was at stake, and in Egypt that meant life. Cleopatra resolved to keep a watch upon her emotions.

She adorned herself. True, it was not yet time to give a banquet, for today Cæsar was only presenting his officers to the Queen of Egypt: Romans, who first broke in and then did homage to her in her own palace. It seemed to her that they were both curious and confused; for on that day no one in

Alexandria knew which of the three powers was reigning; even the Romans were not sure. What had begun in yesterday's twilight in so fantastic a manner, today, seen in the hard light of noon, seemed to have become bold and unmeaning, and she asked herself how many would be silently laughing at it all.

In the evening—when she had invited Cæsar alone to her table—she found him gallant but reserved; quite incidentally he told her that on the following day he would read the king's testament to the people, and reinstate his children. So that no fresh parties should be formed in the palace, he would then and there restore Cyprus to the two younger, and by this gift he would prove Rome's friendship to Egypt. That was all —and again he expressed his admiration of her Sidonian silks.

She was taken by surprise, and said nothing. When had her imperious will encountered such treatment? Her father had enjoyed no real power, and she had despised him accordingly. At first she had listened to her ministers; but when she saw how stupid they were she had taken her own decisions. But the Roman who now sat facing her, and who kept on looking up from his golden plate and gazing at her with his dark, searching eyes—this foreigner, whose mind was still unknown to her—informed her of her fate as though he, Cæsar, were her master! Did he draw this privilege from his own poor legion, now guarding the palace and the harbour? Did he draw it from his fame, or from her surrender? She persisted in her silence; and he, of course, was aware of it, and he did not interrupt her thoughts. If she compared his decision with her own calculation, even she, for the moment, could see that no other was possible. But that he should *tell* her all this, instead of asking her what she proposed—this was almost more than she could bear. Twice she began to ask a question; twice the words died in her throat; and since none the less her lips had opened she met his inquiring gaze with a smile.

VII

With a crash the enemy broke into her idyll. Hardly had the frigid proclamation been made in the Gymnasion when the palace was in arms to frustrate it. Pothinus revenged himself, eunuch-wise, by secretly spreading the report that the queen was a harlot who had surrendered her power to her Roman lover; that the famous Cæsar was a valiant bedfellow, but a feeble commander, and that his men were few and loath to fight. One blow, and Egypt would be free of Rome for ever!

Since Cæsar could not venture to attack the army of Achillas in the east of the Delta, and did not feel that he was strong enough even in the capital to seize the treasury, he sent orders to Pelusium, in the name of the young king, that the army was to be disbanded forthwith. Achillas, for all response, had the two Egyptian messengers put to death, and marched upon Alexandria. One morning an army of twenty thousand foot-soldiers and two thousand horse stood before the gates of the metropolis, and before long they had entered the outlying quarters of the city. Now the master of the world, cut off from his sources of power, must perforce accept battle on a distant shore, against an enemy whose strength was five times his own. He held less than a fourth part of the palace, and the harbour, and he had a small fleet; against this, the young king and the eunuch were his enemies. The eunuch continued his intrigues among the people and in the palace. One day he had wooden platters and goblets laid upon Cæsar's table, and in response to Cæsar's questioning glance he shrugged his shoulders: all the gold in the city had presumably been appropriated by the Roman officials! Then, as he proposed to poison Cæsar at a banquet, and the Roman was warned by his barber, Cæsar had him put to death without more ado, and set a watch about the young king. At the same time he sent messenger after messenger to the shores of the Mediterranean, asking for reinforcements.

Before long he found himself completely trapped. On the land side the besieging hosts cut him off from the water; on the seaward side they barred the narrow entrance to the harbour, and when he sought to break through he lost more of his few men than he could afford. Yet now, in the moment of danger, he was a younger man. Let fire be thrown into the ships! And ninety Egyptian ships were burned at the foot of the Pharos, grain-ships among them; a warehouse caught fire, then a second, then a third, and by the afternoon the flames had reached the library, and there burned all that the State and the intellect of Rome had learned from her greater model; there burned the source of all the doctrines of wisdom and of beauty which for thousands of years had made the Mediterranean the artisan of race and fatherland. But was he who destroyed it a barbarian soldier, who had won to power merely by the stupidity of force? Some obtuse party leader, the enemy of intellect? No, he was Cæsar, the subtlest of all the Romans; Cæsar, who had drawn nourishment from the breasts of the Greek spirit in order to raise himself so far above his kind that his name would be immortalized as a synonym for power. It was he who all unconsciously destroyed the pedestal on which he stood. The scholars and poets, their arms uplifted in horror, stood on the hill behind the palace; there they saw the four hundred thousand rolls, the greatest library on earth, the immortal palladium of their knowledge, the treasures of their inner life, go up in flames, and they could do nothing to prevent it. Cæsar had no time to give thought to the matter.

For Cæsar was ubiquitous. It came to a naval battle in the outer harbour. He stood on one of the galleys, issuing his orders. The galley was rammed, and all on board escaped in the boats. Cæsar's boat was overfilled; it sank. Now he was in the water, swimming towards another boat. The hem of his purple cloak fast between his teeth, in his left hand he held out of the water a few rolls that he wished at any cost to save; and so, swimming with his right arm, hampered by his cloak, ducking every few moments to avoid an approaching missile, he struggled through the water; the cloak he had to drop at last, but he still held the rolls as he clambered into another boat; a man well on in the fifties, fleeing from the harbour to the palace. Four hundred of his men were drowned; the battle was lost. His purple cloak was fished out of the water and stuck on a boathook by the jeering Alexandrians. At the same time ominous reports were spreading to the effect that the Pompeians, after the first shock, now that they knew that the victorious Cæsar was trapped, were everywhere mustering afresh under Pompey's sons. Instead of defeating the remaining supporters of his only rival after the great victory, the mighty Dictator had to waste his resources, here on the verge of the desert, on the channels of the Nile, and even in the streets, by fighting an enemy of his own making, an enemy whom he execrated yet could not escape.

And then, one morning, it was discovered that Arsinoë had suddenly disappeared. The younger sister of Cleopatra, appointed by Cæsar the mistress of Cyprus, she had fled by night with her governor and lover, Ganymede; and he, making a thrust at the opposing army, slew Achillas. The two parties began to negotiate in order to gain time. And the latest news was that reinforcements of Jewish and Persian troops were on the way.

A little patience: help was at hand! Then, at last, Cæsar was able to envelop the Egyptian army, engaging it on either side. Now the Romans were victorious: on the channels of the Nile, the inlets at the mouths, and in every corner of the Delta; ships with all lights extinguished, so that the enemy were unaware of their passage, ships newly arrived, put ashore in the swamps between the mouths of the Nile. On this outlying verge of Egypt, which belonged wholly neither to the river nor to the sea, day after day a confused battle was fought, and the exhausted power of Egypt retreated before the swords and the sweeps of the younger race, into the labyrinth of its own morasses.

The little king, who had borne himself valiantly at the last, was drowned in the Nile, dragged down by the weight of his golden armour. Arsinoë returned to the palace a prisoner. The last of her councillors had been killed. For the second time

Cæsar made his entry into Alexandria, and this time the citizens, clad in mourning, prostrated themselves before his lictors' rods and his eagles. The war was over; it had lasted the whole winter. Spring had come.

VIII

That winter Cæsar and Cleopatra had come to know each other. That she lived with him he announced for posterity in the only sentence in which he inscribed her name; it is in his *Bellum Alexandrinum*. "Cæsar restored the Queen Cleopatra because she had been loyal to him and had always remained with him in headquarters."

In these cold words, written by a hand that wielded the pen as though it had been a sword, in this report for the Senate, the people, and history, wherein the author immortalizes the commander, is contained the first chapter of a romance from which a new world was to arise.

Cæsar had seen many women: the lovely Cornelia, who was said to have been the one love of his youth, whom he first knew when he was seventeen, and lost when he was three-and-twenty; the blooming Pompeia, Sulla's grand-daughter, who betrayed him with Clodius; the insatiable Servilia, who had sapped his strength until he was in danger of physical collapse; the noble Calpurnia, with whom he had lived and shared his honours for a decade; and incidentally the wives of senators, foreign princesses, and camp-followers, as opportunity offered and as his fancy dictated. One had held him by her sensual arts; another by her gaiety; a third by dance and music; others by intelligence or courage; and he had turned from one to another so often because only a mosaic of images could approximate to the dream-image of his youth.

But here, for the first time, when Cæsar was approaching the term of his manhood, he had encountered an apparition so surprising that his dreams could never have prepared him for it; a woman who seemed to unite all antitheses by the power of her sex. Valiant, inventive, bold, and cunning, for every plan that failed she had three more in reserve. Objective and unmoved in battle and in danger, when the day was over she was so changed that she might have been another woman; dismounting from her horse and doffing her helmet, she seemed to have changed her sex. If he wanted information concerning a canal by which he could reach an arm of the Nile, she was able to furnish it. If his horse fell under him, and a second and third were not to his liking, she found a fourth which excelled his favourite charger. If a sea-captain should ask what he was to do with his heavy sails, she knew of a shed in which they could be stored. If the war-council asked whether a man who offered his aid could be trusted, she knew his character. On the verge of the desert she could recognize a camel-rider long before a single Roman could distinguish him. At a thousand paces she could smell whether a ship was caulked with Greek or Roman tar and, lying flat on the ground, she could estimate, by the quivering of the soil, the strength of the enemy horse. After a few days in the field he had formed the habit of looking about him as though listening for the voice of a heroic son; in a few weeks' time she had become the general's adjutant, minister, judge, and spy, and even his adviser.

Cleopatra

When quieter days had come he found a changed woman, a châtelaine who ruled with a firm hand the hundred slaves of her household, as she ruled the million of her subjects who then inhabited the capital. He watched her then from a distance, saw how swift her decisions were, and how just—as far as her longing for revenge permitted; saw that she was never weary, but was ready for all contingencies, with the readiness that was the daily price of omnipotence. His youthful son had become a queen, cold as the consort of a Pharaoh.

Yet at night she was neither one nor the other. With a few lamps and carpets, always correcting with her own hands the preparations made by her slaves, she would transform a tent, such as they sometimes shared towards the end of the war, and, above all, the palace, which only a few hours earlier had been a heavily beleaguered fortress, into a place where all trouble was forgotten. Cæsar, at such times, conscious of his Julian race, which ascribed its origin to Venus, felt as though transmuted, for now he was wholly the son of Mars, and it was Venus who unbuckled his sword-belt. With instinctive swiftness her body had divined what the luxurious and fastidious man desired; so that her lustfulness excelled his own. Yet their nights were often disturbed by a cry, a crash, or perhaps a mere rap at the door; for in the worst of those weeks, when the enemy was only a few hundred paces from the palace, there was no such thing as security.

These were the very things that welded them together: the daily peril, and the thought of the power which they were both defending, here and in Rome; the menace of a destiny to be exorcized only by a valour that was almost ecstasy, and which might well lead to disaster; the constant listening to the din of the approaching enemy, the constant hoping for the help whose approach they could not hear; the flickering light of life that never shone with its full radiance, safe from the winds of heaven, but was always on the point of being extinguished in the tempest, only to blaze again with re-doubled passion. Aye, it was the breath of war that had flung together the greatest general and the most extraordinary woman of their time, in such embrace as the ageing man had never before known, and as the young woman was never to know again.

This spiritual ecstasy, which always accompanied the ec-stasy of the body, this clash of two bold yet constantly aston-ished souls, led each of them to ponder deeply on the empires which they ruled, and to reflect how far it was possible for the rulers of these empires to unite. Cæsar, without uttering his thought, felt that the dream of becoming another Alexander, before whose possible fulfilment he had paused, as though startled, was now beginning to realize itself, here in Alexan-der's own city, in this alliance with the wonderful young creature who had come to greet him as a last queen of Hel-lenic blood. Without uttering her thought, she understood what was passing in his mind, and in her desirous imagination she wove into a new, firmer pattern the threads which had always instinctively bound her to Rome—a bond which she had often regarded with distrust, often with hatred; until at last, out of the dream of two human lovers, the lord and mis-tress of human lives, emerged the image of a world-empire.

Yet her aspirations, like his, remote from the ambition of both, purged of any concrete purpose, grew in those self-oblivious moments of accomplished lust when love verges upon hatred and the soul makes the decision between them. Like a wild young mare, Cleopatra had hitherto borne a rider only in moments of fastidious play, and only to throw him off and forget him in her swift flight back to the open air and freedom. Now the dreaming gaze that had replaced the searching glance, the slow breathing, the silently appreciative relaxation of the ageing man had awakened her heart to unfamiliar emotions; there were minutes in which this descendant of the gods tarried beside her, motionless, which made her suddenly riper by years, and her dreaming fancy asked whether she was not in truth his daughter.

And as in his arms she anticipated—what she was too young to feel—the tardy lust of an experienced woman, so he, by her boyish readiness, felt as though transported back to his earliest ecstasies, to the days when he was as young as she was now. Hovering above the earth, as though floating upon the clouds, in the twilight of the sexes and the generations, these hidden ecstasies unfolded themselves, the procreative dreams of a pair of warriors, and the premonition of world-embracing schemes.

When the winter was at an end she told him that in the summer she would bear him a son. Cæsar heard this with emotion, but in his embarrassment he smiled and asked her how she could be certain of the sex of the child. She gazed at him solemnly and repeated, very definitely, that the child would be a boy.

IX

Now, when the war was at an end, Cæsar restored her to the throne. She was joint ruler with her youngest brother, a child without ability, who in accordance with the custom of the Pharaohs was also proclaimed her husband. Arsinoë was Cæsar's prisoner; Cleopatra hated her with all her heart, for Arsinoë had dared to flatter herself that she might usurp the throne. The millions in gold were ready to hand, and Egypt, which the Dictator might have proclaimed a Roman province, was still independent; yet in truth was more closely allied to Rome than the proudest of her citizens dreamed, for the Queen of Egypt was to bear a son to her lover, the Roman Dictator.

Now that the winter was past and the seas were calm, the Roman ships came sailing to Egypt with dispatches for Cæsar. What was the news?

The world was waiting for Cæsar. Rome and Italy, Athens and the Isles, all the cities of the Mediterranean were waiting for him, desiring or dreading his advent. The curule seats from which the Pompeians had fled were unoccupied; the Senate was deserted; hundreds of high officials and senators were in hiding among their friends in the little coast towns. In Italy the last relics of security seemed to have disappeared, for no one knew who was really in power, and how he was disposed to employ that power. Was Rome still a republic? What new powers would the Dictator demand after his overwhelming victory? True it was that Antony, his representative, was trying to enforce order by the strong hand, but who could say whether his decrees really came from his vanished master? And the wealthy were still strong enough, and the aristocrats resolute enough, to profit by the split in Cæsar's People's Party; at least, as long as he was absent.

And here was Cæsar sitting in the foreign palace; before him was standing yet another messenger with letters, and another, who was describing his journey; and Cæsar listened with negligent expression, rarely unclosing his thin lips to put a question to them. He heard how Antony and Dolabella, his most trusted servants, had fought a battle in the Forum, because one of them had stolen the other's wife; how his statues were being set up all over Italy; but how, at the same time, the sons of Pompey, and with them Cato, the brother of his sometime mistress, were arming to avenge themselves for Pharsalus. And how thousands of marauding soldiers of Cæsar were enlisting with the enemy, because they despaired of receiving the pay which was owing to them, and the land which should have been allotted to them; for the leader who was thus in their debt had apparently disappeared. The world, indeed, seemed to be without a leader. The ageing Cæsar, on that alien shore, must appear to himself like Zeus, a Zeus who had deserted Europe; and now Eros was telling him how the people yonder were at their wit's end, terrified and paralysed by his lightnings.

And yet how long had he, as a struggling soldier, fought for this woman, and for power! He had had his eye on the Forum, on the house of the Supreme Pontifex, ever since Alexander's fame of old had shone like a lodestar in the heavens of his youth. To be the master there; alone, without a second consul to share his power, without quæstors and ædiles, without the two hundred senators, the innumerable advocates to whom he must render account in the name of the Republic! This had been his goal. Now it lay open to him; his place was waiting for him, the seat of kingly power; only the name of throne was lacking. Why was he hesitating? Why did not Cæsar sail for home on the swiftest of his vessels?

In the noontide radiance of his world-wide fame, immediately after the victory of Pharsalus, this mightiest man of his age had gone knocking about an alien continent with a single legion, like a mere adventurer. He might easily have perished, and nothing would have been left of Cæsar but the fragment of a reputation. And in the East he had remarried: at first because he was restless and curious, then because he had to, and because he was in love.

But now! What could now hinder him from bringing home the harvest—bringing it home to Rome, without which there was no real fame or power? Cleopatra? The woman robbed of half her charms by pregnancy, month after month becoming more inactive? Would not the pampered connoisseur of women make his escape from her, now, in good time, in order to preserve unflawed the image of Aphrodite? What was preventing him from hastening towards the supreme consummation of his career?

Nothing was preventing him, save his expectation of an heir. Cæsar was resolved to see his reputed son with his own eyes before he left the shore of Egypt.

But she, resourceful as always, had devised a way of ensuring that he should not grow weary in these three months beside a woman who was growing ever more heavy-footed. She equipped a vessel and invited the master of the world to accompany her on a voyage up the Nile.

X

Thalameyos, the royal ship, such a yacht as no Pharaoh had ever possessed, was a floating palace. In the Egyptian banqueting-saloon the carvings in cedar and cypress were reminiscent of originals to be seen on the banks of this oldest of all rivers. Elsewhere the queen's taste had prevailed, and all was Grecian; just as her Greek ancestors had assumed the style of the Pharaohs only on a few set days of festival. Aphrodite and Dionysos were there, in a chapel whose walls and floor were all of mosaic, and in Cæsar's bed-chamber was a frieze with scenes from the Iliad—scenes to incite the ageing hero to new achievements. There were sumptuous decks for every hour of the day, and a little garden; and a whole system of linen awnings sheltered the travellers from the sun, which now, in spring, and in this rainless country, was blazing down more fiercely with each day of their voyage upstream. Slaves and dancing-girls, actors, comic and tragic, the most experienced cooks, with the most fantastic implements, accompanied the floating palace; some on board, as it sailed or was rowed up the Nile, some in little boats. All that could cheer the spirits of her pampered friend, all that could stimulate or soften him, had been provided by the queen, that his leisure might become a festival.

[64]

That Cæsar should permit himself an interval of leisure for the first time in his breathless career, was her triumph; instinct and ingenuity bade her devise means of so stimulating a continually active mind, far from its accustomed and remembered ways and interests, that it would find a few months of idleness endurable. At the same time, she must offer food for his unresting intellect; so that scholars and inspectors followed the ship, or rowed out to it from the little towns of the Upper Nile, in order to explain Egypt to the Roman.

For the ageing Cæsar could not endure three days of that pleasant idleness in which he had spent his youth; a single day on which he issued no commands was no longer consistent with his way of life.

In four hundred Nile boats a few thousand legionaries followed him. He had no wish to attack anyone or make any conquests. But who could say what surprises the Arabs of the desert ranges might not reserve for them—what attempts might not be made to overpower these amazing travellers? There was far less security in Upper Egypt than there had been a thousand years earlier, in the great days of Thebes.

On this voyage from modern Alexandria to the Nubian frontier, Cæsar saw the whole history of Egypt unrolled before him; for the Nile was Egypt.

With the amazement of the ingenuous—that is, the disinterested—observer, and yet with the critical spirit of the experienced organizer, he beheld the legendary river, and saw how its rise and fall, its width and its flow, together with the variable height of the banks, determined in the remotest corner of the country the amount of grain that would be harvested, the taxing and selling of which had made Egypt wealthy. His eye, when he stood in the bows of the vessel, soon detected a badly kept canal, but he concealed from the queen the involuntary smile with which he watched her, swearing like a trooper, dismissing the headman in charge of the canal. In the North, as far as Britain even, Cæsar had built so many bridges and dams in the course of his campaigns that problems concerning sluices, water-wheels, and Archimedean screws were bound to interest him. Since no country on earth depended so completely on the intelligence of its ruler as did this land without rain, men of constructive mentality, from the days of Rameses and Joseph, had whetted their inventive faculties on this problem of water, and Cæsar was not the last to do so.

And he felt that he would not be the last. When he saw, at the foot of the Pyramids, the end of the road by which Alexander had returned to the Nile from the sanctuary of Amon, Cæsar felt that he had found his place in a cycle of four thousand years, and was astonished to find how near he was to Alexander; he seemed to be following in his actual footsteps. Instead of diminishing as Cæsar left his city, Alexander's magic influence increased with every day of the southward voyage. Before the gigantic halls of Amon and Osiris he felt the surprise of the army engineer who asks himself how such lofty columns could have been erected without machinery. But where the Ptolemies had approximated to Greek forms, in the temple of Edfu, and upstream at Philæ, the Roman saluted his great prototype again, and accepted the encounter as an omen.

He was impressed by all that was told him by the priests, in Greek, or by the peasants for whom he sent, through their interpreters. He was constantly asking himself how he, Cæsar, would have ruled this country, and what improvements he would introduce if he should rule it tomorrow. The names of the peoples who had wandered of old from the Nile to the Red Sea by the two ancient highways made him think of the way to India, and once more the Persian Alexander stood before him; and next moment he saw Persia as the hereditary foe of Rome; he had a vision of Crassus, who had allowed himself to be defeated there, and of the whole Persian enigma. But then he reverted to the methods of Egyptian commerce, at the height of its prosperity; day by day, as they voyaged up-stream, a wealth of practical details stimulated the intellect of this modern Pharaoh, and the method of fastening the saddle-cloth on the camel which he rode was for him as worthy of remark as the potter's wheel in a village above Thebes, on which were shaped the pitchers that were destined to raise the water to the level of the fields.

To the unresting general and dictator, now completely divorced from his normal occupation, this voyage up the Nile revealed itself as a great school of Oriental life.

XI

But Cæsar was also a guest in this country and knew what was due to the queen of this floating palace when, after a luxurious repast with the officers, she sat beside him in the midst of her cushions on the port side of the vessel, watching the changing colours of the sunset over the Libyan desert as the daylight faded and the heat of the day abated. Muffled in the shawls which the careful hands of her slaves had wrapped about her, she lay there in the favourite position of her childhood, propping her chin in her hands and turning her brown, falcon's eyes to the silent man who sat beside her on his cushions, trying, by lifting his head, to conceal from her the baldness to which he could not get accustomed. He knew then that she was waiting for a story.

On those evenings he may have told her the whole story of his life—in selected episodes, of course, for there were whole regions of his mind which were withheld, even from this woman in whom he had such confidence. Perhaps he had asked her for some delicacy which was served at their evening meal; and then, of course, he would tell her how but recently, in the civil war, he and his men had eaten roots and for days had gone without water, because Pompey had managed to cut off their supply. It was just before Dyrrachium, the only battle he had ever lost. That was a thing worth seeing, how the legions had come to their general's tent and had begged that they might be punished! The whole Ninth Legion was disbanded as a punishment! Were there often mutinies? Sometimes; there had been one in Sicily. He had gone down to them and shouted at them: Quirites! But they had shouted back: We are soldiers!

Did they love him? she asked.—Oh, yes, as long as he was victorious.—And did he love them?—Individuals, yes; the man who came to him with a helmetful of clear spring-water. . . . Yes, in the desolate North the Roman soldiers had shown what they were capable of! Ten years they had been with him in Gaul, and never defeated; they had seldom grumbled, there was little need to punish them, and so long as one gave them bread and decent shoes, and occasionally women, they were content and trusted their leader. But they must see their general himself fighting when things were looking dangerous; for example, in the forest battle against the Nervii, or lately in Epirus.

Again and again he remembered Pompey. He had not then made the best use of his victory. Was he growing too old, too easygoing? Ought one to retire from active service at fifty? He could have done anything after that victory; in that war without battles even Pharsalus could have been avoided. Was Pompey perhaps too spoiled by fortune? He had always been rich, always famous; he was noble among the noblest; so everything had come his way. On the other hand he, Cæsar—so he soliloquized for Cleopatra—had always been out of favour; at every step upwards he had been checked by Roman society, for which very reason he had had to find support in the people, climbing painfully, step by step, so that he was forty before he had a province to rule, and what a miserable province, among the barbarians! Why was Pompey the one darling of the gods and the Senate? There were times when his resentment kept him awake at night. Already an old man, and yet not the master of Rome! To end his life in party squabbles, like those advocates and adventurers! That prospect, and the thought of Alexander, who had triumphed when so much younger, had filled his heart that evening—was it only three years ago?—when he stood before the Rubicon, in Rimini, hesitating for half an hour as to whether he should risk the venture and march on Rome.

It meant that one was proclaimed the enemy of the fatherland! Yes, yes! Even if they had not put it to the vote! How the senators had derided him! Was Cæsar hoping to conquer the great Pompey? *He* was no Ambian or Suessonian chieftain, lurking in the oak forest!

She wanted to know if he had first consulted an oracle. He smiled. The number of his horsemen, the skill of his marksmen, the strength of his rearguard, his commissariat: these were his oracle. A few heroic lieutenants: these were his priests. Antony? He was the best of them! When Antony had ridden out of Rome disguised as a slave, to join him just beyond the Rubicon, he had shown him to the cohorts in order to fill them with indignation against the party government that had made it necessary for a valiant man to escape in such a guise!

Cleopatra listened. There was a metallic hardness in his voice as he spoke of Antony's escape; the old resentment, the old hatred of the parties had revived as he told the story. The parties!—and he could not master them because he needed them. She had questioned him about Antony before this; and always a light came into Cæsar's eyes; it seemed that he could overlook Antony's failings because they could not be divorced from his virtues. Since he was one of the two Romans whom she had formerly seen at close quarters—she did not choose to speak of the other, of Pompey's son—since Antony, the captain of horse, had made such a favourable impression on the girl of fourteen, she wanted to hear more of him, to know what he was really like. Cæsar always spoke of him as of a wild, headstrong son, whose unruly life one pardoned because of his loyalty and valour; and while he was commonly chary of praise, he had nothing but good to say of Antony.

But when she asked him whether Antony too could become

a king, he replied with an emphatic negative. As a second in command, under a stronger leader, Antony was incomparable; but for supreme command he had neither the patience nor the coolness. There was no moderation in the man, for which reason he no longer had the confidence of the people; even now, one might be sure, he was racketing about Rome, pardoning and proscribing in Cæsar's name, just as the whim took him, or the charming Cytheria suggested; even now he was probably being borne through the streets in the same litter with her, drawn by a pair of tame lions!

Cleopatra listened. Cæsar's voice was merry now, as it seldom was. Yet at this moment it was not Cæsar whom she saw before her, but that other, whose Bacchic head had filled her with unrest in the old days, and who now seemed to be ruling Rome in obedience to the whims of a singer. A pair of lions? In a litter? What crazy things they think of in Rome! Life might hold all sorts of things in store . . . for which a man of Cæsar's age would have no use. But all sorts of things might happen to her, sooner or later, because she was so young. . . . Through whom? Life was just beginning, and when she had given birth to the boy it might very well begin a second time! Yonder, in the rock-tombs, where the last rays of the sun were still glowing, veiled in their linen swathings, were the queens of this land. Once, perhaps, Hatshepsut had been drawn along the Nile valley by a pair of tame lions, riding in a covered litter with the high priest, and while the people fell to the ground before Isis re-arisen her holy lover stroked her knee, but she controlled her features and would not smile.

Cæsar could not know whither the suddenly kindled fantasy of the pregnant woman had wandered; he noted only

[71]

that she was absent-minded, and asked himself whether Antony, years ago, had perhaps had his way with her. Why had she questioned him a third time about Antony? He was younger—aye, indeed, nearly twenty years younger!

Cæsar rose and went to the bows of the ship. He saw in the heavens his own star: there shone Venus, from whom he was descended.

It is strange, she said to herself, when she found herself alone; it is as though his future destiny were stirring within him, as my child is stirring in me.

Had she prayed to all the gods that the child would be a son? Perhaps one ought to inquire according to the Persian usage; Cæsar is so taken up with Persia. He has been very silent these last few days. At times one would think that here he is no longer sensible of the distant burden and the power that are waiting for him; then he is merry; then it seems as though he felt young again. But he suddenly grows gloomy once more; he eats little and drinks nothing; his cheeks look sunken, and it seems as though he were afraid that his sickness would come upon him. Six months, and not a single attack; perhaps the whole thing is merely talk. But often one doesn't know whether he is thinking or merely dreaming. Sometimes he murmurs to himself, repeating numbers. And at other times he may be silent for half an hour, without even glancing at the river bank. What is passing in his mind at such times?

Last night, when he was groaning in a nightmare, until I shook him gently, and he started up awake, he stared at me hard, and when he had come to himself he laid his hand on my body and murmured something. It was not mere politeness when he questioned the physician as to the date, and then decided on a longer voyage. He wants to hold his son in his own hands, for he has great things in store for him.

Has it ever been said, she thought, that the sons of elderly men are weaker than others? The first childbirth is supposed to be difficult; one may die of it. The physician will be super-humanly careful; he knows that they will kill him if I die. What will Cæsar's nephews in Rome do if a genuine heir should make his appearance? If he goes away and does not return, a father will have to be found for the child. But what needless anxiety! Cæsar wants this son of his; how could he de-sert the child and his mother! For a thousand years no child in his mother's womb has had such a future!

Strange! Cæsar was thinking, as he stood in the bows of the ship. There are times when she has a gesture, a movement of the hand, exactly like Cornelia's, thirty years ago. Then one suddenly sees how young she is. When Cornelia gave birth to Julia she was no older. And Alexander's wife . . . she, of course, was no older. Are such women too young to bear strong children? If my Julia had lived longer as Pompey's wife there would have been no civil war. Would that have been desirable?

He had been fortunate long enough, had Pompey; even his sudden death was to be envied. Someone ought to have stabbed him a few months earlier, when he was still at the height of his power. Then, of course, there would have been no Pharsalus. But what was really desirable? To be born to a great position! Not to knock about for twenty years, buying the people, buying senators, buying soldiers, buying women, to get to the top at last a weary man, with a bald head and

aged limbs! Above all, not in this most scatter-brained of cities! Germany and Gaul were conquered; one had fought
thirty battles there; and after nine years one came home victorious. And what was the talk of Rome? The banishment of
Cicero!

To be born with a crown! To be a king at eighteen! Then,
indeed, an Alexander might have the world at his feet at
thirty.

And Cæsar, standing in the bows of the ship, gazing into
the darkness, continued his reflections. . . . It seems as though
she no longer realizes that all men bow their faces to the
ground before her. Innate majesty, when it is majesty like hers,
cannot be matched by personal success. Are not these tropical
kingdoms happier than our cold republics? And yet her fore-
father, who crowned himself here in Egypt, was only a mid-
dling lieutenant of Alexander's. Has any schoolboy ever
learned the date of any battle that he won? Yet now, three
hundred years later, his descendant is still seated on the same
throne!

One must do something final. Deification is cheap and
commonplace; it binds no one; it operates in an unknown
heaven, and when one likes there's an end of it; even the sons
of the gods are not certain of reverence. No deified general
has ever yet founded a dynasty. People think of the crown as
something permanent; inheritance from father to son; regular
recurrence; the eternal chain. But has she not sworn to me
that the child is a boy? If she really gives birth to a son . . .
where in all the world is a queen of older blood, of a dynasty
more brilliant, more famous, than this Greek woman, strayed
into Egypt and so doubly rich? Are we to look for the mothers

of our sons among the shaggy Sigambri or the mist-shrouded Picts? No, the new lord of the world must be of Eastern blood, of Alexander's line! He will transfer the power of Rome to the East. East and West—one must bind them together with a crown, even though it be a ring of iron! The evanescence of adventure must be exorcized in a son! Another ten years in which to train him; no longer is needed. Above this land of Egypt Venus shines softly, night after night. We Julians are descended only from the gods. My son shall be the offspring of a king! One must do something final.

XII

A fortnight after the floating palace had returned to Alexandria, Cleopatra, who was then in her twenty-third year, gave birth to a son in the palace of her fathers: the son which she had promised to her lover. She called him Cæsar, but the people of Alexandria named him Cæsarion ("little Cæsar"), and in the inscriptions he was Ptolemæus Cæsar. On the temple walls Cleopatra had it recorded, as the Pharaohs had done fifteen hundred years before, how the god Amon had appeared to her as a procreative force, and how the gods rejoiced in this new child of a god. As for the priests, they told the people that Amon had assumed a human form in the person of the great Roman, Cæsar, whose line had sprung from Aphrodite, in order to cast his shadow over the divine queen. The sceptical Alexandrians laughed; that was a tale for old women and children.

Perhaps the two mortal parents smiled when the proclamation of the priests was submitted to them for their signature. But Cæsar did not smile when his son came into the world, for the plans of half a year of scheming depended on the birth and the sex of this child. He remained beside her until he saw that she was out of danger. Urgent messages called him to Rome, where Antony appeared to be excelling himself in his escapades, and everything seemed to be in a state of dissolution. But before he returned to Rome he must deal with the Persian in Asia Minor, who was fighting the Roman generals there as once his father had fought them. The captive Arsinoë was sent to Rome, where she must be kept for Cæsar's triumph. Three Roman legions remained in Egypt. In order to avoid leaving an officer of high rank in Egypt, Cæsar placed a liberated slave in command of the troops. Whether they remained as guardians or as custodians, as allies or as oppressors, depended solely on the queen's attitude to Rome.

When Cæsar left her she seemed to him as young as when she had risen to her feet from the unrolled carpet. Now he left his son with her in pledge. It was agreed that in the following year she should join him in Rome, in order that she and her lawful husband, the boy Ptolemy, might conclude a solemn league with the Roman people and Senate. In the eyes of the Egyptian priests, Cæsar also was her husband, though the voluble Alexandrians were scribbling on the walls epigrams about this Roman Amon. Some said that with this son of Cæsar, Egypt had finally sunk to the level of a Roman colony; others saw in the child the symbol of an alliance; others again feared for the fate of Egypt if harm should befall Cæsar.

When Cæsar set sail for Rome, Cleopatra was crouching in her favourite window-niche. The ships glided out of the harbour; Cæsar, she knew, was on the largest vessel. She knew what he was thinking at this moment, for his thoughts were her own. As she was straining her eyes to distinguish him, so he was trying to make out her figure at the palace window. Each was thinking of the other's adventure, which, it seemed, would determine the fate of the world.

An exiled queen had saved herself by her genius and her charm. And therewith she had undergone initiation, as a lover, a comrade, and a mother; all this in a few months, at the hands of a man almost thrice her own age. A victorious general, who had staked his powers and his life, was rejuvenated by love, and had become the father of a son. Substantially, both had striven for the same amalgamation in order that their son might inherit the earth.

From the bold conception that embraced the Mediterranean they reverted to the secret hour of their first ecstasy, and a deep melancholy seized upon the tall, thin man in the shadow of the sail, and the little queen at the window, as they saw how quickly the distance between them was increasing; and each, at that moment, was touched by the fear that destiny might be parting them for ever. Silently, with mournful eyes, he gazed from the stern of the ship toward the palace window, uncertain of what the future might hold.

But she sat in her wide window, with her feet drawn up, her hands half folded between the marble wall and her brown curls. She was confident of victory and of the future; she was smiling.

Zeus

Who does not know Cæsar even without my stammering?
... How truly great, pure, and good he is! Mighty, powerful,
without fear of opposition! Immovable, irresistible! Wise,
capable, exalted above circumstance, knowing himself the son
of Fortune, wary, quick—the epitome of all human greatness!

—GOETHE

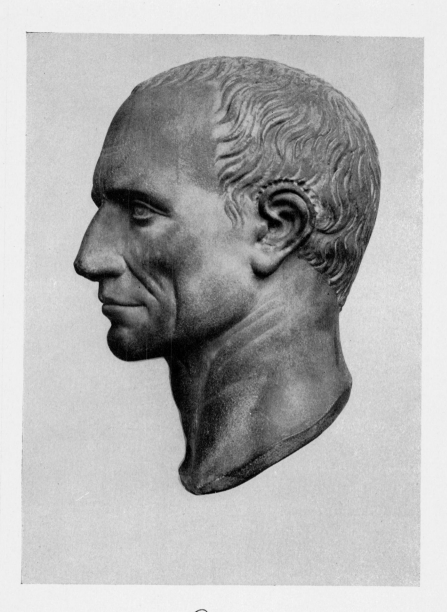

Caesar

CHAPTER II

Zeus

I

THE summer was sultry in Rome, and one accustomed to
the sea-breeze that distinguished Alexandria, surrounded
by water, from all the other ports of the Mediterranean, was
doubly oppressed by the hot air of the Italian capital, which
came up from the adjacent marshes, and was stirred only by
the rare thunderstorms. The wealthy Romans fled from the
city at this season, spending bucolic months in the Alban
hills, where they could comfortably pursue the intrigues and
financial schemes of the capital in the shade of laurel and
cypress, while the poets, pampered with wine and women, immortalized their hosts. True, Catullus was dead, who could
say such naughty and spiteful things so beautifully, but in his
place they had Virgil, very eloquent in his florid way, and
young Horace—but one never knew which party his graceful
verse was intended to support.

After all, it was a chancy business, wasting money on one's
posthumous fame; one's pecuniary sacrifice to one's mistress
brought a more certain reward. In the long run everything

[81]

was a matter of money. Since the days of one's forefathers had a poor man ever become consul, or even ædile? To borrow enough money, to buy votes, and then, when one had the power, to acquire the amount borrowed and scrape a fortune together into the bargain! Cato had lived like the ancients, atoning for his lack of money by his moral self-complacency; but such people end by committing suicide. What could Pompey and Crassus have done without money? And now, Cæsar even? In the matter of subornation he was excelled only by his officials. The Republic was old and tired; one must be quick to take one's place amongst its heirs.

There was a feeling that the twilight of the gods was at hand, and Roman society amused itself as best it could in town and country. All were extravagant, though no one was rich nowadays; all thirsted after the supreme consummation of pleasure, since no one knew what the morrow would bring forth.

But this summer no one had left the city, because Cæsar had remained in Rome. He had just returned from his African victories, and he had defeated the last Pompeians in a glorious battle at Thapsus. The Pompeian leaders were dead or wounded; the surviving sons had escaped to Spain. In the meantime his party, on the first reports of the victory, had proposed that he should be made dictator for a term of ten years: an innovation in Roman history. However, on entering Rome he had made a great speech to the people, swearing that he was no tyrant and would never become one; he would accept the dictatorship only for another year, and the same with the consulship. The sceptics smiled at this, but for the moment the general mood was one of idle rejoicing.

For the Romans were looking forward to two great sensations. In August, Cæsar would hold his triumph, and among the half-million spectators there would be a stranger: the Queen of Egypt had come to Rome from the South even as Cæsar returned through Spain from the North. Yes, Cæsar had now two wives in Rome, and a son! Who, at such a time, would be exiled in the Campagna! No one who was anybody could afford to miss the sight of Cæsar's foreign mistress!

For Cleopatra the year that had elapsed since her parting from Cæsar had been as quiet as for him it had been full of commotion and victory. She had suckled and weaned her son, and now, in his second year, on the voyage to Rome, he had begun to stand on his feet when the ship did not roll too much. After so many storms she had found a way to appease the land, or at all events, the few hundred men who influenced its destiny. Behind the shields of the Roman legions, in the reflected light of their powerful protector, and in the enjoyment of a certain sense of stability, the Alexandrians had begun to look kindly upon the ambiguous matter of their queen's love-affair and marriage, and since everyone was profiting by the trade with Rome, they soon began to feel that the Roman general was really the god Amon in disguise, and their crown prince a son of the gods on both sides of his house.

But she, his beloved, when soon after his departure she heard of his brilliant victories in Asia Minor, had ascribed them—as though he had never been victorious in the past—to the rejuvenating power of love, or to the son which she alone of all women had borne to Cæsar. His reports told her much, but through her agents she tried to learn all that he was doing in his absence. She must know the name and the aspect of

every woman who came into contact with him, and on what
terms he stood with his wife; indeed, she had spies for that
very purpose in Rome. She had heard how, on returning to
Rome, fourteen months after his victory at Pharsalus, delayed
by that magical interlude, he had quickly set all in order, or
had at least pacified the city; and in two months' time he was
off again, to conquer the heirs of Pompey. Only now, on returning to Rome for good, had he sent for her; now, when
he might hope—though so much too late—to rule in Rome as
master, and as the Alexander-dream of his youth had foretold:
namely, to rule alone.

Alone, but for his heir. That had been the inspiring thought
of this year of separation, and when of an evening in the field
he remembered the young and lovely women of Rome, or compared them, after his return, with the woman who had borne
his son, both remembrance and comparison drew him back to
her, and he realized that his longing for the child was blended
with his yearning for the enchanting mistress of those warlike
months. Moreover, he was now impatient to show himself to
her, his second wife, in the splendour of his triumph, which
he had postponed for a year, and in this respect he was resolved, as master, to crush any possible opposition.

With all the pomp of the Republic, surrounded by senators
and officials, Cæsar had received the allied queen of the Egyptians with her fraternal consort, the twelve-year-old Ptolemy,
and their court, the alien splendour of whose raiment and bearing filled the Romans with jealousy and amazement. In his
sumptuous gardens on the left bank of the Tiber, where today
the park of the Doria-Pamphilii climbs the Gianicolo, the master of Rome had made ready a villa, equipped with all the lux-

ury with which Cleopatra's guest on the Nile sought to repay her hospitality. He saw to it that this or that detail was embellished before her arrival, and in some cool little chamber an easy chair may have been introduced, or a curtain provided, in memory of the floating palace on the Nile. It was only when he visited her alone on the evening of her arrival, carried in his rapidly moving litter from his austere house on the Forum to this home of fantasy, that he became fully aware of the double life which he was now beginning, and which had the charm of novelty even for his over-experienced age. When he called to mind her figure, as he had seen it on the occasion of the State reception, it seemed to him just as boyish as it had two years ago, when the carpet was unrolled. But in this half-hour one desire was supreme: to see the boy, face to face. According to her letters, the child had his father's features.

When the litter halted beneath the ancient ilexes, in the red, hazy glow of the July evening, there was no one waiting at the iron gate; it seemed that all her servants had been ordered to withdraw. He dismissed his own, entered the gate, and walked up the wide garden path towards the villa. Faintly amused, he glanced into the shrubbery; perhaps this was some new whim of hers. It amused the Dictator, who was accustomed, wherever he went, for all to await him with timid or curious glances. Half-way to the house he heard a faint hiss, as though someone were calling him, yet did not wish to betray himself.

On a semicircular marble bench, in the shade of the great pines, Cleopatra was seated, with the boy standing beside her, so that his head reached up to her shoulder; as she embraced him so, it seemed that she could not rise to her feet, but she

[85]

smiled such a greeting to Cæsar as no legion, no theatre could offer him. In astonishment his gaze passed from her to the child, and back to her own face. Not a trace of her was there, but the child was exactly like himself. Seldom can there have been such a likeness between the features of a child and the furrowed lineaments of an ageing, hard-bitten warrior. This likeness was no faint reminiscence of Cæsar's own childhood; it was the grey-haired Cæsar of today that seemed to be mirrored in this childish face. And the child, with his black eyes, gazed with astonishment at the strange man.

Cæsar tasted the full happiness of the moment which the gods had granted him after so many perils; and yet he was keenly aware of its transitory nature, and he inhaled its beauty with the sense of farewell that thrills us at sunset when we do not know whether another dawn will be granted us. Now, as when they had parted, he lapsed into a melancholy that refused to be banished, although for courtesy's sake he tried to smile.

Once more she was the victor, in the strength of her youth. This powerful personage, whom she had seen for the first time that morning in the pomp of his Roman dignities, now sat beside her in a lonely park on the outskirts of the city, gazing with his searching eyes at the heir whom she had promised him, and turning that gaze back to her with the secret challenge which she had detected already that morning behind his compressed lips. Yes, he was king of Rome. The dream was beginning to near its fulfilment.

II

The temper of Roman society could not have been worse.
All made haste to visit the villa beyond the Tiber in order to
see and criticize the foreign queen. To some she seemed, as
an Egyptian, to belong to the race that worshipped animals,
although she looked every inch the Hellene she was by blood.
Others made merry over the descent of this so-called queen,
from a Ptolemaic bastard and an unknown mother. They reckoned up the debts which her father, the consistently drunken
Fluteplayer, had left behind him, and asked, mockingly,
whether by any chance she had come to pay them. For ten
years past people had spoken of Cæsar's wife only in a tone of
disapproval, but now they suddenly began to pity her, as the
true, neglected wife of the Dictator; or they spoke with false
compassion of the queen's imprisoned sister, who had been
languishing here for a year, in order to be dragged in Cæsar's
triumph.

All the women, and some at least of the men, were agreed
that the queen was really not at all good-looking; less beautiful, at any rate, than a dozen aristocratic Roman ladies. The
only thing which both men and women admired in her was
the cleverness with which she had persuaded this man, who
was now half-way through the fifties, and had long been regarded as infertile, of the parentage of a child who had evidently been begotten by some enterprising adjutant. Since
everybody was confident that such a thing could not have
happened to him, the pressure generated by the presence of

this overpowering personality was to some extent relieved as by a safety-valve.

At the same time there gathered about her a crowd of rival flatterers; a legitimate Queen of Egypt, apparently recognized by the Dictator as his official mistress, was, after all, a more important person than her father had been: a king in exile, lavishing his gold and contracting debts in order to regain his throne. Since Cæsar might do the most surprising things—to-morrow, or next year, who could say?—one could not sufficiently honour his confidante; so far from his union with a foreigner making the notion of a monarchy more unlikely, the pair of them, when they appeared in company at a banquet, were the very picture of a king and queen: an impression which, in the sceptical minds of the Romans, had all the force of a suggestion, and soon became a positive apprehension.

Yet the thing that astonished all who were not wilfully blind was the tact, the reserve, of the foreign queen, of whose excesses Rome had heard so many tales. In the place of exaggerated richness, they could see only good taste in her fashion of dress, and while this was not the Roman fashion, it was, if anything, more decent. In the two years which she spent in Rome, none of the many letter-writers and poetasters who were ill-disposed to her could ever detect a coquettish look or gesture, a scandalous action, or even an indiscreet word, which might be regarded as confirming her bad reputation; so complete was her reserve in this foreign environment, so tensely was her mind directed toward the one purpose, which could be achieved only in Rome.

Privately, as she endeavoured to find her way through the

network of Roman intrigue and greed, she was no more impressed by Roman society than it was by her. Here she was spurred on by the natural curiosity of the Egyptian, who from her childhood upwards had looked towards Rome, puzzling herself to discover the secret of Roman power over her own country. Moreover, it amused her now to buy the support of great people who had once refused her father money; and here she made use of the man whom he had left in Rome— Amonios, a true Levantine bloodhound, who could whisper to her the hundred secrets of the related or hostile families at the heart of the Republic.

But her real aim, which she followed with passion, was to discover those individuals who had influence with Cæsar, or might have influence in the future; and from the manner of his intercourse with one and all she estimated the depth of his roots in this Roman soil. To all these influences and interests she, with no helper but her son, must oppose her plan of world-rule; as a remote fixed star she must detach the comet from the orbits of a thousand planets! But to do this she must ascertain the nature of these planets, and their attractive power over the comet.

When during her first weeks in Rome she received her visitors in the garden on appointed days, and fashionable Roman society seemed to be growing accustomed to her cool refinement, Antony was not among her guests. He was angry with Cæsar, for the latter had censured him severely on his return from Egypt, and Antony had become too great a man for such treatment. There were a hundred things which, in Cæsar's opinion, Antony had done wrongly as Cæsar's representative, and which the magnanimous autocrat would soon have forgotten; but the fact that he had bought the palace of the murdered Pompey, and had wrongfully taken possession of his Greek statues and his wine-cellar—paying for neither—was a grievance against his government which the old Pompeians ought never to have been afforded. On this point Cæsar was insistent; but Antony refused to take orders; the result was an altercation and estrangement. Cæsar did not again appoint him consul, but preferred his rival, Dolabella, whom Antony hated; here jealousy was the trouble. And now Antony was going about the city and spluttering threats; soon there was talk of a scheme for murdering his friend and master.

When Cicero paid his respects to the queen, entering the villa from the garden in which she usually preferred to receive her visitors, there was a searching mutual inspection, and they felt that they distrusted each other. Is this man still a friend of Cæsar? Cleopatra asked herself. Cæsar had fallen silent when there had lately been talk of Cicero. In the Catiline trial he had not dared to attack Cæsar, and subsequently he had borrowed money from him. Cleopatra had heard that he had once been condemned to "honourable exile." But what did "honourable" mean in Rome? And who, of all the people weaving their intrigues in the garden that evening, had not at some time been exiled? In Asia Minor, they said, he had made money like the rest of them, in spite of his moral speeches. How else would he have paid for his fine villa? But then she smiled, and when he spoke, in brilliant periods, of a certain original manuscript which was said to have been saved when the great library was burned, she promised him that she would send to Alexandria for it immediately. Then her pupils dilated, and a moment later she was welcoming two tall young men.

He never comes alone! thought Cleopatra, forcing herself to offer her hand to the thinner of the two. She found this youth of seventeen repulsive, but Cæsar spoke of him amiably. It was Octavian, with his friend Agrippa. What was there in this nephew to meet with Cæsar's approval? she thought, examining him anew. His deportment was bad, his complexion spotty—he was always pale and never properly washed—and his light-brown hair was badly brushed as usual. Moreover, he was always nervous about his health; and one could see at a glance that he was a bookworm. And his glassy eyes had a greedy look that spoke of secret vices. If his grandfather, the old moneylender of Velletri, had not been such a leech, his father could never have married into Cæsar's noble family, and the boy would have been of no greater consequence than his friend—who, like him, kept on staring at her bosom.

I know your secret wishes! she thought. If you cannot plough Cæsar's field now, you will try at all costs to get hold of the crops! With a sudden intuition she turned to a woman slave, sent word to the nurse to bring the sleeping child, and held it under the snuffling nose of the pallid youth. He did not see the arrow that shot from her golden-brown eyes across the pillow—an arrow aimed at his heart. Octavian, Cæsar's seventeen-year-old great-nephew and his protégé, merely stared at the features of Cæsar's son. The shadows of coming events, unguessed and inscrutable, but predetermined, flickered among these three human beings, while the harsh Agrippa waited for the moment to introduce himself.

[91]

He grudges him his life, thought Cleopatra, gazing down at her child with silent, half-open lips. If he had dreams of becoming the heir of a childless Cæsar, then he must hate Cæsar's son. We must double the guards outside the pavilion.

Then a new and more unexpected visitor entered the room, and while the two young men took their leave of her she held out her left hand to the new-comer, for she was still carrying the child in her right arm. The stranger gazed earnestly at the sleeping child. They would criticize her in Rome, thought the queen, for receiving her guests with the child in her arms; she had never done such a thing before, and only her hatred of the youth who hated her child had induced her to do so to-day. But now, since chance had so strangely served her purpose, she kept the child a little longer; for the man who stood before her was himself reputed to be Cæsar's son. It was Brutus.

Him also the queen received with equanimity only because Cæsar had spoken in his favour. Barely thirty years of age, his virile bearing and his earnest and searching glance should have pleased the woman of four-and-twenty. But when she imagined him in love—and she imagined a man in love if she wanted to form an opinion of him—she was conscious of a certain aversion: she felt that Brutus would never surrender himself to anyone.

He is surely not Cæsar's son, she thought, although his eyes are so like Cæsar's. If he is, then Cæsar has been as wholly submerged in the nature of an alien woman as I have been in his. And then, as though she felt that she must separate the two, she gave the child back to the nurse, and listened to Brutus, who had the singular habit of never discussing society, but only principles. Today he advised her to educate the child on Pythagorean principles, so that he might learn to account to himself, in the evening, for each day of his life. The queen appeared to be listening to him; she nodded from time to time, but she saw in him only a zealot, who had saved himself, in his righteousness, for what sinister motives? Another of these turgid Latins! thought the Greek woman. Is there any moral problem he has not settled for himself? First he turns to Pompey, who slew his father, because law and order and what not were on his side. Before the battle, they say, he was copying extracts from Polybius instead of looking to the saddles of his cavalry. Yet Cæsar gave express orders that he was to be spared if he was captured in the rout, and when he went over to the victor he was given a brilliant reception! In return he takes a wife from the most dangerous section of the city: Cato's daughter, the widow of an archenemy! Why, there is the matron in question—pretentious creature!

Brutus had begun to speak of Varro; he was asking the queen if she had read his essay in condemnation of Eastern luxury, and recommending a return to the old Roman simplicity. She replied that she had not, and asked him to tell her more; but instead of listening she was thinking: What a tactless Roman! Tactless, the whole self-righteous family! All the same, when he was governor of Cyprus he lent my people money at forty-seven per cent! But Cæsar, of course, forgives this man everything. It is as though he felt himself honoured by the condescension of this lordly Pompeian! Only recently he said that he intended to make him prætor! When I looked at him in surprise he smiled, saying that one must forget old enmities! What a wretched life it must be—without revenge! That's the way to breed conspiracies! We had enough of that at home; and these moralists are the most dangerous. Cæsar must be warned—even if the man is his own son! But the ravenous Servilia—she had such a hospitable heart that no one really knows whether Brutus is Cæsar's son. Cæsar thinks so, but Brutus, who wants everything to be proper and lawful, refuses to admit it. What ill-feeling on every side! How many enemies Cæsar has! Has he a friend left?

III

For many mornings Cleopatra sat as model for the Greek sculptor Archelaus. Since the work has not survived we do not know what she wore on these occasions; but as the statue was commissioned by Cæsar it cannot have been very much. Only a single bust remains as an authentic record of her beauty; all the coins are bad, the descriptions meagre, so that she has suffered at the hands of history the same fate as Alexander, who lacked nothing in life but a great poet, as she lacked only a great artist. But imagination is all the freer for that. Whether the statue was begun too late, whether the sculptor was too often disturbed in his work by caprice or social exigencies, it was seen by the Roman people only in an unfinished state, and under extraordinary circumstances.

In these first weeks, at a season when the heat of summer was wont to depopulate the streets, all Rome was living in a state of lively expectation. The queen preferred to have herself carried through the streets by a few servants only, unrecognized and unattended. She knew, of course, that Cæsar was having her watched, but she behaved as though she were ignorant of the fact. While in Alexandria she never gave a thought to the lives of the poor and the slaves, and was hardly aware that she, with all her royal magnificence, was standing on their unnumbered heads, here she inquired into the life of the little man, for here Cæsar's power was dependent upon his vote, or at least upon his mood, which the hostile parties might reverse, or at all events endeavour to reverse.

At such times, when she alighted unobserved in some obscure corner, to loiter, with a single slave, through the more sordid quarters of the capital, how narrow the streets seemed, how crooked, and how hilly! Brick walls that one could not look over, much dirt, and little light; a people rich only in children, huddled together in a stench of decaying refuse. Only three of the streets of Rome were practicable for horses, and since all the traffic was crowded into them, heavily laden wagons were permitted to use them only at night. She could hear them rumbling and thundering as soon as the sun had set; she learned that every night, by the light of flickering torches, loads of marble, and bricks, and timber were tumbled off the carts, and she marvelled at the strength of the nerves of the Romans, who were able to sleep through it all.

How many of all these storehouses had been filled by her own country! Here were linen and glass from Alexandria, herbs and spices from India, and whole warehouses full of writing-paper, whose fibres had all been grown on the Nile! But between all the warehouses—as her father had told her when she was a child—whispered and glided the miracle of

Rome, the water that filled their baths and cisterns, for which they seemed to be always athirst, and which was carried in pipes even to their dinner-tables.

Among the warehouses she saw the homes of impoverished knights, which during the calamities of the civil war had fallen into the hands of enriched adventurers. The wealthiest baker in Rome gave political banquets in his palace, and the conversation at such banquets interested even Cæsar. She learned who was buying goods from Syria and re-selling them to Gaul; who lent money for ransoms, and who really furnished the freeholds with which the ex-legionaries' insatiable hunger for land had to be appeased. She saw the marble palace of the equestrian Marmurra, who was striving to emulate that of Lucullus, and before which were placed, on a feast-day, the thousand long tables at which Cæsar's People's Party had a hundred oxen served up to the electoral societies. Everything seemed to be overcrowded in this hot, feverish Rome; only the temples were deserted.

So in the streets of Rome Cleopatra saw what she had hitherto known but imperfectly and untruly, and what her huntress's nature grasped better through the medium of her eyes and her nose: the tottering of an ancient republic, the sophistication of democracy, the decay of noble principles, everything lapsing into venality, until only a pale shadow of the ideal of equally privileged citizens tempered the will to power of a handful of adventurers. The more she compared these men with Cæsar, the more he gained by the comparison.

Were there still gods in this Rome? So the queen asked herself. Even in her capital, faith had vanished, but there a secret understanding obtained that all should still respect the ancient forms. Here, in the streets of Rome, she found the worship of Mithra beside that of her own Isis, a sort of communion service in honour of the son of the Persian god beside Egyptian processions in which milk was allowed to drip from a gilt breast. Perhaps she may have heard in the theatre the applause that invariably followed the lines of Ennius, which declared that the gods care nothing for our griefs; or she may have been among the audience when a belated survivor of the old Rome shouted at the mummer who related, with a grin, the crimes of Diana: "May the gods vouchsafe you a daughter who commits all these crimes!"

In this mood of decadence a spirit of fatalism was general: the gods would never lift a finger to help their worshippers! The only things one could trust were comets and meteors, earthquakes and unnatural births. Had not Cæsar said in the Senate, speaking as Supreme Pontifex, that death was the end of all things? This was spoken from his heart to the man in the street. Throw yourself like Cæsar into the intoxication of adventure, cried the man in the street; he's the man for feasting and for gold, and if into the bargain he does a bit of conquering for the Republic, one can always prolong his dictatorship! What he manages to mop up he gives back to the people; he is more generous than Pompey, Crassus, and Sulla put together!

How shrewd he was! In this luxurious city he had just introduced a law against luxury, and while he stinted the fashionable women in their gorgeous litters of a tithe of their display of purple silk and pearls, he pleased the artisans by his law, since he lavished games upon them, and even introduced, in the new Circus, crocodiles which he had brought from the

Nile, and men who but yesterday had greeted the death of a gladiator with frantic applause were now stilled by the plaintive trumpeting of the elephants.

Cleopatra returned full of amazement from her wanderings through Rome. Having grown up in a world to which poison and the dagger were familiar, and which was untouched by the influence of Platonism, she was now repelled by the spectacle of a society and a nation that gave their lust for gold and pleasure old names which had no longer any validity, so that all was as though tarnished by a murky breath of imposture. Cæsar seemed to her the only person who shared her own cynical innocence, and if here and today she had met him for the first time she would have learned to love him for this sovereign freedom. Merely because she saw that he was weakened by no doubts he seemed to her a born king, and therefore her mate.

Brutus, however, who had to justify himself before his conscience when he turned his political coat, she hated because of his morality. When on the Capitol they showed her, beside the ancient kings, his ancestor, that Brutus who had overthrown the last King of Rome, she began to dislike the very sight of the Capitol.

IV

But Cæsar's triumph began with an omen at which Cleopatra, who was always looking for omens, trembled.

Slowly his chariot drew nearer, encompassed by the shouting of the mob; she could see his head lifted high above the rest, and while the charioteer curbed the four bay horses, Cæsar gave the Roman salute. In the sunlight his features seemed old and grey, but his naked arm was muscular and rosy. Were not his eyes seeking her on the tribune, where she sat near Calpurnia, Cæsar's wife? Suddenly, when he was distant no more than a hundred paces, she saw him stagger, then leap to the ground. The crowd gathered round him, shouting; the axle of his triumphal car had broken! Messengers ran off, shouting; he had to wait for a second chariot, but in an astonishingly short time another was brought up, and the horses put in.

But as he passed the tribune in the new chariot, and the eyes of thousands were fastened upon his face, his gaze met that of Cleopatra, for whose sake he had postponed this triumph. He laughed. Cæsar laughed up at her, then pointed at the man whose heavy steps were clanking before his chariot, and as his bold, black eyes met hers again he seemed to be calling to her: "Was it the chain of the conquered king that broke? The chariot for me today; for him tomorrow, death!" His look so ravished her that she trod underfoot her premonition of ill, as one treads out a spark.

The delight of the people was endless when that evening forty elephants with torches bound upon their backs followed Cæsar's chariot to the Forum.

Cleopatra's thirst for vengeance was sated only on the day of the second triumph—for Cæsar, who had never yet celebrated a triumph, now organized no less than four within a few days. Of these the second was the Egyptian triumph; and its sole purpose—according to the official interpretation—was to do honour to the lawful queen seated in the tribune, and celebrate the defeat of the opposing party. First her impatient eyes rested on the pictures of her slain enemies, Achillas and Pothinus, as they were carried past her; Achillas and Pothinus, who had once driven her from the throne; then just in front of Cæsar's chariot, which did not break down on this occasion, came Arsinoë, the second of her disloyal sisters. Alas, that the moments fled so fast—that the sight was vouchsafed her for only a few brief minutes! Cleopatra stared after her, savouring her revenge, hardly noticing the mournful giraffes which followed, now shown for the first time to the roaring crowd. Her attention was given wholly to her fettered sister.

Suddenly the image of her uncle in Cyprus rose before her eyes; her uncle, who, when she was a child, had preferred poison to Arsinoë's fate. For the second time in her life, at the age of twenty-four, Cleopatra was conscious of the full meaning of shame and of honour, of triumph and of suicide, and with the somnambulistic premonition of genius she felt, at this moment, the touch of a destiny still remote. She did not hear the impudent songs of the veterans marching in the triumph, which contained allusions to her and to Cæsar, so that the crowd roared with laughter, and Cæsar laughed with them. She saw only the bowed neck of her hated sister, who kept looking at the ground, as though seeking to escape the eyes of the mob. When on the following day Cæsar told her that it would be a wise move to spare Arsinoë's life, she could not understand him. When, finally, on the last day of the triumph, caricatures of Cato were carried in the procession, the queen overheard the indignant whispering of a few patricians who were seated behind her on the tribune. She was glad then that Cæsar today was no longer so wise as yesterday; glad that he had angered the cold and impassive aristocrats; and she was most of all delighted when in the evening he began to harangue the people, for at the close of his solemn triumph he appeared with slippered feet. This disdain of the mob seemed yet another proof of the king in Cæsar. For Cleopatra's statecraft was sometimes overcome by a passionate longing to make sport of everybody—people and magnates, priests and ministers, bakers and armourers—to treat them with disrespect and show them that they were a pack of eunuchs!

The great day for such extravagant moods came early in September, just after the triumphs. Cæsar had built a new temple for the mother of his line, Venus Genetrix, and he consecrated it with popular feasts which outshone all that had preceded them. In the Circus his gladiators fought not only with one another, but also with wild beasts, and to an impoverished Roman knight, the first of his rank to degrade himself by appearing on the stage, he gave a golden ring, thus restoring, after his performance, the dignity which he had forfeited as an actor. He had tragedies performed in every quarter of the city—in four languages, for the benefit of the numerous foreigners—and finally he offered the people the unprecedented spectacle of a naval battle, in which Egyptian ships fought one another on an artificial lake outside the city. In such a tumult of rejoicing was the temple of Venus inaugurated.

But what did the noble Romans behold who attended the ceremony of consecration? The statue of Cleopatra as Venus! To the heads of the Republic Cæsar offered the Queen of Egypt, his mistress, in her divine origin, as she was worshipped in her home. Indeed, in order that he might see this with his own eyes, and show it to others, he even lost his greatest virtue—patience—for the statue was not yet finished, and the lovely model seems to have pleaded with him in vain.

He had affronted all the traditions, whether sacred or profane. Clodius had once set the likeness of a prostitute in front of Cicero's house, to serve as a statue of Liberty, and Pompey's lovely Flora had been the model for the image of a divinity, but what was that compared with this freak of Cæsar's? Today everyone understood—and the majority realized with dismay—what the statue of the deified queen in the temple of Cæsar's family divinity meant! Indeed, to make it plainer he issued a coin among the people on which Venus and Eros could be recognized as Cleopatra with Cæsarion in her arms.

With this graceful conceit, which revealed the poet in him, Cæsar prescribed to the citizens of his capital the manner in which they were to think of his mistress, and hinted at the opinion which they were to hold of his plans. A little later he had a law introduced in the Senate which allowed him, in the Oriental fashion, to marry several wives.

With the mature common sense in which he excelled the youthful queen, he had foreseen the unpleasant results which might follow a divorce, and had therefore chosen this novel means of legitimizing his son by Roman as well as Egyptian law. So, working from above and below, he laid the religious and juridical foundations of his dynasty.

For to found a dynasty of his own blood was now, eighteen months before his death, Cæsar's most heartfelt desire. Before it could be fulfilled he had yet to venture on one great and unique enterprise.

Cleopatra's nervousness increased, and with it her watch-
fulness. The more Cæsar ventured, the higher beat her heart,
but her misgivings increased in proportion. Had Cæsar still
any friends? The distance which divided Cæsar and herself
from Roman society seemed to be rapidly increasing this
autumn. The statue of Venus had offered the malcontents a
welcome grievance. It was now evident that after four Roman
marriages, of which the only issue was a daughter, who had
long been dead, the Dictator had chosen a foreign woman to
be the mother of his race. What more natural than that he
should crown himself the king of this queen? He had already
had himself appointed sole Consul for the year, and at the
same time he had renewed his dictatorship for another year;
so that he had powers which even Sulla had not possessed!
Expectation grew tenser as fear increased, and with expectation a general sense of uncertainty and suspense. There was a
strained expression in men's eyes, and their mood was in-
flamed and irritable: Rome was confronted with the monarchical peril, and was afraid.

And not Rome alone. In Spain all the malcontents among
the soldiery had mustered under the sons of Pompey; so that
four years after its beginning the civil war was still in progress. Suddenly, just as his world-embracing plans were at last
on the verge of realization, the Dictator had to take the field
again, to lead Romans against Romans. This interruption of
all his plans meant a fresh separation from Cleopatra, who

was morally unprotected when Cæsar left Rome. He was wont to conquer his enemies, that she knew. But what if an arrow or javelin found him out? The years had not taught him to spare himself in battle! Was he still strong enough? It was winter; the roads on the slopes of the Apennines were rough; at Thapsus, in his last battle, he had suddenly been seized with cramp. The lovers parted with heavy hearts; the gulf of the generations that lay between them, growing ever deeper with the years, could be bridged, it seemed to them, only when they were together. When they were parted she seemed to him remote and as a figure in a dream; and to her he seemed an old man.

They tried to keep in touch with each other by a network of communications; but they both knew that each had surrounded the other with secret spies, at whose appearance they probably smiled. Might not the lovely queen fascinate some young Roman; might not another princess captivate the great Dictator? For the time being intellectual pursuits appeared to fill his leisure sufficiently, for on the journey to Spain Cæsar wrote the *Anti-Cato*, an attack upon the republican ideology which Cicero had glorified. Then he became the general once more, and plunged into battle.

Meanwhile Cleopatra was fighting for him in Rome. Had Cæsar any friends left? Was he not making a capital mistake in always endeavouring to forget his enemies? The old Pompeians, of whose cold glances the foreign woman had been conscious from the time of their first meeting, quietly drew together, for the upshot of the new civil war was still uncertain; it was allowable for anyone to hope. Cleopatra's agents were everywhere; they listened to the malcontents disputing in the streets, and followed the taciturn into their houses; and the queen had all the popular epigrams explained to her, however racy the vernacular. She was always trying to detect the mood of the popular quarter, and to compare it with that of society.

In society she tried, cautiously, to note the fluctuations of the war spirit. What was Cicero doing and thinking, whose voice was still among the most influential? He had always kept out of the lion's path. Now he congratulated him on his new essay, which was quickly circulated in Rome, in order to exhibit the generosity of a great author to a dilettante general. At the same time he resolved to play the second Aristotle to this second Alexander, and he wrote him a letter, expressing the hope that, like the Greek, he would rule Rome only as the first of her citizens. It was a State document, written, really, for posterity, and for the sake of his posthumous fame, but at the last moment, on the advice of a shrewd financier, the famous author preferred to withhold his historic letter.

Cleopatra knew all this; she knew everything; and what she knew she wrote to Cæsar, who, inquisitive as all dictators, diverted himself in the field with the gossip of the capital. She knew that Brutus was constantly taking counsel with his brother-in-law Cassius. And what were their two wives planning, who still seemed to live in the shadow of Cæsar's sometime mistress, Servilia?

When Cassius entered the villa beyond the Tiber—for it was now too cold to sit in the garden—Cassius, with his sharp features, his resolute voice—their eyes met, and flashed, and met again. This iron man would perhaps have pleased Cleopatra, and the lissom Greek would surely have fired his senses had not the shadow of Cæsar fallen between them—of Cæsar, for whom she was fighting an invisible battle, for she had long known that Cassius hated him. And really the lions were to blame for this hatred. When the Greek city of Megara, after Cæsar's victory at Pharsalus, had refused to open its gates to his legate, so that the catapults got to work, the famine-stricken citizens finally released a pair of lions which Cassius had brought from Africa some time before, and had left there, intending that they should finally fight, in his name, in the Roman circus. But now Cæsar's officials declared that the recaptured lions were their property, and refused to surrender them. Cassius held their master responsible; how dared this consul, this Cæsar, steal the symbol of power from him—from him, who had rescued the fragments of the Roman army in Persia while Cæsar was aimlessly sacrificing thousands in Gaul! He would never forgive him!

Once more a forgotten enemy! thought Cleopatra, as she noticed Cassius, who was standing against a pillar. Another Pompeian too promptly pardoned! When he was serving under Pompey did he not burn, at Messina, thirty ships of Cæsar's fleet? Besides, she thought, his eyes are eloquent of his jealousy. Doesn't Cæsar see it? Doesn't he want to see it? To all these young men he seems too old to possess so much; one grudges him his young mistress, another his son, a third his lions! And they all have the same look in their eyes when the liberty of the citizen is mentioned. Formerly, when Pompey was in command here, they were all enthusiasm for their Dictator, who trod this same liberty underfoot; indeed, this Cassius had even fought against Cæsar at Pharsalus! A pack of turncoats, whom he received again after the victory! If he had only destroyed them all, instead of becoming reconciled to them, he would not be fighting again today! That his plans for ordering the world tomorrow make him forget his enemies of yesterday—that he lives too swiftly to hate—in short, that he is not revengeful—that is the only failing that distinguishes him from us kings and queens!

Now she saw Cassius approaching a tall man of some forty years, whom she distrusted as much as she distrusted Cassius: Decimus Brutus, the other Brutus, now quite a favourite of Cæsar, who had made him an admiral, young though he was, for on the voyage to Britain, and later, in battle against the Veneti, he was said to have fought magnificently. Twice had Cæsar appointed this brilliant officer, who, of course, had always been of his party, to be governor of Gaul, and by so doing had enabled him to make millions. So what could there be suspicious about him? Nothing but his increasing arrogance. Cleopatra had once caught the glance with which he had followed Cæsar as the latter passed by him. It was a glance full of disparaging criticism, and the scornful little twitch of the lips that had followed this glance, though it lasted only a second, had revealed to Cleopatra his hatred of Cæsar, while it increased her own hatred of him, for she could not avenge herself on one of Cæsar's favourites.

Now, however, her gaze was withdrawn from the group of men, for a tall, proud-looking, black-haired woman was approaching her, seeming, as she did so, to assume a more than ever rigid bearing. This was Octavia, Cæsar's great-niece, whom the queen detested as much as she disliked her younger brother Octavian, the youth with the bad complexion and the cold eyes. The woman began to discuss yesterday's contest, and when Cleopatra laughed at the recollection of the rhinoceros which had spitted the criminal, the pious Octavia covered her eyes with her hand. In the meantime each of the two women wondered whether the other was not older than she, whether black or brown hair was really the more attractive, and what exactly it was in the other that attracted the men. Everything about "the Egyptian," as her friends called her, was alien to the self-righteous Octavia, and everything about Octavia was repugnant to Cleopatra; and yet their feelings were quite different.

Upstairs, in the reception-rooms, they asked each other, with factitious smiles, for the latest news from the Spanish front.

VI

When the victorious Cæsar returned in the spring, it seemed to his lover that the skies were cloudless. He had annihilated the enemy in the battle of Munda, and he seemed like a man refreshed. She had heard of the beginnings of a love-affair with the wife of a Mauretanian king. If what she had heard was the truth, he must have forgotten the foreign woman quickly, for if a gloomy lover had left her in the winter, the man who returned to her now was as though rejuvenated. There must have been hot fighting at Munda, for one of his confidants told her afterwards that Cæsar had stridden on ahead of his wavering cohorts, but in the evening he had said, quietly: "I have often fought to win a victory; today I was fighting for my life."

But the great event of which the Forum and Roman society were full on Cæsar's return was not his victory, which was accepted as the usual thing, but his reconciliation with Antony.

Cleopatra had heard much of Antony in Rome; amongst other things, that during the last few weeks he had turned from the moderate party of the Cæsarians to the active left wing, thereby depriving these eternal malcontents of their last excuse for remaining faithful to the constitution. Antony —so Cleopatra may have thought—was like a complaining mistress, who sides with the critics of her lover as long as he is present, but when he has gone to the wars again, and those who sit safely at home have begun to find fault with all he does, a moment comes when she can no longer endure his absence, and one day she runs after him and throws herself into his arms. In the two campaigns which Cæsar had fought against the Pompeians, Antony had held aloof; every dispatch had excited him; if he was told of an officer's blunder, he knew that it was one which he would have avoided; and he could not bear to watch Cæsar's triumph, for he ought to have been riding close behind him! But now, what with the last great victory at Munda, and yet another victorious homecoming, it was too much for Antony! He had ridden forth to meet the homeward-bound Cæsar, remembering the day when he met him out on the Rubicon, when they began the great adventure of their lives together—and now all Rome was telling how Cæsar had taken him into his wagon, and had journeyed with him for a whole day.

The solitary, ageing Cæsar, who saw clearly enough that the crazy Dolabellas who followed him had no love for him, was no less a gainer than Antony by this reconciliation. Antony won back the only man who could have his unstable character from disaster; Cæsar won a friend.

When he spoke of this to the queen he watched her tensely, to see how she accepted the statement from his lips; but all his doubts were dispelled. Though in the floating palace on the Nile he had been vaguely jealous of the absent friend, and had traced this jealousy back into years long past, now made stronger by his new fame, the Dictator, his power for the first time undisputed, felt that his mere presence was enough to overcome any rival. Moreover, he could not separate the only two persons whom he trusted; he felt that he must bring them together, and he did so.

It was spring once more when the two men went to meet the queen beyond the Tiber, midway down the cypress avenue that led from the gates to the villa. All three were deeply moved.

Cæsar embraced her slender form with the unreserved gaze of the possessor. He felt that his happiness was enhanced by the adulation of his younger companion. Owing to the fatherly affection that he cherished for Antony, he believed that the latter would regard his adventure with filial respect; at the same time, he took pleasure in the thought of his extraordinary situation, and he felt how little hold age had upon him. He was so confident that he even forgot to watch the man and woman before him.

Antony saw before him simply the woman whom he had contrived, on every opportunity, to gaze at from a distance, and often more closely than she was aware; but whose long, slender hand he touched for the first time today, whose glance and smile and fragrance he could now at last drink in. Ten years ago, at the banquet-table of the king, her father, she had been fourteen, and he was too full-blooded not to prefer the woman of twenty-four that she was today. But while he was conscious of her merely as a woman, it never occurred to him that he, who had possessed so many women, might try his luck with this one. Just as in Cæsar's presence he could never have modified any order of his, so that presence today was a sufficient command that he must honour the woman who belonged to Cæsar.

Cleopatra, whose charm a moment later had restored her two guests to their normal mood, was the only one of these three persons to see and understand the other two, because in the supreme moments of sexual tension she forgot herself —as she had forgotten herself on the day when she rose from the unrolled carpet. In a flash her wakeful senses compared the virility of the two men whose four eyes were fixed upon her.

The handsome captain of long ago had now a more debonair expression. He was a man of thirty-eight years, more of a Hercules than ever, his head was covered with curls, and his full cheeks were framed by a brown beard; he was visibly sure of himself, and on the best of terms with gods and men. All that part of herself that was, in fact, the survival of her ancestors, the part that now and again sought to slip the yoke, felt itself drawn, in the presence of this lusty male, to such delights as could hitherto tempt her, until she drove them away, only in the heat of summer. But the other man, tall and thin, whose bony frame had so little power of awakening lust—this man whose skin was tanned and weathered by years of campaigning, whose spare cheeks, hard chin, and prominent nose looked as though their touch would bruise one—from this man, bald as he was, and twenty years older than the other, there seemed to flow such imperative power, and he seemed to possess, in the place of lustful instincts, so mighty a generative impulse, that the woman's intuitive mind, in spite of all its innate curiosity, could not for a moment be in doubt. Of these two men she felt that it was he who was the king.

In these few moments Cæsar had unwittingly won the greatest of his victories, a victory over his friend and his mistress, over the man and the woman of his choice.

VII

But this new friend had a wife of his own, and Fulvia the queen could not endure. She could not understand how a mere burgess's daughter could aim at sovereignty, and while her own ambition, amidst the conspiracies of the pretenders, had raised her to the throne, and in the last two years had enticed her in the direction of a power whose scope would be unlimited, her sense of royalty lifted her so high above all other people that for her the citizen and the slave were equally remote and alien. Cæsar she regarded as the one exception, but he, after all, reckoned his descent from Venus. Why, in this republic, did all the old families make such a boast of their antiquity? They were all related, these so-called great Roman houses, just as their most prominent members, men and women, had all intermarried, divorcing each other and contracting new political marriages. Now that she had been a year in Rome it was not the immorality all about her that astonished the queen, but rather the fact that almost all love-affairs were decided by money, and all divorces by party interests.

In Fulvia, to quote an ancient writer, there was really nothing feminine apart from her body. "Her ambition was to govern those that governed, and to command the leaders of armies." Nevertheless, she had no attraction for cold, ambitious men of her own stamp; she had married three libertines in succession, and now, the mother of four children, the offspring of these three marriages, she was no more than midway through the twenties. Whether her first or her second husband had been the more vicious was a question for society gossips; Durio, at all events, the bosom friend of Antony, lost a fortune to his friend, and then his wife into the bargain; but Antony had married her only after Dolabella, the third of the boon companions, had deprived him of his own wife, Antonia. All such matters had decisive results, for the man who had influential connexions by marriage found it easier to become ædile or consul, and the man who had been divorced or betrayed voted in the Senate with the enemies of his enemy.

The deeper the queen probed into the party politics of Rome the greater the contempt she felt for the origin of a power that was based upon the ballot, and had to be continually repurchased by bribery and inheritance, marriage, divorce, and adoption. Everything tended to link her own policy directly to Cæsar's overthrow of the constitution and assumption of kingship.

Yet she was too shrewd to trust anyone but Cæsar. She accepted the friendship of Antony, even of Fulvia, because they both hated Cæsar's enemies, and distrusted the men and women who had seemed to her suspect, when his new friends were still resentful of Cæsar, and therefore of her. Now she saw that her instinct was justified; she learned that Antony hated Cicero because Cicero had sentenced his mother's second husband to death; and further, the great moralist had slept with Tiro, his favourite slave.

When one evening Cæsar had told her of Antony's dissolute revels—how on the morrow of the marriage-feast of Hippias the comedian he had vomited during his address to the people in the Forum, how on another occasion he had sent singing-women to sing outside the houses of virtuous families, and waken them out of sleep by their unchaste songs—the Dionysian hero of these stories pleased her a hundred times better than Cicero and Brutus—and she told Cæsar as much. Cæsar, of course, smiled, adding in a fatherly tone that Brutus was a profound philosopher, and that Antony had led the left wing to victory at Pharsalus. But Octavian, his nephew, he never mentioned, for he had read the queen's aversion in her silence, and as a nobleman he was resolved to protect his family from criticism, even from hers.

But now, before his eyes, and in accordance with his desire, a new family had come into being, and when the queen saw his gaze resting on the boy, who now, in his third year, as an ancient author tells us, was "ridiculously like" his father, she knew what his plans were, even though party questions might seem to take precedence of them. In the shadow of the hundred intrigues that surrounded her, who was set by Cæsar's sheltering hand on an island that none could reach—spied upon by curious eyes, protected by her one friend—in this second year of her Roman life Cleopatra was growing more arrogant. Her villa and her garden were seldom open to visitors;

the stranger received by Roman society had become a queen surrounded by her court; Cicero, in his letters, called her simply "the queen."

In her expectation of Cæsar's overthrow of the constitution, for there was now nothing to prevent it, she had made away with the last formal obstacle to her marriage. We can prove nothing, but the fact remains that her brother, the young Ptolemy, disappeared about this time, apparently in the autumn of her second year. He would assuredly never have facilitated the marriage of his lawful wife by divorcing her; he would rather have led the party of her Roman and Egyptian enemies. Why spare him? He had never been her husband; her childhood was already past when he was born, twelve years later than his sister; his mother was unknown, his father was a monster, and there was no such thing as family affection among the Ptolemies; so what should prevent Cleopatra from doing away with the boy who stood in her path? The fact that he was her brother? But what moral law should have deterred her, since the gods of Greece and Egypt, on whose legends she had been reared, had been wont to kill their blood relations as readily as the Roman patricians in whose midst she was now living?

Ptolemy disappeared. Cleopatra's path lay open before her.

Yet there stood a shadow between these two, though they might seem destined to rise to the dazzling summit of mortal happiness. It was the shade of Alexander. Cæsar resolved to follow it.

Ever since his youth he had seen in Alexander his only pattern, but everything about him was legendary and inimitable. In Rome one was elected Consul, together with a colleague, perhaps a few times in succession, but always for only a year. What could a man do in one brief year! If one conquered a province, or even three, as Cæsar had done, one remained there for a few years as proconsul, but sooner or later the central government turned one out. Had Sulla been omnipotent, or Pompey? Had not the parties ground them down? No Alexander could spring up in a republic.

Only when the long civil war had subordinated the citizens to the soldiers, and the laws to the arbitraments of battle— when the victory of Pharsalus had lifted Cæsar higher than any Roman potentate before him—could he begin to weave the romantic longings of the youth into the policy of the ageing Dictator. In these three years he had rapidly approached the achievements of Alexander. It was on the Nile, beside Alexander's tomb. and in the floating palace on the Nile, that the spirit of the Macedonian had seemed to come to him and call upon him to complete what he had but begun at Pharsalus. The thought of Alexander's desert ride to the oracle of Amon had filled him with a sense of exaltation, and had shown the sceptic what was possible even in his enlightened age. The founding of the capital at the westernmost point of an Oriental empire was confirmed by the example of Rome, whose situation, almost against his will, had hitherto always driven him northwards.

His most receptive season had been passed, and his first battles fought, in the camp of King Nicomedes, as whose darling he was still derided, now that he was old. What wonder that now, towards the end of his career, the South had seized upon him again, with all the embellished memories of his first youth—the South, the spirit of the Mediterranean, the warmth and the blue skies that seemed to caress the mind and the limbs of the bald-headed, haggard old soldier, healing him and bringing back his youth! On the Nile, in the most luxurious country in the world, he had asked himself, in astonishment, why he had wasted the best decades of his life in Teutonic forests; why he had lived amongst the barbarous peoples of the Alps, and fought the sullen Britons in the isle of mists. For down in the South were Ephesus and Tarsus, glittering, and blessed by the grace of the ancient gods; the sun-steeped islands cooled their arms in a gentle sea; Crete and Cyprus, Antioch and Athens, invited the foreign conqueror to a feast of wit and intellect, invited him to taste of a riper civilization instead of making a parade of his austerity. Alexander and the Mediterranean were calling the old soldier eastwards.

For no rest is vouchsafed to the conqueror. The valiant warrior who in his youth heaps victory upon victory and conquers nations does not go unpunished; the shadows of his victories follow him as women followed Don Juan; they will not let him grow old quietly in a peaceful community. Having founded his power upon the sword, he must draw it again and again, since the world demands constant repetition from its heroes. If he wished to win a crown, to found, like Alexander, a world-empire and a dynasty, now, when he was nearing his sixtieth year, his old victories would no longer suffice. The Republic, he felt, would sacrifice its last liberties only to fresh victories; would surrender itself only to the conqueror of Persia, just as in the old legends the virgin who was all but conquered continued to exact from her hero the most perilous adventures.

For Persia, the scene of Alexander's triumph, was also the great and eternally unconquered rival of Rome, the only rival which the omnipotent Latin republic had to suffer once Carthage had fallen. For half a century now campaign had followed on campaign; Sulla and Pompey were victorious for a time. Lucullus and Crassus were slain. There were ten thousand people living in Rome who had had to suffer the death or slavery of their kinsmen at the time of the last catastrophe; it was barely eight years ago. Old Crassus had allowed Pompey's triumph to go to his head; and with only forty thousand men he had attempted to conquer the Persian Empire. He saw his son's head carried before him, transfixed on the point of a lance, by the victorious enemy, and he too fell at last, contemptuous of death. But the eagles and the standards had remained in Persia, with the bodies of the slain, and since that day he who thought to win the people's favour must plan a war of revenge against the Asiatic foe.

Only the civil war in their own country could have interrupted these preparations. Today, since Cæsar alone was left, the people expected of him the very task that he, in the depth of his heart, was longing to take upon himself. At the same time the shrewd calculator perceived his advantage, for despite all the glory of his Spanish conquest, his legions were still unpaid, and these legendary countries were said to be overflowing with gold; for India bordered upon Persia, and India in those days was held to be a sort of fairyland. Motives of every kind—political, romantic, dynastic—were pointing out the road to Persia, the hereditary foe of Rome.

As a general, Cæsar had carefully studied the reasons why Crassus had failed. Crassus had been intimidated by the rumour of the gigantic bow, from which the Persians discharged their arrows at a range never yet attained; they met him on a forced march, which seemed as if it would never end, for month after burning month the enemy withdrew farther and farther into his boundless territory. Cæsar, whose most recent campaigns had lasted only a few months, now allowed himself three whole years, for the goal of his vast plans was not the Euphrates, nor yet India. After subduing Alexander's East he intended to march through Hyrcania, to the Caspian Sea, crossing the Caucasus into the land of the Scythians, whose neighbours were the Germans; then, attacking the Germans themselves, he would return home by way of Gaul, so that the Roman Empire would then be bounded only by the ocean. For such stupendous purposes he began to accumulate a store of gold, acquired by the sale of land; he established great armouries in all the Mediterranean ports; and presently the whole of Italy was once more astir. But no one was busier than Cæsar himself, for this plan of world-empire taxed his highest faculties to the utmost. In this connexion Plutarch speaks, in his wonderful style, of Cæsar's "jealousy of himself, a contest with himself (as eager as if it had been with another man) to make his future achievements outshine his past."

Cleopatra watched him with astonishment, and with misgiving. If it was his plan to found his dynasty on his world-empire, instead of the converse, the most intrepid of women, once the Amazon had become a mother, might well fear a thousand dangers. She knew that it was idle to question Cæsar, and precisely because he trusted her as he trusted no one else, she dared not seek to tie him down to a definite statement. She knew what he was aiming at; he was thinking of the crown, and of Cæsarion; yet there were times when it seemed to her that he had not yet come to a decision as to the sequence of his future actions.

And at this time there was something that the Romans regarded with astonishment and misgiving: a flood of orders from Cæsar's cabinet, flowing forth into the farthest provinces. Had he a premonition that this year was to be his last? Or was it merely that he felt that, having conquered the last of the Pompeians, he could now, for the first time, rule as a monarch, obedient only to his own conceptions? He seemed to be possessed by a quite unwonted impatience, which was urging him to take everything into his own hands: finances, reforms, reconstruction, and the world-war. One morning the Romans learned that Cæsar was planning to intercept the Anio and the Tiber, just outside the city, by deep canals, and so to divert their course that they would flow into the sea at Terracina. Another morning it was said in Rome that Cæsar intended to drain the marshes about Pontinum and Setia, thereby creating fertile soil for thousands. On a third morning it was reported that Cæsar meant to build over the whole of the Campus Martius, and also to erect, on the Tarpeian Rock, a theatre more splendid than that of Pompey. During the following weeks Varro was commissioned to establish libraries in every quarter of the capital, containing books in many languages. At the same time Cæsar instructed certain engineers to draw up the plans of a new Roman port at Ostia; the sea would be held in check by breakwaters, docks would be built, and all the dangerous invisible reefs and shoals would be levelled.

But his mind was ranging far beyond Rome; he was making the most gigantic plans. He was planning a compilation of all the laws—the first *corpus juris*—and also a great road across the Apennines. His eye fell upon the Peloponnesus; he resolved to pierce the isthmus of Corinth and to rebuild the city; it rested on conquered Africa, and he decided to resuscitate Carthage, because it had been destroyed when Corinth had fallen. What could not be accomplished in this one long year! The Egyptian astronomers who came at Cleopatra's bidding to devise a new calendar had vouchsafed the ruler of the world a year of fifteen months, so that they might fall into step with the sun, and end the temporal chaos of the last hundred years. In order to construct a new calendar for the thousands of years to come—the calendar which we possess today—Cæsar made the last year of his life the longest of all years. It was as though history was unwilling to part with him.

IX

But if all these things were born of a creative imagination, they were also the offspring of his political wisdom. Only because he combined imagination with statecraft was he Cæsar. He proposed to give bread to tens of thousands of unemployed workers by ordering them to erect great public buildings for themselves. Freedmen and artisans of every kind flocked to his colours, to fight in the coming year, and also to work on his building schemes. He exacted a forced loan from the cities; he nationalized all duties; he passed a law compelling the rich to buy land of the State so that he could pay three hundred sesterces to each of the forty thousand legionaries to whom he had promised land and money before the battle of Pharsalus; but since he was a king he added a hundred sesterces as interest.

And all this money did not really exist! It might be in Persia, perhaps in India. Since at the end of this, as at the end of every civil war, no one was contented, but all were conscious, despite their relief, of a certain disappointment, the victor was driven to make fresh conquests, and the more of a monarch he became, the more zealous he appeared to be to win such popular favour as no longer seemed to be needful once he bore a crown on his head. Cleopatra, as she watched and marvelled, could not determine whether he made all these plans because he held the people in affection, or because he despised them.

A new and final triumph, in celebration of his victory in

Spain, had alienated many, even among the people, for the victory was a victory of Romans over Romans. After Pharsalus, when he found himself in a similar position, Cæsar had forborne to hold a public triumph. Rome was beguiled with a banquet at which twenty-two thousand tables were laid, and at which, for the first time, Italian wines were provided, followed by such gladiatorial combats and games as had never been seen; but this time he allowed five thousand real soldiers to appear in the enlarged circus, and after them men of prætorian rank fought to the death, and finally the sons of princes from Asia Minor danced a war-dance. While Roman society was still feeling perturbed by such signs of arrogance, Cæsar declared an amnesty for all Pompeian veterans, and restored their confiscated estates to their sons and widows; indeed, in one of the temples he set up a statue of Pompey, his great enemy, whom he had but now finally conquered in the persons of his sons. This was such a noble inspiration that even Cicero wrote that by setting up this statue Cæsar had established his one firm foothold.

It was just these inspirations of his that astonished the queen. In her cynical innocence she, who since her childhood had practised the hereditary method of protecting her life by revenging herself on her enemies, began more than ever to fear for her friend when she saw him persist in forgiving his enemies. What—when he set out upon his great campaign, did he mean to leave all these malcontents in the rear, these men who came flocking to him only by reason of their greed for gold and position? Was it possible that he should appoint this Brutus and this Cassius prætors, instead of dispatching them, at the very least, to the remotest provinces as proconsuls? Cleopatra resolved to warn Cæsar. Not through Antony, for he would have blurted out the warning, bungling the whole matter.

It was on one of those winter evenings which Cæsar, a year ago, would probably have spent in solitude, shivering in his Spanish camp, so that this year it pleased him to enjoy them all the more frequently in the villa beyond the Tiber.

After the din and bustle of the day, after the hundred faces, servile or bold, watchful or pleading, which had passed before his eyes, he found himself longing for the sound of her voice, the golden-brown glance of her eyes, which no longer flashed when the evening had come, but only shone; for the refinement of her dress and her perfume, her lamps and her divans; and when he had seen his son for a moment there was an interval of rest and silence, which he seemed to inhale in slow, deep-drawn breaths. Even on this occasion she waited a long while before she spoke her warning, choosing her words coolly as she sat in her chair before his reclining figure. In its cold objectivity this warning would have sounded like a military dispatch had it not been spoken in her voice.

He heard her unmoved; it was then, perhaps, that he uttered the words which Cicero and Appian have cited as spoken by him at some time during these last months: "I have lived too long already. Better die once for all than be always waiting for death."

Yet such words only expressed such a mood of depression as must from time to time come over one whom singularity seeks to ransom from time and death. We may conclude, from his confidence in Cleopatra, that he then roughly outlined the dangers that threatened him. Or did he suddenly

leap to his feet with the agility of a youth, to tell her of a conspiracy in which he himself had taken part as a young man,
together with Crassus and two other friends? They were going to enter the Senate-house, armed with daggers, and at a
signal they would kill all the senators whose names were on a
certain list; the signal was to be given by Cæsar, who would
fling his toga from his shoulder, baring his breast. Crassus
was to have been Dictator, and Cæsar commander of the cavalry. But at the last moment the cowardly Crassus was afraid
to come!

On a second occasion the conspiracy was against himself!
And Cæsar told her how at a later date, at the time of the
Catiline conspiracy, he had spoken, in the same Senate, against
the sentence of death which Cicero had demanded. A few
infuriated senators had rushed at him, sword in hand, and the
unarmed man had been saved only by the action of those who
stood beside him, who threw themselves in the way of his
assailants. It was long before he entered the Senate again. All
this he told her only to make her understand that no one was
better acquainted with such tricks than he; there was no need
to warn him.

The queen was silent. She could allege nothing against
these men beyond her instinct, which often hit the mark
sooner than did a man's thoughts.

When Cæsar was alone again—perhaps while he was still
on his way home from the villa—he recalled to mind, in his
soldier's fashion, the face, the character, the past history of
each of the three men whom the queen regarded as suspect.
Cassius? He has done excellent work during the last three
years. The burning of the ships was a master-stroke. He's too

pale, and too close with Cicero, that's true. And evidently resentful because I am not more intimate with him. But is that a reason for discarding one of the few men of any independence? He'll be prætor next year. Then, Decimus Brutus! He has stood the test of twenty years. Never loses his head; he was still shouting orders to the men when the waves swept over him on the British coast. Indispensable as a commander, second only to Antony; what's more, he's never drunk. A born consul. Already on the list!

And Brutus? That she doesn't understand. Curious! Perhaps a belated jealousy? She wasn't yet born when Brutus's mother and I . . . She's just too young to understand. What it means to think he may be my son, when I felt deeply for his mother, and yet not to know for certain that he is—she's still too passionate to understand. Cornelia—she was my first youth; Brutus's mother was my second; Cleopatra is my third. The convulsions are more frequent. At any moment one might fall dead. . . .

X

During the last months of winter the queen's uneasiness was intensified. The more restless Cæsar grew, the greater were her alternations of hope and fear. The prize for which they were both playing was no less than the world; and almost the only adversary was Cæsar's age. Could a man near the end of his sixth decade conquer the world, companioned by a woman of five-and-twenty, for a son just learning to speak? Was his creative energy still great enough to overcome his uncertain health, the jealousy of the staff, the resentment of the defeated, and the hardships of a tropical campaign? When Cæsar saw the densely thatched brown and raven polls of his officers, and compared with them his own bald head, as seen in the mirror, or in imagination, it seemed to him that he was the oldest man in Rome, and all around him was youth, whose hair and teeth, whose elastic step and slow, deep breathing he could not, with all his omnipotence, recover for himself. And when his long fingers lingered on the brown curls of his mistress, or stroked the soft, silken head of his son, he must have held it against Zeus that only the gods can renew their youth eternally.

What he was venturing now was more audacious than Alexander's feat, because he was undertaking it so late in life. In vain he looked for other examples, for a predecessor nearer to himself in years; there was only the one, whom he, as the second, must follow. No one was urging this dictator, who after thirty years of preparation had at last attained to monarchical power, to bring the dishonoured Roman standards home from the Euphrates. Now he might rule in Rome for the twenty years of his old age, protected by his troops, unimperilled by external enemies; he could marry his queen and educate his son, and a submissive Senate, in an imaginative moment, might confer the kingly title upon him and his posterity.

But the Alexander-dream was stronger; it was stronger because two human beings had dreamed it. For here was no sly, foreign ruler seeking to seduce the Roman potentate by her charms in order to become a still greater queen. Here, he knew well, was a woman whose mystical longings reached

out toward the stars, though at the same time she was resolute to drain the cup of every earthly pleasure. Both had
been steeped in their youth in the legends of their people;
the Greek studies which had inspired both Cæsar and Cleopatra, in years of childhood passed on different shores of the
same Mediterranean, were deeply rooted in their hearts, and
to both of them Fame seemed a messenger of the gods.

But all this did not affect their objective statecraft, and on
a lower emotional plane both reckoned up exactly their profit
from their alliance and their conquests. Cæsar knew by what
percentage the Egyptian fleet and the treasure of the Ptolemies would strengthen him in his Persian enterprise. But the
world-historical aspect which the dream of his youth had assumed in a ripened intellect was urging him to fulfil his destiny and hers in the grand style that was prescribed for them
by the astonishing nature of their meeting and its results. For
Persia was now no longer a mere province; it was the great
symbol of the Eastern world, which was now to fall into the
hands of the West, and only then would the kingly title acquire its mythical power. Cæsar, shaping his life as an artist,
was making the winning of the crown a difficult achievement.

The fact that he was about to imperil the crown yet further by a three-year campaign was bound to alarm Cleopatra,
both as queen and as mother. While he was alive she had far
more than a treaty of alliance in her hands; she had the great
pledge, the boy, by virtue of whose existence he meant to
make himself immortal. She had no occasion to fear his in-
constancy in love; he was too old for infidelity, and she was
too beautiful. But between the going forth and the returning
of his armies were the whizzing of a thousand long Persian

arrows, the waters of a hundred rivers; fevers rose from the steaming marshes; and then there were the conspiracies at home. The universal hostility that surrounded her, which she had seen increasing for the last eighteen months, the jealousy of former collaborators, the network of envy on which the women politicians were at work, the general resentment of the younger generation—which in this cynical age knew nothing of reverence—at having to serve a spirit that towered above them, and the occasional marks of decay in Cæsar's countenance—all this went to nourish her doubt as to whether it would still be possible to reach the great goal.

That he recognized Cæsarion as his son all Rome was aware, but there was no documentary proof of his paternity. To her this would have meant more than a Roman marriage, for Cæsar was her husband in Egyptian law. Last winter he had drafted a bill which would allow him to marry several wives; but it had not yet become law. Was this carelessness? she might have asked herself. Were there political reasons which had inhibited the two intentions? She did not know that in these last weeks Cæsar had reopened his testament, and had modified it by a codicil in which he adopted his great-nephew Octavian as his son.

This codicil, whose historical consequences Cæsar could not have foreseen, can only have been conceived in view of the possibility of sudden death—in war, or as a result of his convulsive malady; it betrays merely the forethought of a wealthy private citizen, who in this unpolitical testament divides his personal estate, and the designs of a powerful individual who wishes to provide for his family the possibility of serving the State in eminent positions. It was the left hand that Cæsar held out to his past, to his family, to his fellow-Romans, and his compeers; the right hand pointed to the future, grasping at a crown that was never intended for his great-nephew. Cleopatra could not be mentioned in a will that was valid only for the interval before marriage and coronation. For what power and position could a Roman dictator without a heritable empire devise to a wealthy Queen of Egypt? She was mentioned in only one clause, and then not by name: Cæsar appointed several guardians for a possible second son, who might be posthumous. What other woman could be his mother, seeing that the ageing Calpurnia had never borne children? The whole document was one of those testaments whose seal the testator himself hopes to break.

What dispositions could Cæsar have made as regards the succession? He had recently had himself appointed consul for a term of ten years; this was an innovation in Roman history; but it abolished half the kingly power by omitting the title, and completely excluded the other half, the succession. As the Roman people, since the expulsion of the old kings, had nourished an actual superstition against the monarchy, and as, none the less, everything was urging it on towards the monarchy, someone hit upon an abstruse expedient. Some ingenious individual declared that he had discovered a passage in the Sibylline Books to the effect that Persia could be conquered only by a king. It was therefore decided that Cæsar should be raised to the throne in all parts of the Empire, but that in Italy the name and the emblems of kingship should be prohibited. The only thing of which no one dared to speak was—the succession.

And could he, who was about to enter upon a campaign

that would probably continue for years, have any wish to leave behind him in Rome a foreign queen, so that she might rule in his stead, and require the people to bow down to her son as the heir to the throne, even before they had played for the people the prelude to the new dynasty? Would not the foreign woman, as a lonely regent, have intensified all that resentment on the part of the genuine Romans which must in any case have followed the formal end of the Republic? Yet it was not possible to postpone the Persian war; the preparations had been carried too far, the general tension was too great, and the enemies at home had become too powerful.

Cæsar did not know, though the queen suspected, that these internal enemies were beginning to close their ranks, or he would not, in these last weeks, have exasperated them still further. Yet he did so, inasmuch as he showed himself, adopting in all respects the fashions of Cleopatra, as the king which he would not yet declare himself to be. Now he had coins minted that bore his profile; on a festive occasion he rode in an Egyptian chariot, with a crown of golden laurel-leaves on his bald head; he accepted a golden chair in the Senate, and even a statue on the Capitol beside those of the seven ancient kings.

At the same time, under the influence of his Egyptian model, he had his bust set up in the Pompa Circensis, amidst the images of the gods; a resplendent couch was made ready for him in the great temple, and in public prayers the "Genius of Cæsar" was invoked. Like Alexander, he was granted the privilege of burial within the city. In these last weeks he was like a man who is still parted, by a dividing wall, from the woman he has long wooed, and is unable to sleep.

He was surrounded by a thousand grudging enemies, who noted with satisfaction that the most lucid and most patient of potentates had at last become capricious and arrogant. Every day the Romans had some new story to tell one another. On one occasion he appointed a handful of unknown individuals to the Senate—they were actually Gauls—on another he conferred important offices on the sons of proscripts. Another time he said that Sulla was a fool to relinquish the dictatorship. And on a fourth occasion he declared: "My word is sufficient; it is law. The Republic exists only in name." And when a people's tribune failed to rise to his feet as Cæsar passed, he rebuked him in public.

But when the whole Senate, together with the consuls and prætors, approached him to offer him the life dictatorship, he himself remained seated. This behaviour created a profound sensation, and many of the senators left the hall. According to Plutarch's account he attempted to rise to his feet, but was held back by Balbus, who said: "Will you not remember that you are Cæsar, and suffer them to pay their court to you as their superior?" It is a fact that he immediately had himself carried to his own house and, baring his neck, he cried: "Now anyone who so desires may cut my throat!" He even put forward his fits as an excuse: "In my condition one cannot retain one's composure if one has to address an assembly on one's feet; one suffers from giddiness and spasms, and loses consciousness."

With tense anxiety, and sometimes with alarm, Cleopatra noted these uncertain gestures. She could but regard them as symptoms of failing vitality, for it was precisely his sovereign self-confidence that had formerly lent them such flexibility.

If she questioned Antony, the one man she trusted, she received only a brusque soldierly reply. For Antony was flourishing in his master's favour; in this last winter it was Antony who enjoyed Cæsar's fullest confidence, and he alone had access to all the Dictator's plans for the coming war. He was even appointed joint consul with Cæsar; his brothers were elected, respectively, prætor and people's tribune, and when his friends rifled the State treasury Cæsar said nothing. For Antony, Cæsar's *coup d'état* could not come too soon; he even tried to provoke it. For in February the monarchical crisis was intensified by three incidents:

Once, when Cæsar was making a solemn progress through the streets, and certain of the bystanders hailed him as king, he replied: "I am not king, I am Cæsar!" On another occasion, when he found that his statues had been adorned with royal diadems, and that the people's tribunes had removed them, he deposed one of the tribunes, calling him, scornfully, the new Brutus, because the old Brutus had overthrown the monarchy; and also a Cumæan, which was to say, an ass.

On the third occasion he sat on a golden throne in the Forum in order to watch the young men racing through the streets at the pastoral festival of the Lupercalia: an ancient observance, when the men struck at one another with thongs of hide with the hair left upon it. Antony, who was always delighted to play a new part, joined the young men, half naked and equipped with a tail; and taking a diadem wreathed with laurel, he ran with the rest. When he came to Cæsar's throne he held the diadem up to him, and hailed him as Lupercus, a sort of Jupiter Amon, and as king; but perhaps as king merely of the festival. Whether this was an inspiration on the part of the Dionysian Antony, or whether it was done according to agreement, the fact is that the onlookers of Cæsar's party clapped their hands, but the myriad-minded people looked on and was silent. Thereupon Cæsar refused the wreath—or was it a crown?—and at this the people applauded him. Antony offered it a second time, and Cæsar, again amidst the general applause, repeated his gesture of refusal. But then he had the diadem taken to the Capitol, and he caused it to be written in the calendar that on this day Cæsar had twice refused the crown.

All these proceedings must have filled Cleopatra with misgiving. Here men were playing with a symbol whose reality was bred in her bone; to her it was sacred. It was now that she heard Cæsar utter words that reflected the deepening twilight of his soul. "Death," he said, "is less terrible than men imagine. After all, it is a misfortune which one need not experience twice." These strangely sceptical words, which might have been spoken by a *moriturus*, were elucidated by an even stranger remark, which Plutarch has recorded. When someone warned him against Cassius, he said: "I do not like his pale looks."

Secretly, then, Cæsar was busied with thoughts of death and the possibility of a reverse of fortune. At the same time, the queen learned that he had dismissed his bodyguard, and would allow none but a few lictors to accompany him. Familiar from her childhood with poison and dagger, she was aware of something that had escaped Antony: she knew that a conspiracy might grow out of these petty incidents.

She could not know that such a conspiracy was already in being.

XI

The men whom she distrusted so greatly were not the only conspirators, but they were the leaders. In the end, nearly eighty senators appear to have been involved in the conspiracy, for those engaged wanted to show the people afterwards that the indignation against the Dictator had been widespread. To save the Republic and the liberty of their fathers, which it seemed would be lost after a victory over the Persians, was the motive which impelled them to expedite the murder, for it was settled that Cæsar would leave Rome on March 17th. In the Senate, which he had summoned for the 15th—the first session for a long while—the conspirators would find their last opportunity. There were surely men among them who were acting for the sake of liberty; but not the three leaders.

Three high officials, in their thirties, members of old families, three men upon whom Cæsar had showered his favours, but who nevertheless were consumed with ambition, neither they nor the others were actuated by motives of personal or ideal vengeance. There was no one among them who sought to avenge the death or banishment of a son or father, for Cæsar nearly always pardoned his enemies.

Decimus Brutus, whose career was without example—and all that he had done he owed to Cæsar, had accomplished under Cæsar—like Brutus, who stood in the confidential relation of a son, can have been actuated only by the desire of the second to become the first. So long as Cæsar was only his general or his consul he could endure his superiority, for Cæsar was much older than he; one would follow him, and before long one would be a general or a consul oneself; but a Cæsar who was drawing near to the throne was moving away from him, and blocking his upward path by the creation of a dynasty. For Cassius, on the other hand, envious and grudging by nature, a defeated Pompeian whom Cæsar had pardoned, it was unendurable that he should owe his enemy gratitude; yet he had to suffer his forgiveness. He justified himself to history by the incident of the lions, which seemed to give him a key to the soul of a Cæsar such as Cassius wished him to be.

Brutus, however, in whose moral reputation the whole conspiracy found support, was—as appears from Cicero's letters —one of those conceited men of honour who obscure and yet embellish their all too human feelings by ethical motives, and so contrive to mask their every desire with a mission. If he had lent money in the provinces at usurious rates of interest, he had done so, of course, for the good of the fatherland; if he solicited high office he believed that he was sacrificing his studies for the good of the State. Was he about to slay Cæsar? It was the spirit of the ancient Brutus that had summoned him to action; the ancient Brutus, bearded and peevish-looking, with his prominent, leathery ears, who stood amidst the statues of the Tarquinian kings to whose overthrow he had sacrificed his own children.

The truth was that in Cæsar Brutus hated the man who claimed to be his father. The patrician's conception of family purity was intolerant of the tarnished reputation of his mother, who, now an old woman, was still living at her son's side. A

Brutus must be begotten in lawful wedlock, for only so could he be descended from the famous regicide and liberator. The old, long-enduring love-affair between his mother and Cæsar, once the talk of the town, was today a half-forgotten legend, to be effaced for ever if it clashed with the son's faith in his legitimate father. With a nobler soul, a more lucid mind, a keener vision, Brutus might have been Cæsar's son indeed; for if Cæsar adopted a great-nephew, who was of good blood on only one side of the family, he would surely have adopted the man whom he believed to be his own son; especially if the latter had given him the love and admiration that he owed to the character and the genius of his father.

But Brutus's self-righteous morality, which must be for ever justifying itself, made it possible for him to hate his natural father, even if in so doing he must betray his legitimate father! For the latter was slain by Pompey, so that his spirit should have called upon his son to avenge his death in the ranks of Cæsar's army! Far from avenging it, when the breach occurred between the two triumvirs he went over to the enemy and for two years fought against Cæsar, until the latter triumphed at Pharsalus. And then, instead of loyally following the sons of Pompey, Brutus for the second time went over to the ruling power, as soon as he had learned that Cæsar was willing to receive him. Now he must revenge himself upon the object of this twofold betrayal in order to recover his shaken self-esteem.

True, he was well aware that in killing Cæsar he was killing the man who had defeated his father's murderer; he was killing the man who had forgiven him his first betrayal, and who had afterwards bestowed every imaginable favour upon him. But all such feelings were silenced in Brutus's heart when he

[137]

reflected that in Cæsar he would kill the man who had seduced his mother and had expelled him from the ranks of his
glorious forebears. And was not the manner in which Cæsar
was doing violence to liberty a confirmation of the fact that
he could not be his father? Once the man lay stretched at his
feet, the problem was solved for ever; the eternal question
would be silenced; Brutus would have proved by his deed that
he sprang from the line of Brutus the regicide.

To follow him thus far—what should Brutus have done? He
should have gone up to Cæsar in the Senate; he should have
cried aloud, invoked liberty, and struck him down; he alone,
man to man. Then, indeed, he would have been no hero, like
Cæsar, for he would have fallen upon an unarmed victim; but
he would at least have been a man. But what in truth did he
do? He was one of a score of cowardly assassins who, delib-
erately counting on their numerical superiority, fell without warning on an unarmed soldier who had fought his way
through a hundred battles. He was contemptible, and even
two thousand years later no wrong that Cæsar may have done
to the cause of liberty can excuse the pitiful deed of Brutus.

XII

One of the last evenings before the Ides of March Cæsar
spent with the queen. He was in high spirits; his melancholy
mood had left him. The rolling of the drums, the pealing of
the trumpets, the tramp of the troops as they filled the roads
of Italy on their march toward the ports, the fulfilment of a
plan long cherished and long elaborated in solitude—all this

renewed the youth of the general who had always been happier in the field than in the city, though in his hours of resig-
nation he tried to believe the contrary. The excitement of departure, the ending of this mundane idyll, the promise of a
new, intoxicating adventure, put fresh life into him.

Cleopatra's plan was this: soon after his departure she
would return to Egypt, and there, by means of the Syrian
troops and dispatch-bearers forming part of his mighty army,
she would keep in touch with him. For now the last great
blow was to be struck, the last battle fought, beyond which
lay the fulfilment of his dream.

It was her dream no less than his, and in such a rare hour
of leisure as this he rose once more to his full stature, free of
all the cloaks and trappings of the multifarious day. On this
last evening, it may be, they passed in review the scenes of
their life together in Alexandria, each reminding the other of
things forgotten, each completing the other's memories, as
lovers will who seek to mitigate the dread of new perils by
looking back at dangers successfully overcome. Today, more
than ever, all depended on Cæsarion; they seemed to see him,
grown to young manhood, keeping guard over the Alexander-
dream.

But even on this last evening Cæsar saw, behind her smile,
the distraction that for weeks had been threatening to estrange
them. She had heard of bad omens; all Rome was full of
rumours; people were talking of solitary birds that had settled
at night with loud outcries in the Forum; of sacrificial victims
that were found to possess no hearts; of sudden lights in the
heavens; and in such omens the queen's own instincts found
confirmation. She could not tell these things to the man who

was on the point of taking up his sword anew. But he himself told her certain things: that for some time past the horses which he had dedicated to the gods beside the Rubicon had been refusing to graze; that the Ides of March were dangerous to him; and that yesterday a flock of birds had carried a twig of laurel into the Curia of Pompey. Was it not so? And Cæsar laughed.

But the queen did not laugh with him; so he tried to distract her by subtler means. Did she remember the Chaldean who before the gates of Babylon had counselled Alexander to delay his entry until the morrow? But why wait? Had she, Cleopatra, ever shown fear in those devilish weeks in Alexandria? It was the foreign city that oppressed her. Euripides had sung: "He is the best seer who gives prosperous advice!" Cæsar promised to spend his last evening with her.

On the following evening he dined with Lepidus. Decimus Brutus was of the company; he was silent, savouring his knowledge of what was to befall the master of the world on the morrow. Perhaps it was he who turned the conversation to the subject of death; we have it on record that there was talk of death. Cæsar was signing some documents which had been brought to him as he sat at table. As he was reading them he heard the question asked: What kind of death was the best? "A sudden end," he said, as he signed the paper before him.

Next morning the eighty men who had concealed their short swords and daggers beneath their togas were trembling; he only, who carried no dagger, did not tremble. But he felt unwell; the terrifying dreams that Calpurnia had related to him, her pleading, and his desire to comply with her wishes on this, the last day before his departure, kept him at home; until Decimus Brutus came, sent by the conspirators, and sought to persuade him to attend the Senate in spite of Calpurnia's pleading; for what would the senators say if, after he had summoned them, they learned that his wife's dreams could cause him to change his mind? But as Cæsar still refused to accompany him, Brutus (according to Plutarch) offered a last inducement, apparently invented on the spur of the moment: today, immediately before his departure for the seat of war, the Senate, in accordance with the plan which had been discussed, intended to confer upon Cæsar the title of king beyond the bounds of Italy. This decided the question, for it was intimately related to his own schemes.

So as he was borne in his litter to the Curia of Pompey he did not hear the cries of a slave who sought, with excited gestures, to give him some message or other; nor did he read a roll of papyrus which Artemidus, a Greek scholar, forcing his way through the crowd, had thrust into his hands with urgent words and signs, indicating that he was to read it immediately. This roll, containing the names of the individual conspirators, and warning him of their intentions, was the only document which he had in his hand as he entered the Curia; he had intended to read it immediately after the session, for the philosopher's excitement had made an impression upon him. When a senator accosted him as he entered the building and detained him for some time, speaking in low tones, the conspirators believed that they were discovered, and some of them sought to escape. At the same time Antony, whom they wished to spare, was detained in the outer colonnade.

When Cæsar had entered the Curia and had taken his seat in the throne-like chair, Cimber, as previously agreed, was the first to approach him, interceding for the recall of his banished brother. When Cæsar put him off, being anxious to proceed to more important business, a number of the conspirators came forward in support of the appeal; some kissing his neck and breast, as though in homage, in order to ascertain whether he was wearing a secret breast-plate. Cæsar, seeing himself beset, sought to push them all aside with a sweep of his right arm; but Tullius clutched his toga, so that it slipped off his shoulder, exposing his breast under the thin tunic. This was the signal agreed upon. Cæsar cried: "This is violence!" and sprang to his feet. "Now"—so Appian relates—"Casca, who stood nearest to him, stabbed him, thrusting at his throat with his sword, but it glanced aside and wounded him in the breast. Cæsar tore his toga out of Cimber's clutch and seized Casca's hand, leaping down and gripping him with great violence. While he was wrestling with Casca another plunged a dagger into his side, which was bared as he twisted round. Cassius wounded him in the face, Brutus stabbed him in the loins." "Some say he opposed the rest"—so Plutarch tells us —"and continued struggling and crying out, till he perceived the sword of Brutus; then he drew his robe over his face and yielded to his fate."

He fell at last pierced by three-and-twenty wounds. At one moment two of the senators had attempted to come to his aid; now all fled from the building. No one was willing to hear what Brutus had to say; the conspirators themselves, losing their heads, quickly made their escape. The dead Cæsar was left alone in the empty hall; none looked down upon his body save a marble Pompey, his great enemy, murdered before him. Later two of his slaves took up his body in order to carry it to his house.

Now nothing remained in the hall save the roll containing the list of the conspirators.

XIII

Cleopatra, beyond the Tiber, may have heard the news a few minutes later than the rest of Rome. She had been expecting some evil to befall Cæsar. Now, instead of lamenting or uttering accusations, the young queen at once realized the danger of her position, and acted in the interests of her son, who was also Cæsar. In those days the metallic brilliance of her nature shone with a more heroic light. While hundreds of influential Romans fled from the city, the unprotected woman remained. At any moment she might be murdered, but for a month she remained in Rome. The only man she trusted, Antony, was also the man whose interests corresponded with her own.

If Antony, during the next four days, was able to find an unexpected opportunity in the danger which he had escaped, this was due mainly to Fulvia, his wife, whose restless and inventive mind had at last found the field in which she could play her hazardous game—and she played it for years, until her death. Fulvia was perhaps the only Roman citizen who was a match for Cleopatra in the approaching conflict.

In the first confusion, which was doubled by the conspirators' lack of forethought, only one man acted. Antony, who had fled from the Curia and had thrown defences about his house, invited Cassius to supper on the evening after the murder; Brutus was dining with Lepidus, another friend of Cæsar. Antony seemed to concur with all the conspirators' wishes; he agreed that they should be granted an amnesty, and that they should be publicly honoured. He could venture to do so because he had in his possession an instrument of power which no one else possessed. On the night after the murder, accompanied by a few slaves, he had gone unobserved to Cæsar's house, and had obtained from the distracted widow Cæsar's papers and his movable property, in order, so he said, to put them both in a place of safety. Then, hastening to the temple of the Ops, he removed the treasure of the State, which was worth five million of our dollars. But the others, terrified by what they had done, made off in disorder, possessed of nothing but their freedom.

Among Cæsar's papers was his testament.

When Antony had glanced through the testament he sent a messenger to the queen, begging her to come to him. The street was lit by torch-bearers, but they ran quickly from house to house; the doors grated and swung open and were quickly closed again; no one could know at what corner a dagger awaited him. This Greek Amazon was surely the only woman who ventured into the streets of Rome that night. But now she was in Antony's house, reading the testament. Three great-nephews inherited Cæsar's fortune, Octavian, the eldest, receiving three-fourths of it. In case one of the nephews should fail to inherit, Decimus Brutus was to replace him as heir. If a son should be born to Cæsar after his death, several of his friends, who were among his murderers, were appointed to be the child's guardians. Cæsar's gardens beyond the Tiber, and with them the house in which the queen was living, were bequeathed to the Roman people. Every Roman citizen inherited three hundred sesterces. In a codicil, Octavian was declared to be Cæsar's adopted son.

There they sat facing each other, Cæsar's friend and Cæsar's Egyptian wife, unable to reconcile themselves to his testament. Since they had not met to chide the dead, but to save their own lives, they barely had time to ponder the meaning of the document, nor did they fully realize the bitterness and the irony of the fact that some of the conspirators benefited by the terms of the will. The one provision to which they both had to reconcile themselves was the last—that concerning Octavian!

Why did they not destroy the document? Why did they not have another written and sealed that very night? During the next few weeks Faberius, Cæsar's private secretary, forged for Fulvia dozens of papers in Cæsar's name, and with his assistance Antony fabricated senatorial resolutions, amnesties, and notes of hand, transferring and acquiring fortunes. It was not possible that they should have failed to realize the tremendous opportunity offered by the fact that Octavian, at the age of nineteen, would find himself the central point of a party which was ill-disposed to them. It would seem that these three people, who had met to pass the night in consultation only a few hours after Cæsar's murder, were restrained by a sort of piety at the sight of his signature.

To several of the conspirators, whom he invited a few nights later to a banquet—a shrewd idea of Fulvia—Antony showed the genuine testament, and over the wine he persuaded them to consent that he should read it to the people on the occasion of the funeral rites. Brutus and Cassius were foolish enough to agree. For with the single clause that made every Roman citizen Cæsar's heir he excited the people's anger against the conspirators and shaped the history of the next few years.

Cleopatra rorced herself to think only of Cæsarion. The dream was over; this must have flashed across her mind in the first few minutes. But the precious pledge of the dead—the boy—still lived, and now that his father was gone she must prepare the way that he would one day tread—even if he then possessed no more than this visionary privilege, that he was Cæsar's flesh and blood. Was Antony his rival? When she looked at Fulvia she was inclined to suspect that he was. But for the moment they were both the rivals of the pale Octavian. What would he do? He was now in Apollonia, attached to one of the legions that Cæsar had sent on ahead to Greece, surrounded by his tutors, who were to instruct him further in philosophy. At the same time, he was a junior officer, for in the last war he had acted as Cæsar's adjutant. If this had been her own country Cleopatra would have sent out her emissaries then and there, to kill him as he sailed for Italy. Then the history of the world would have followed another course.

For the present, they both decided to fight him. The queen had need of Antony, in order to legitimize Cæsarion; Antony needed the three-year-old boy, that he might rule in his name and prevent the youth of nineteen from ascending the throne.

So in the night after Cæsar's murder a silent alliance was concluded between Cæsar's friend and his mistress, between Antony and Cleopatra; and perhaps she remembered for a moment that happy summer evening when Cæsar had first introduced his trusted friend. The tide of life was high in them, and they were both deeply moved as they clasped hands on parting. Antony gave her a second squad of soldiers to escort her through the dark streets that led to her home and to protect her in her lonely villa.

A few days later, thanks to Fulvia's cunning, Antony's position was so surprisingly strengthened that he was able to confront the Senate—for he was, of course, consul—with the official statement that Cæsar had recognized the child of the Queen of Egypt as his own lawful son; and he adduced the evidence of Oppius, Cæsar's powerful financial counsellor. By so doing, Antony made all that he hoped to achieve, as civilian and as soldier, dependent on the romantic existence of Cæsar's son, as whose guardian he had without more ado seized the reins of power. It was a master-stroke. No one opposed him, and no one spoke of Octavian.

But Octavian came! On receiving the news of Cæsar's death he hastened to Rome, and a few weeks later he stood at Antony's door; that is, he sat in the entrance-hall, for Antony kept him waiting. And when Octavian explained, in his quiet, astute voice that he had come as Cæsar's heir, and demanded all Cæsar's papers, and all his gold, he found in his rival, who was twice his age, a sort of general berating a lieutenant. He must not get it into his head that such a youngster could be Cæsar's heir! And thereupon—according to Appian—Antony left Octavian and walked out of the room.

A frightful blunder—and Antony was to suffer for it!

Octavian was able to visit the queen also just before her departure. He knew very well that her son was his rival, but today his cold, fascinating eyes were seeking only to ascertain what she herself thought of him. He encountered a penetrating gaze; her huntress's eyes were searching for some sign of his blood-relationship to Cæsar. To her relief she could discover no trace of such relationship; he was outwardly the descendant of the man whom she privately called the Velletri money-lender.

All was still unsettled, up to the very day when the queen took ship with her great retinue. Everything was calling her back to her own country; her son's life was not safe, for many were beginning to find him an obstacle, and abroad in Rome she encountered angry looks, for the man in the street was saying, derisively, that the gardens in which she was still living now belonged to the people by the terms of Cæsar's will; above all, her enemies at home might cause a disturbance now that the man was dead upon whose power she had built the future of her country.

On a morning of mid-April Cleopatra stood at the stern of the ship that bore her eastward, gazing, for so long as it was still in sight, at the Italian coast. Her mind was full of her last glimpse of Cæsar on the day of his funeral. Once more she saw the mob take charge, in obedience to the voice of some unknown onlooker; and instead of carrying Cæsar's body to be burnt on the Campus Martius they began then and there to build his pyre. She saw how soldiers and sailors, citizens, children, a hundred thousand strong, laid hands upon anything within reach that seemed inflammable; they tore off their outer garments, the men discarding their weapons, the women their jewels, the musicians their flutes, in order to sacrifice all that they possessed to the hero whose body the flames were consuming, and whose soul would take rank among the gods. Never before had there been such a funeral pyre, built by a people's devotion; and now, as she saw it rising before her, as she seemed once more to smell the smoke, she saw herself also, standing at a window, too far away to cast anything into the fire.

Then—so she thought, as she saw the town of Ostia growing smaller—from her window she cast a dream into the flames, a dream as great as the fire, as great as the man whom the fire was consuming. It was the Alexander-dream; and the jewels, the coloured pomp, the robes and the throne and the diadem, all burned in the mighty fire that the people of the Republic had lit for their dead consul, because they had not been willing that he should become a king.

With a heavy heart she mused on the fickleness of fortune, on kings and the kingly heritage, loathing more intensely than ever the rule of the mob as the pyre smouldered out before her eyes. As the vision faded, the Italian coast disappeared. Here, on this vessel, a sleeping boy was all that was left of Cæsar's power.

Then Cleopatra went to the bows of her ship, gazing southwards across the sea as though she could already glimpse the shores of the land that was her home.

Dionysos

For men are violent, and are always possessed by their latest notion, and an obstacle will readily divert them from their path. But a woman is skilful in devising means, and following the devious path she adroitly reaches her goal.

—GOETHE

Antony

CHAPTER III

Dionysos

I

WITH mute resentment the magnates of Alexandria received their queen. She had spent two years out of Egypt in order to conclude a treaty with Rome; where, then, was the treaty with its ritual seals? What had the people and Senate of Rome promised the Egyptians? The mighty Republic was in a state of chaos, the man on whom she had staked the fortunes of her country was dead, the son whom she had borne him was fatherless. And worse was threatening. If the conspirators remained in power, would they not make a clean sweep of Cæsar's policies? And what would become of Egypt then?

Cleopatra was able to show that the anxieties of her ministers and the accusations of her enemies were groundless; she adduced the statistics of the trade with Rome, which during the last two years had reached an unprecedented level. She spoke of the legitimization of Cæsarion by the Senate—the work of Antony—and when she was still confronted by a sceptical silence she demanded, impatiently, what other heir of Ptolemaic blood they had in mind—for the last survivor, Arsinoë, Cæsar's prisoner, had disappeared in the confusion of the past few weeks, no one knew whither. But they had all made so much money out of Rome that she quickly succeeded in dispelling their doubts as to the future.

Yet she herself was full of doubts. When after two years' absence she returned to the echoing, vaulted chambers of the palace, she was appalled, at first, by her loneliness. Here she had seen her father, drunk and sober, ruling and playing the flute; here two brothers and two sisters had grown up at her side; and although there had been much strife and hatred there had been at least continual movement. There, at the great table, she had feasted with Antony and her father; that was now eleven years ago. Cæsar was lying on these very cushions when she tumbled out of the carpet before his eyes. Was it possible that only four years had passed since she had first encountered the flash of the black eyes beneath the kingly brow?

Now she was back in her old, deep window-niche; she had drawn up her feet, and leant her head against the marble wall; for it was warm: the month was May, and the air was windless. Down there in the great eastern port, where she saw that new ships were making ready for sea, while others were running into harbour with shortened sail—in this ever-busy outlet to Rome Cæsar had swum from the sinking ship to the boats of his rescuers, holding in his teeth the purple cloak that grew heavier and heavier and at last escaped him. And yonder, to the left, his trireme had glided out to sea; she gazing after him, he gazing up to her, for neither knew whether this might not be an eternal farewell. Today the last farewell had been spoken.

Inasmuch as Cleopatra had never revered a father, never lived on terms of friendship with a brother or consort, she now felt trebly forsaken, conscious of the chill that surrounded her in the place of her first love-affair. Now she could have wished even Pothinus, the cunning eunuch, or the younger Ptolemy, or even the drunken Fluteplayer back again for an hour, so that she might dream herself back in the old days, although she felt no longing for them. Back in her native environment, waked out of the great dream which for years past had lifted her out of the world of her ancestors, Cleopatra found the city of her fathers too restricted, the empire too small, and its splendours meaningless. It was not Rome that she missed, for there the outward forms of the Republic had always repelled her; she was saddened by the first loss that had impoverished her life, the first intrusion of destiny in its despotic aspect. What she missed was the man before whom she had humbled herself, who had been at once father and teacher, lover and brother: Cæsar, and she must now have the courage to live without him.

But now little feet were pattering through the halls of the palace; they had not yet learned to stand when she had sailed for Rome. By a miracle a Cæsar restored to youth had been given back to her, and this woman who had never in her life shed a tear was now near to weeping, not in sorrow, but for very happiness.

A hundred times she had tried to reckon on what night of

those first warlike weeks she might have conceived the child:
whether in the palace or in camp; on the cushions yonder, in an
interval of silent gazing, or the night when they heard the music
of the troops, and a few women were shrieking outside amidst
the soldiery. Or it might have been on a certain afternoon,
when the enemy had at last given way, and Cæsar had told
her the story of earlier battles. Flushed with victory, his right
hand extended, speaking in broken phrases, he seemed to be
sunk in a day-dream of the future; but then, as he once more
realized the presence of his silent listener, he suddenly threw
himself upon her with the swiftness of youth.

Today, recollections of these hours of love came back to
her. The place, the presence of the child, and above all her
loneliness, which she had not realized on board ship, while
she was busy with her plans, were waking memories such as
her less voluptuous and infrequent relations with Cæsar in
Rome were little likely to call forth. Now her naïve and sensual nature told her that she needed a man; but when she ran
over the elegant young men of her court it seemed ridiculous
to think that one of these could be Cæsar's successor. It would
be easy to find a young slave, and easy to silence him if he
dared to chatter.

Dismissing such thoughts, as her manner was, with a toss
of her curly head, she turned to the boy, lifted him up, and
pointed to the ships; and when he asked her whither they
were sailing she told him that they were all bound for Rome.

II

And there came to her from Rome couriers and agents, spies and moneylenders, bringing her, like the links of an uninterrupted chain, news of the events upon which her fate depended, and that of her country; in all the Mediterranean no one was so well served with news as the Queen of Egypt. While her subjects were continually striving to send their wares to Italy, bringing back from that country hardly anything but gold, she herself sent nothing thither, but she was indefatigable in collecting information as to the achievements and the conflicts of the Italians, for she was anxious to draw the diagonal to the Roman parallelogram of forces, and only from the chaos of a hundred reports could she deduce the probable truth, and only from this the decisions which would be taken by those concerned.

Not in vain had she studied Rome. Formerly, despite her father's descriptions, her sensitive mind had perceived the Roman people only as vague and misty figures; but now she could imagine exactly how everything happened, the expressions and gestures of the actors, the stresses and pauses of their speech. Even more than the men, the women of Rome, whose decisive influence she had learned to realize, came to life before her eyes.

There was Servilia, Cæsar's sometime mistress, who today, another Niobe, symbolized, in her family alone, the civil war; she had a son and a son-in-law in the camp of Cæsar's avengers, and a second son-in-law with the conspirators; and then there was her Brutus. So two of her sons were fighting against each other, each on the wrong side. Cleopatra realized the shock which this elderly woman must have suffered when Cæsar was murdered by her own son, and it may be that on comparing Servilia's lot with her own she was touched with a compassion which was really foreign to her nature.

Above all, her agents followed every movement of Fulvia, whose hatred and love of power would for the first time be fully kindled by the new and portentous situation. In her early youth she had seen virility and talent squandered without result, and even with Antony she had hitherto been able to do no more than induce him to be reconciled with Cæsar, so that of recent years she had been forced to play the part of the wife who discovered all that was happening round about her, in order to warn her husband, the favourite of the man in power. But with Cæsar's death, and indeed on the very day of his death, she took a hand in a greater game, for she alone could curtail the exuberant Antony's pleasures, knocking into him, in return, the great ambition of becoming not the second man in Rome, but the first. As a beginning, she had won his brother Lucius for her cause; together they would convert the only too self-indulgent man, transmuting his joy in life into a purposeful effort, which had hitherto been inhibited by the sight of his great leader.

Not that Antony underestimated himself. In his soldierly way he spat at the mention of the young Octavian, and he would not have taken orders either from him or from Lepidus. As for the conspirators, one had only to make their position impossible, and then defeat them. Look where he would, there was no one above him. But such a man had far to go before he could change the course of history. This Dionysos had not the power of Zeus, to project his visions upon space and time. But such was the male desire of Fulvia, who did her best to make life uncomfortable for him, and indulgence contemptible, by pointing her Dionysos to the vacant throne of Zeus. To Antony, smarting under her pricks, it suddenly seemed that he had only to imitate Cæsar in order to equal him.

The news which Cleopatra had received of Fulvia's autocratic behaviour filled her with uneasiness; her woman's instinct immediately divined the danger that threatened Antony, and therefore herself. Though her dream was over, she must be the ally, not the enemy of Rome. This was a fundamental principle which had been instilled into her ever since her childhood. An Antony who was a consul and a general making war on the conspirators was the Antony she hoped to see; but an Antony who began to climb into Cæsar's place, who sought international adventure and played the dictator before he had won a single victory, was a danger to himself and to her.

To her especially, since a powerful Fulvia would drive all other women away from him, as she had attempted to do already, and she had certainly distrusted the Egyptian as profoundly as Cleopatra distrusted the Roman matron. That they both hated Octavian had not been a sufficient basis for friendship. This Fulvia, at the age of twenty, had already been twice a widow, and today was no older than Cleopatra. She had exhausted every refinement of pleasure in her first two marriages, and she seemed, by nature and by reason of her experience, a rival to Cleopatra, and the recent happenings in Rome had apparently roused her to active enmity.

Would not this woman do everything in her power to make her husband, now raised to the dictatorship, see in his own son a better successor to Cæsar than this distant Cæsarion, whose mother was making such claims for him? Surely, Cleopatra concluded—for she had read Fulvia's glances when she had met her on social occasions—surely Fulvia would rather see the childless, ageing Calpurnia ranking as Cæsar's widow than the young Queen of Egypt, with her inconvenient son; especially as Cleopatra the woman might easily take her husband's fancy. If Cleopatra saw in Antony her only friend in Rome, she already saw in his wife her future enemy.

All the information she received spoke of Fulvia's decisive influence. The naïveté with which she kept on producing, month after month, fresh documents bearing Cæsar's seal and superscription was bound to bring together those who were betrayed by the fraud, even though they could not yet venture to speak openly. The private secretary continued to fabricate posthumous pardons and proscriptions in Cæsar's name, and everything, in the last resort, was a matter of money, as though the laws and the resolutions of the Senate were put up to auction. Cæsar's fortune (some five million dollars) was just enough to enable Antony to pay his debts and buy, with a lavish hand, all who would support him in his bid for power.

Yet Antony was by no means master of the situation. In the end, he was driven to extremities by the consuls, who were more or less on the side of the conspirators. Defeated at Modena, he was obliged to flee from Italy, while in Rome his wife was accused of fraud by Cicero, whose speeches were unanswerable. For Cicero, that eternal weathercock, who on the day after Cæsar's murder wrote that he regretted only one thing—that he had not been invited to this banquet of the gods—wrote, only a month later, a most emotional letter, in which he did homage to the genius of Antony. But a few months later still, he had realized the true greatness of Octavian as compared with Antony. Since his intellect was always striving to produce material results, though he was lacking in the naïve brutality that engenders action, Cicero's super-subtle wriggling, while it did not obscure his genius, was often injurious to his reputation, and in the end it brought him to his death.

Cleopatra, on the other hand, refused to allow bad news to shake her sympathy for Antony. Her instinctive nature, far more confident than Cicero's, was ensured against the tremors of the intellectual by a physical passion, whose name was Cæsar, or now Cæsarion. Her enemy, in Rome, as in the outer world, was still Octavian, this other Cæsarion. She had realized this even before the murder, and she continued to realize it for fourteen long years, unto her death. At the same time, her interest in Antony's fate was increasing; as long as he was Octavian's enemy it continued to increase; but there were times when the two were friendly, and then even Antony meant nothing to her.

But the defeated Antony of whom her informers told her— this was a man after her own heart. They told her how he fled across the Alps, in search of the legions of his old friend Lepidus, whom he had helped to make his peace with Cæsar; how, dressed in black, with dishevelled beard, and splashed with mud from head to foot, he had appeared before the troops, acting the part of the faithful Cæsarian persecuted by a wicked world. Only a brook lay between them as he spoke.

They all knew him and loved him, and as he sought to win them by his eloquent speech, Lepidus, at his wit's end, had the trumpets sounded in order to drown his voice! And when Fulvia made speeches in the open market-place, seeking to inculpate Octavian—complaining that he, Cæsar's heir, did nothing to avenge Cæsar's death; that instead of paying Cæsar's legacy to the people he was seeking to take Antony's life —when she heard such reports there were moments when the distant queen felt even a liking for the savage Fulvia. How plainly she could see and hear all the tricks and falsities of Rome—she could almost smell them oversea! How in Rome each of the four parties tried to draw the others out into the open, and then attempted an amalgamation; how Cicero eloquently warned them against unloosing a sixth civil war, though he himself had not done so badly out of some of the other five; how the cold Octavian, as the youthful heir, left the doors of Cæsar's house wide open, in order to please the people whom he despised, and yet retained the inherited money, just as his grandfather the moneylender would have done; and how all were paying court to the omnipotent veterans, hoping to buy their swords and their arms! All these things were amusing to the woman who heard or read them in Egypt.

But a few weeks later further letters spoke of the desire of these legions to make terms with Cæsar's successors, for they were unwilling to fight their comrades. Cleopatra turned pale at the news. What could she do, she who was irrevocably opposed to Cæsar's murderers, if his natural avenger went over to his adopted son! And yet the thing was actually happening, only six months after Antony's defeat and banishment. Still, in the north, the enemies met, together with Lepidus, in order to form a new triumvirate. The old triumvirate which Cæsar had concluded fourteen years earlier with his rival Pompey and the wealthy Crassus furnished the model for this distrustful union of dictators, all of whom wanted to gain time and betray their rivals by spurious treaties, in order to choke them off quickly at the earliest possible moment; a comedy for subjects who were useful, after all, as soldiers and tax-payers, to glut their leaders' greed for power with blood and gold.

But what a decline in personality! In the place of Cæsar, a little nephew; in the place of Pompey, the great aristocrat, a dissolute lieutenant-general! And yet each of the three who had revived the old covenant assuredly regarded himself as the future Cæsar. Octavian had even prefaced his own name by the names of Gaius Julius Cæsar; thirty years later his world was beginning to believe that there had never been a Cæsar before him.

In speechless bitterness Cleopatra listened to the report of one of her sleuths concerning the conclusion of the new triumvirate; how the armies had assembled on the banks of a river in the neighbourhood of Bologna in order to act as witnesses and sureties; how Lepidus was put ashore on a little island, from which he signalled to either bank; how Antony and Octavian had themselves ferried over, and how before the eyes of their cheering cohorts each felt the other to make sure that he had no weapons concealed upon him. Indeed, the soldiers, who still believed that relationship was a bond, sent a delegation to the newly reconciled opponents, urging the desirability of a marriage; Octavian must marry Fulvia's daughter by her first husband, a child who could not be more than eight or nine years of age, and Fulvia, who had always based her hopes upon Octavian's bad health, and had long prayed for his death, must now embrace him as his twenty-six-year-old mother-in-law. Octavian, who was twenty, must surely have thought how much more interesting it would have been to marry the mother.

Cleopatra herself had faint hopes of this marriage, but hopes of a very different kind; she had only to imagine these three men on their island in order to see that their alliance would be of brief duration: the easygoing but rather hot-tempered Lepidus, who wanted only to be left in peace, the loose-living Antony and the frigid Octavian, who wavered between an ostensible temperance and vicious excess; nervous and sickly, timid and therefore cruel. And these men, all three of whom were inferior to Fulvia in energy and imagination, were sharing Cæsar's empire as though it were their family inheritance.

The long inventory which the three men immediately drew up—they proposed to have two thousand of their wealthiest enemies murdered—had no terrors for Cleopatra. She was gratified to hear of Cicero's death: how the soldier had pulled his head out of the litter and had slowly sawed it off. But that Fulvia had afterwards spat on the head of her dead enemy and had transfixed his malicious tongue with her hairpins seemed, to her queenly mind, contemptible. How all had taken to flight in order to save their lives, how senators disguised themselves as slaves and emptied latrines in order to escape detection, how others distributed all their wealth at the last moment, in order to leave nothing for the bailiffs, and how wives had their hated husbands included in the lists—all this Cleopatra learned from her Roman reports. But she felt sickened by such doings when she realized that the motive at work was not the blazing lust for revenge, but a cold avarice, and when she pictured, at the back of all these murders, the plebeian faces of the two hundred thousand mercenaries whose brute force was needed if the rulers were to rule.

The queen, accustomed to take vengeance, might even have begrudged Fulvia the fact that she saw so many enemy heads roll in the dust. A wealthy neighbour, Rufus, who had formerly refused to sell his house to Fulvia, had to surrender it now, and when Antony, to whom the severed head was brought while he sat at a banquet, said that he did not know the man—he supposed this must be his wife's affair—Fulvia seized the head in an ecstasy of revenge, and had it set up in front of the house for the sake of which she had had the man killed. Her power was increasing, for now she ruled in Rome with Lepidus, whom she had subjected, while the two other potentates sailed for Greece in order to inflict a final defeat upon Cæsar's murderers.

In this conflict, which was soon to shake the whole empire, even Cleopatra, on her distant shore, was compelled to take sides. Her heart recognized but one party; but when the war for Cæsar's succession reached even Africa the interests of her country were in jeopardy. What would she do if Cæsar's murderer, Cassius, who was now with eight legions in Syria, resolved to obtain as much gold from Egypt as Cæsar had obtained five years earlier? One of the other party was near enough to protect her, but his name was Dolabella, and although he was the foe of the conspirators, he was also an enemy of Antony. When he appealed to her for help, the queen gave him the four legions which Cæsar had left in Alexandria to protect the interests of Rome. But the man who came to fetch them betrayed her, or was captured by Cassius; at all events, these twelve thousand Roman soldiers, at the orders of the Queen of Egypt, fell into the hands of one of Cæsar's murderers.

A frightful position! Had she not reason to dread the arrival of her enemies? Already this Cassius had sent her his orders: she was to supply him with ships, and her governor in Cyprus actually gave him some. She made haste to strengthen her fleet; but who would protect Egypt, and the open port of Alexandria, if Cassius should now take the old desert route from Syria, which for thousands of years had been trodden by the conquerors of Egypt, and last by Alexander? She could see him standing before her, yonder, across the Tiber; leaning against the right-hand column of her atrium, measuring her with a glance that took in Cæsar also. What if the insolent whim should take him to look a little more closely at this mistress of the Cæsar who had fallen to his dagger? The Nile was lower than it had been for decades; there was famine in consequence, and the plague was raging in the capital. Her reply to Cassius was only an evasion which might gain her a little time.

But it seemed that the gods were not on the side of Cæsar's murderers. Just as Cassius was pressing her, he was summoned to Macedonia by a hasty message from Brutus, who was making ready to fight a decisive battle against the triumvirs. Which side would be victorious? Cleopatra did not know which was the stronger, or who was the better general.

As a matter of fact, the outcome of the battle of Philippi

was quite indecisive. Two generals had confronted each other, of whom one was as nervous as the other; Brutus, who in his fatalistic impatience struck too soon, defeated Octavian, who was so terrified by the onslaught that he hid among the reeds; Brutus would have won the day if he had given vigorous support to the army of Cassius, who had just been defeated by Antony. It was late in the day when Antony, opposed by his defeated ally, Octavian, as well as Octavian's victorious enemy, contrived none the less to win the battle, until his vanquished enemies fell by their own hand: that Brutus and that Cassius who had dared to slay great Cæsar.

Once again, as the news came from oversea, it aroused the same emotions in Fulvia and Cleopatra. Both were amazed, or enraged, by the leniency of Antony, who should have killed Octavian out of hand! But of the two women only one was engrossed in that moment when Brutus turned against himself, with the same hand, the same sword which two years earlier he had plunged into the loins of the defenceless Cæsar. This suicide, which was followed by a dozen other suicides of conspirators, counted for Cleopatra as the true revenge; in this the gods had spoken.

For beyond the changing aspects of the future, amidst all her foreboding thoughts, Cleopatra never lost the vision of the star in which she trusted. Soon after Cæsar's murder she could even see it in the sky with her bodily eyes, in the form of a gleaming comet.

III

One day—it was six months after the battle of Philippi—there landed in Alexandria an extremely elegant Roman, hitherto a stranger to the queen; an inscrutable person, half-philosopher, half-pimp. His name was Dellius, and he was Antony's messenger.

When the Roman Empire was divided among the triumvirs, Antony had stipulated for the East. Thither his nature drew him, for there was very much of the Greek in him; thither his youthful memories, and lastly Cæsar's legacy. Not that he intended forthwith to set out on his conquest of Persia; he was not sufficiently the Alexander for that. But Cæsar's papers, which Antony had taken from his house on the night of the murder—a mass of notes, figures, maps, sketches, such as a general puts together on planning a great campaign; the names of ports, of routes to follow, the numbers of horses and oxen, estimates of the forage needed, all bundled together anyhow, and for that reason all the more stimulating to a successor—this singular patrimony of Cæsar, which had fallen into the hands of his first officer, exerted a mysterious power over the heart and head of his devoted heir, as though it were at once a symbol and a warning. One day, thought Antony, he would make something out of that. But first he intended to conquer the south-eastern coasts of Asia, the islands and peninsulas of his youth. It was thither that his nature drew him, not to the cold barbarians in Gaul, and Cæsar's belated confession still echoed in his ears: that he had been too long away from the South. Here many precious things were waiting for him, the loveliest slave-girls and the sweetest wine.

This time, to his surprise, there were even princesses for him in the South. For the petty kings in Cappadocia and Phrygia vied with one another in the banquets which they prepared for the Dionysian general; but indeed, to keep such a monarch waiting outside his tent was in itself a moment worth having lived for, and later, when he threw back the veils of the queen of such a king, he felt that now in truth the banquet had begun. So Antony made his progress through the isles of Greece, and since no Roman enemy was left there now, nor foreign enemy either, he could well put a world of his own between himself and the army, a world in which dancers and comedians moved to the strains of harp and flute, while the spears, no longer weapons, were wreathed with ivy.

It was in such a lustful mood that the comparison of these women with Cæsar's beloved filled him one day with vexation, and he resolved that here also the second Roman should become the first. But the shadow of Cæsar still lay heavy upon him. Had not Cæsar sent for her to appear before his judgment-seat before he saw her? And had she not now sent Cassius her four legions? The reports that she had put about in this connexion might be true or false; one thing was certain, that at Philippi he, Antony, had been forced to sacrifice many of his men to these troops of Cæsar—and through her fault!

But he could not simply accuse her as she deserved; Antony's respect for this woman was too great for that. So he left it to his gallant envoy to find a form of address that would be something between an invitation and a summons. And Dellius had hardly been presented to the queen before he

[169]

threw up the sponge; he foresaw what must happen, and the best that he could manage was to quote, with a smile, a line adapted from the Iliad, advising her, as Poseidon counselled Hera: "Fare in thy finest raiment forth to Cilicia!"

Cleopatra smiled and awaited a summons. Several letters reached her, and she did not refuse the invitation, but she showed, by her regal attitude, that if she paid the triumvir a visit she would regard the voyage as a pleasant excursion; and in short, she would consider the matter. Once more, as seven years ago, when Cæsar had summoned her, she sat alone; yet this time not in a sorry tent on the edge of the desert, but in her cool palace, considering her decision.

"Never against Rome," had the Fluteplayer, her father, advised her when he was sober. Was it destiny that no Alexandrian had ever pleased her for long? Or was it only a matter of taste? A second Roman! Antony was not Cæsar, that was clear. She would never again in this world find Cæsar, unless in Cæsarion. But had not this bearded Dionysos much that Cæsar lacked? How would it be to sit beside him while two lions drew them through the streets? There were many things that she had never yet tried; but her blood, and certain highly seasoned verses, aroused her curiosity and showed her the way.

She was as confident that she would be victorious as Cæsar used to be before a battle. But if he wanted her, then she, as his guest in a strange port, would not long defend herself; he was too strong, and she too beautiful. Even to anger Fulvia was a pleasant goal; this alone would have repaid her for the journey. So she drew her conclusions beforehand, and in the end she was making, of her own accord, a voyage which would probably end in an adventure. She knew, before all things, that he was the only man who had truly loved Cæsar, and that being so he could not be indifferent to Cæsarion.

But how should she appear before him? One could not roll oneself up in a carpet a second time; especially if in the meantime one had become a mother. Something would surely occur to her, she thought, and she made her preparations.

At the same time, the colder half of her nature was making its calculations. She must be the friend of the Roman administrator of the southern Mediterranean; she must please such a man. And this decided the matter, for her pride made it difficult for her to sail across the sea to a Roman simply because he had sent for her. So, in order that she might feel as regal as when she had sailed for Rome, she gathered together gold and slaves, jewels and ornaments; she had a whole houseful of magnificent treasures packed in hundreds of chests, which were carried down the steps from the palace and into her ships on the brown, sweaty, gleaming shoulders of innumerable slaves. Twelve triremes were filled with them, and the ancient writers were lavish with the names and descriptions of curious works of art, in order to describe what the queen took with her when she sailed for Tarsus.

During the voyage to Asia Minor Cleopatra, in her practical fashion, rehearsed yet again in her mind what she might expect from this second Roman:

According to all that she had heard from Cæsar, from his enemies, and later from her agents, Antony was as good-natured as his mother had been, and as unreliable as his father; for the home from which he came had been endangered by the extravagance of his father and saddened by his mother's tears. He had not had much of an education; he had fled from his studies in Athens, preferring a life of adventure in Syria as a captain of horse; and as such he had come to her father's royal table, when his eyes had met those of the child of fourteen in that strangely earnest glance. Later still, when he was thirty, he had been discovered by Cæsar.

If Cæsar had singled him out, and had finally given him his utmost confidence, it was because he felt that here he was on firm ground. It was so rare to be secure against jealousy, and as for loyalty, was there such a thing? And this devotion, once it was found, was even rarer when combined with great ability in the field and a courage that knew nothing of caution. In these respects it seemed to Cleopatra that he was indefectible; and the decisiveness with which Antony had made his preparations for avenging Cæsar's death during the excited conversations on the night of his murder was in palpable contrast to the diplomatic waverings by which Octavian, the heir elect and the proper avenger, had gradually approached Cicero and others of his enemies.

To be sure—thought the queen, on board her trireme—to be sure, he was also something of a comedian; that was why he used to mix with the players. She could hear him still, as she had heard him at Cæsar's funeral; now raising his voice, now sinking it to an artificial whisper. With what theatrical skill he had exhibited the waxen effigy of the murdered man, pointing to its twenty-three wounds, and at last, as a brilliant climax, outspreading the bloody toga! Yet his were real tears, for he loved Cæsar. Yes, he and she were the only people who felt, beside Cæsar's corpse, that they would not look upon his like again.

What droll ideas he has, great child that he is! When he

came home after his reconciliation with Cæsar, and it was once more reported in Rome that Cæsar was dead, and that it was a hostile army that was approaching, Antony hurried on before, disguised as a slave, threw a black cloth over his head, and went to his wife—it was Fulvia herself who told me—with a letter from Antony. Fulvia screamed: "Is he alive?" Antony pointed sadly to the letter; she opened it and read it. Antony promised that he would never again sleep with the lovely Cytheria. Then he tore the cloth from his head and romped about the room with her!

On another occasion he had made one of his friends a present of half a million sesterces, and when, with a look of reproach, the exasperated steward laid the money before him in a heap, Antony said: "Is it so little? Go and fetch him twice as much!"

And as Cleopatra thus reviewed the character of the man toward whom the ship was bearing her, she realized, as she recollected each anecdote, that none of these stories could have been true of Cæsar. For because Antony was so much less a king than Cæsar, he could be more of a comedian, more of a child, and a spendthrift. For that very reason he seemed the man to please women.

Women? Fulvia was the obstacle; since Antony was quite unreliable the influence of the fierce Fulvia was bound to cast its shadow over him and prevent him from forming other connexions as long as she was at hand; Cleopatra asked herself how long this influence would last when she was far away. But then, again, she remembered Fulvia's hatred of Octavian. Here was the point in respect of which the three of them were agreed. Once Antony could be recalled from his vinous good

[173]

humour to warlike energy, one could do anything with him.
That Fulvia had long ago recognized, and Plutarch's psychological genius realized it a century later, when he wrote: "Antony had passed through the school of petticoat government
before he fell into Cleopatra's hands. And the latter had every
reason to be grateful to Fulvia, who had already broken him
in for her successor, and handed him over well accustomed to
obey."

The great biographer, in Elysium, may have noted the smile
with which Cleopatra read these trenchant words of his!

IV

Antony sat in a wide market-place, his great sword at his
side—the sword that hardly ever left him—very loosely girt, for
he could not endure the stiffness of anything that reminded
him of uniform; leaning back in the curule chair which had
made its way from Rome into the colonies. He was sitting in
judgment, for as triumvir he had the right of life and death.
True, no one had conferred it upon him, save indeed a puppet
Senate. But he had also conferred it upon himself, by virtue
of the power which had given him half the Roman Empire;
for little enough had fallen to the lot of Lepidus, the third of
the trio.

Antony was in Tarsus, still a flourishing port on the Gulf of
Alexandretta, at the eastern corner where it joins the Mediterranean, opposite the island of Cyprus and ancient Antioch.
From this key-point had marched every army which had sought
to conquer, from the Syrian base, the great kingdoms of Asia

Minor—Armenia, Media, and Persia, then more often called
the land of the Parthians. Tarsus lies a little inland, at the foot
of Mount Taurus, and those who approached it from the sea
had to sail up the Cydnus, a little river full of reeds and papyrus. But then the river spread out into a lake that enhanced
the idyllic aspect of the city.

It was nearly sunset, for the great Lord Antony chose the
cooler hours of the day in the shade of the market. There, in
the midst of his labours, he was aware of a commotion in the
market-place, in front of his high seat; and he saw how the onlookers—first the youths, then the women, and presently the
men of Tarsus, and the Roman soldiers—were gradually disap-
pearing. Since he was inquisitive, like all dictators, he asked
for an explanation. Someone told him, stammering a little,
that a miracle had occurred, a thing past belief: Aphrodite
had come; she was sailing up the Cydnus; presently she would
disembark.

Antony was both a soldier and a comedian; such have no
faith in fairy-tales. And he commanded that the mysterious
lady should appear at once before his judgment-seat. In the
meantime the commotion was increasing; people were running and shouting; music seemed to be wafted through the
air; messengers ran hither and thither; soldiers snatched up
their weapons; horses were saddled and mounted; everyone
had some new report of the wonder, but all were agreed in this,
that the strange lady, with her servants, had made no move.
What did the conqueror, torn between curiosity and anger?
He rose from his chair and went down to the shore.

"She came sailing up the Cydnus"—wrote Plutarch, and it
was from him that Shakespeare had the tale—"on a galley

whose stern was golden; the sails were purple, and the oars were silver. These, in their motion, kept time to the music of flutes, and pipes, and harps. The queen, in the dress and character of Aphrodite, lay upon a couch of gold brocade, as though in a picture; while about her were pretty boys, bedight like cupids, who fanned her, and maidens habited as nereids and graces, and some made as though they were rowing, while others busied themselves about the sails. All manner of sweet perfumes were wafted ashore from the ship, and on the shore thousands were gathered to behold her."

But now, as a lane opened for the Lord Antony, at a sign from Cleopatra curved rods bearing lanterns were raised and lowered, so that the lights formed a variety of arabesques. The evening twilight and the light of the many-coloured lanterns were delicately blended; it was still light enough and already dark enough to reveal but fitful glimpses of the smile on the queen's lips. And as she lay there in indolent calm she lifted her white, slender hand to grasp the rough, brown fingers of the soldier. Half-queen, half-goddess, she greeted him, and the Roman, half a comedian, was doubly qualified to appreciate the *mise en scène*.

That very evening the feasting began. "All the plates and dishes and vessels on the table were of gold," a Greek writer records of the first banquet which she offered to the Roman; "they were set with precious stones, and adorned by the art of the finest masters. Purple hangings, embroidered with gold, covered the walls, and twelve triremes lay ready to receive the triumvir and his retinue. When Antony marvelled at the splendour of a feast prepared with such magical celerity she begged him, with a smile, to regard the haste of her arrival as excuse for any lack; on the morrow, if they would all return, there would be more to please the eye. At the same time she begged him to accept all that he saw, as a present from her. On the following day he found himself the guest at a still more resplendent banquet, at the close of which he was again presented with all that he saw. Each senior officer received the couch on which he had reclined at the table, with golden beakers and golden plates and dishes, and a litter, with bearers; the other officers were presented with silver beakers and dishes, saddle-horses, and slaves. On the fourth day the queen spent a talent on roses for every guest, which covered the floor to a depth of a foot, while garlands hung from the ceiling of the hall."

Very late, when Ares had at last gone ashore, Cleopatra thought: This Roman is some twenty years younger. He seems inexhaustible. It is worth the voyage. The State treasury has suffered a little. But at least Egypt is secure.

V

In the afternoon, when Antony had slept his fill, and the latest banquet had not yet begun, he sat beside the reclining queen on board the floating palace, and told her what had really been happening since they had parted in Rome. As she lay there, her head supported by her hand, she conjured up the vision of Cæsar, seated, like Antony, beside her couch, as they voyaged up the Nile; but she did not tell him what she saw.

This is certain, that in after years she never reminded him of Cæsar, unless it were to spur him on.

In the matter of love, indeed, no such incitement was needed. Antony, who at first was always aware of Cæsar in the background when he acted the part of his successor in the favours of the lovely queen, was unconsciously impelled toward excesses of virility, as though to prove to her and to himself that in this respect at least he was stronger than the insuperable dictator. For it was really the possession of this woman that first lifted him out of his Dionysian revelry. As a woman and a queen she had impressed him greatly on the occasion of their first meeting in Rome, and no power on earth, and no refusal, could have deterred him from making a conquest of her had Cæsar not stood in the way. Now he was free; Cæsar was dead, and he held half the Roman Empire in his grip. Now he could show himself a dictator, like Cæsar, and he lost no time in displaying himself before her at the head of his legions in a brilliant parade. If he saw her smile at this performance, he knew that only as a man could he make a new appeal to her imagination.

There was no more radiant pair on earth. Antony, at the age of forty-two, despite his riotous youth, had still the vigour of a Hercules; Cleopatra, at twenty-eight, was a ripe woman, but still slender; still the Amazon, but an Amazon who had borne and suckled a child. Both were possessed by the feeling that they were now in the dazzling noontide of life; both were inspired by the instinct to offer themselves to the other as elect examples of humanity, and further by the desire of a thousand onlookers to behold the mingling of power and beauty, now invigorated, now lulled, now roused again by the strains of nuptial music: what an encounter of the sexes was here! What a spectacle for the gods of their peoples, who under their divers names were yet the same gods!

Only now, after a week of feasting and of nuptial celebration, did Antony feel altogether a being exalted. Under the sobering influence of a cold bath he reflected that the last and only thing he had needed, in order to become Cæsar, was Cæsar's mistress; but when his thoughts were once more coloured by the warm, dim glow of wine he actually believed that in this woman he had discovered Cæsar's magic key. The void which he had felt about him since the night of the murder, and in which he had only hesitatingly advanced under Fulvia's encouragement, was now suddenly filled by a vortex. There were none of those curious pauses, in which he had listened, between his own orders, for the accustomed word of command; Antony the soldier had become his own master. Yet for Antony the Dionysian there were surprises such as were unknown to the campaigner, and rare enough even in Rome, such as only an Alexandrian refinement was able to offer, and they filled the soldier with silent amaze. At the age of forty-two he even learned to consider the beauty of a woman's mouth: it occurred to him that he had never before seen a mouth so beautiful.

Cleopatra too had felt that a certain emptiness was closing in about her; but in her case it was her blood and not her intellect which had felt the lack of full satisfaction. She had begun with playful perversities, driven to youthful follies by her troubled senses; then she had served the passions of an over-experienced and ageing man; and she felt that somehow she had been cheated of something. Now she was caught up

[179]

in the same vortex as Antony, and while Antony was amazed by the cultured quality of the love which she offered him, she flung herself passionately into the torrent of physical force that seemed to flow from this man. When she fell back, exhausted, the tale of the two lions recurred to her, and life, which had held many bitter hours for her since Cæsar's death, now rose again to the level of her brimming fantasy. Here was a new, a second chapter.

Outwardly, at all events, the first must be liquidated. When Antony, seated beside the reclining queen on one of the cooler afternoons of her visit, had reached, in his narrative, the point which he had first conceived as an accusation, but which he now merely touched upon with a question, she was able, with well-prepared adroitness, to turn the tables upon his arguments. She was supposed to have supported Cassius? To have sent ships and troops to Cæsar's murderer? Those she had sent to Dolabella had been held up by stormy weather. But then she herself had sailed with her ships, as far as the Ionian Sea, in constant peril of capture by Cassius, until fresh storms and her own illness had driven them back! It was thanks that she deserved! What he deserved was to be asked why his people had not helped her more effectively in so perilous a situation!

Whether Antony believed all this is not recorded; but Appian may be right when he says, at this juncture: "He admired her as a miracle not of loveliness alone, but also as a miracle of wit, and felt himself suddenly drawn to her by youthful passion, although he was already in his fortieth year." It flashed into the mind of the accused queen that this was an afternoon for making requests! There were still three persons who imperilled her power at home: Arsinoë, liberated from her prison, after Cæsar's death, by some hand unknown, had fled to the temple of Artemis in Miletus; and that Egyptian governor of Cyprus was still alive, who had of his own accord gone over to the side of Cassius; and lastly there was a young adventurer who posed as the elder Ptolemy who was drowned in the Nile. They must all be killed! Antony nodded, and his soldiers swarmed along the three coasts, and presently they brought their lord, as the customary proof of their obedience to orders, the heads of the slain, which Antony showed to the queen.

Now at last this Ptolemy felt secure upon her throne. Two sisters and two brothers had been slain by her orders or for her sake; she was the last and only Ptolemy; there was no one now beside her, save Cæsarion. As she considered this new situation, she already envisaged the birth of a second son, the child of this second Roman, for under all her Alexandrian refinement Cleopatra had the natural feelings of an amorous woman who longs for children.

When she thought of Fulvia—and of her the naïve and voluble Antony often spoke—she saw a Roman matron of her own age, who had already borne four children to three husbands, and at first she had nursed them herself. Now, of course, when her energy was at its maximum, Fulvia could be thinking only of the State, and power, of Antony and Octavian, and of how she wished Octavian were dead, although he was formally her ally and her son-in-law. For after the battle of Philippi he had fallen seriously ill, and Antony's party had hoped that they were rid of him. At that time Antony's fame was on every Italian tongue, for all had heard of Octavian's cowardice and his personal defeat.

In Rome, Antony continued, the demand of the home-coming legions for the land which they had been promised was constituting a new peril; Lepidus, who did whatever Fulvia desired, had become quite impossible. Fulvia opposed the confiscation of estates by Octavian because they belonged to members of her party; Lucius, Antony's brother, had to produce orders from him, most of which were forged. Fulvia retained two legions which had been promised to Octavian as a sort of pledge, and Octavian wrote obscene epigrams on her and had them distributed in the army.—Out with the epigrams! cried Cleopatra; and then, of course, she began to laugh, and since Antony, with his thundering bass, laughed with her, she made him repeat the malicious things that had been said of his wife until they both shook with laughter, and their slaves, crouching in the corners behind their backs, looked at one another, for they had never before heard their mistress laugh so heartily.

In such moods the quick-witted queen found it an easy matter to persuade Antony, whom she was coming to like better after each succeeding banquet, to pay a visit to her city and her palace. Why remain tucked away in this corner, especially as the winter was coming? True, he had advanced some of his troops towards the north, for it was settled that Persia was to be invaded. He did not say much about this plan, and when he did speak of it she changed the subject; for her instinct told her that this was really but a gesture, inherited from Cæsar, whom he believed that he must imitate, and in-

spired by no inner necessity. She could easily persuade him
to postpone it. And the other danger, the breach with Octavian, was not urgent, to judge from what Antony himself
had told her, for Fulvia could not make war without Antony,
and he had made up his mind to bear with the allies as long
as he could.

And must not Antony's common sense and his spirit of
calculation point him whither this adventure with the queen
was drawing him? Already she was speaking of her return voyage; and yonder in Egypt there were treasures, easier to grasp
than those in unknown Persia! As the lover of the Queen of
Egypt he need fight no battle in order to obtain gold, and she,
who possessed this gold, was luring him on. If afterwards he
should follow the trail of Alexander and carry out the plans of
Cæsar, what could seem a better talisman to him, who believed
in signs and omens, than this very visit to Alexandria? By all
the gods, what should hinder a Roman of poor but honest
birth from being the guest of a queen?

Antony promised that he would presently follow the queen
to Alexandria, in order—as Plutarch puts it—"to fall into every
excess of puerile amusement, and offer at the shrine of luxury
the greatest of all sacrifices, time."

VI

Once more the ancient palace of the Ptolemies rang and
echoed with life. Grooms and armourers, litter-bearers and
fly-flappers, coopers and wine-blenders and many cooks were
busy in the damp vaulted basement; slaves, of whom each

gave his orders to others, so that he might feel his own man; and from time to time they crept noiselessly into the halls overhead, bowing to the ground, and there blows and rewards, questions and commands were showered upon them; and if their masters turned away, there they had to wait—to wait until the evening, or even the next morning, for the great lords had long forgotten them—until some eunuch found them sleeping on the marble floor, and gave them a kick; and they groaned, and softly whimpering went limping back to the damp vaulted basement, to their brothers, who were all still waiting to serve the whims of the gods upstairs.

For at every hour of the day or the night they must always be ready, one and all. "You must surely have a great number of guests?" asked a young student of one of the head cooks (and later on he told the story to Plutarch's father). But the cook laughed at him, saying: "There are not a dozen at supper. But every dish must always be ready at any time, and if anything isn't done to a turn it is thrown away immediately. Perhaps the Roman will sup now, in two minutes' time, perhaps later, or he may send for wine, or otherwise amuse himself, and everything else has to wait. For this reason a number of suppers are always being got ready, for no one can tell when the food will be wanted!"

The Bacchant enjoyed his holiday; he had only a few troops with him, and no uniform. He went about in Greek costume, with white Attic shoes, just as the priests and scholars did; he hunted and fished, or reclined among the philosophers in the Museion, proposing some problem remembered from his student days in Athens, listening to the discussion, dozing from time to time, waking up again, following the argument, debating and settling every problem in heaven and earth, and finally inviting the scholars to drink wine with him in the evening. But always, whether he was afloat or on horseback, or riding a camel along the edge of the desert, the queen was with him, agreeable for any caprice, never weary, never ailing, always ready for anything, as though she had not spent the long morning hours, during which he lay asleep, working with her ministers, settling the hundred matters that awaited decision daily, as though tending to Cæsarion's wants had not already taken hours of the day; although in these crazy times the hours might be reduced to half an hour. For a few months even the child, even Cæsar's son played a minor part in her life, so fanatical was her devotion to this one man. It was the first time she had thus unremittingly tried to please. She wanted to supplant all the Bacchantes in this Roman's memory, all the banquets, the harnessed lions, the Fulvias. She wanted to have him all to herself; for Cleopatra had fallen in love.

This man with the mighty chest, who in a merry mood would throw her light figure into the air and catch it again almost without sinking his arms—this wild man, who here in Alexandria, where no duties distracted him, was almost always desirous of her, so that he would seize and enjoy her at the most perilous moments, barely screened by a curtain from the eyes of her slaves; this general, who would suddenly take her away from the supper-table, and return with her, smiling; this careless satyr, whose effrontery seemed a grace, and whose curses dissolved on his tongue like grapes—this man had completely won her in these crazy months, and whatever she may have inherited from her flute-playing father was drawn to the surface from the secret depths of her being.

If in the fifteen years of her nubile existence she had maintained a fierce reserve because she lacked the right companion, now, in these months of winter, she flung herself into this Roman's orgy as though she must prove herself a match for his vitality. For the first, and also for the last time, in her life she lost for hours on end her sense of beauty and of refinement, and flung herself at him like a wild young animal, or pulled him down to her until he was deaf or blind to all else. For all that, she was never drunk, and if a legend speaks of an amethyst ring whose magical power enabled her to empty whole pitchers of wine without becoming intoxicated, it tells us only what everyone saw—or rather, what no one saw.

It was thanks to this remarkable power of carrying her wine that she was able, in spite of everything, to remain the queen in this—that none of the many officers and Alexandrians who shared her revels possessed her. She was unchaste for only one man; and this man had even his drunken moments when he regretted that she did not sink with the rest into the general sexual chaos. At the same time, the fact that she did not heightened his self-esteem, and recalled him, in sober hours, to the fact that he was dealing with a queen.

Sometimes they strolled through the streets at night, disguised as servants, for the pleasure of waking people up, thundering on their doors until the sleepers came to their windows and ran out to beat them, although they recognized the revellers. "Though some of the Alexandrians were displeased with this whimsical humour," says Plutarch, "others enjoyed it, and said 'that Antony did well to play his comic parts in Alexandria, and reserve the tragic for Rome'!" Sometimes the queen would tease him: since one day when he was fishing he caught nothing, he employed a diver on the next occasion, who had to put fish on his hook under water. The next time he went fishing she herself had a salt fish from Pontus fixed on his hook. Antony roared with laughter, and the story went the rounds of the city.

It was at this time that they founded the "Club of the Inimitables." A circle of wealthy Alexandrians had to entertain the whole society on certain evenings, and each endeavoured to outdo the rest in luxury and fantasy. Fortunes were lavished on a single evening, for the host considered that the queen's friendship would enable him to recover all that he spent. When Antony lay drinking at such a feast he would, of course, begin to tell stories, and it amazed Cleopatra that this immoderate man could talk as enormously as he ate and drank. He would lie there and praise the beauty of his first wife Antonia, and tell how that scoundrel Dolabella took her from him; but he, in return, stole Fulvia from his friend Clodius, long before he married her. Now both men were dead, but here was he, drinking a pitcher of old Rhodian wine, and what they were doing in Rome mattered to him no more than the drops that fell on the floor here. So argued the drunken Antony in the "Club of the Inimitables."

The only person of whom he never spoke was Cæsar.

VII

Yet on the other side of the Mediterranean was Antony's other wife, Fulvia, no less passionate than he, though today, after a youth spent in the company of three libertines, she was less interested in the Bacchant than in the triumvir. All Rome was talking of his Egyptian idyll, and Fulvia could not yet see what threat or lure might call him back to Italy. That he was faithless by nature, and greedy for new women, was as well known to Fulvia as were the charms of the queen. Once he had sailed for southern and eastern waters he might spend years with her and with other women; indeed, he might spend his whole unruly life there without remembering his wife and children. So there was only one means of winning him back, and with him the power he had imperilled, and Fulvia resolved to take it. She resolved upon civil war, in order to wrest her husband from another woman's arms.

This was no devilish inspiration; it was the sudden application of earlier plans; but had it not been for her jealousy she would not have flung herself down this precipitous road. Her plan was this: If by a forged mandate she completed the breach with Octavian, Antony must hurry home to defeat his rival; still less could he remain so far afield if he wanted to keep the peace with him. In either case this news must call him away from the hated Queen of Egypt.

Her letters, and those of her agents, were a strident interruption of the splendid idyll in the Alexandrian palace. In the quarrel over the estates of the legions Fulvia in Italy had taken extreme measures; she had seized eighteen cities of the Empire with Antonian troops, and distributed them, thereby inciting Octavian's troops to revolt, and now, in a *coup de théâtre*, she had fled from Rome, where she was no longer safe, to the fortress of Præneste, accompanied by many knights and senators. There Fulvia, acting as general, had collected weapons and money, men and horses, and had heartened the troops with fiery speeches, until the enemy followed, and shut up the forces of Antony's brother, now consul, and her ally, in Perugia.

Cleopatra's feelings, as she read these dispatches, wavered between contempt and jealousy. She thought of Cæsar's battles in Egypt, in the city and in the country, how she had been his sleuth, his Amazon, and how these battles had been fought for a throne, and that throne hers. But yonder in Italy? What had inspired the citizeness Fulvia to play the warrior? Simply the fact that she wanted her husband! For Antony's sake she ought not to hope that the woman would be defeated—nevertheless, she did.

It was not long before fresh dispatches told of the outcome: Antony's brother, in Perugia, had surrendered; Octavian had spared him, but in revenge had burned the whole city, and presently he held a bloody assize: on the anniversary of Cæsar's death he had four hundred knights and senators executed in front of his temple in Rome! And all this was done two years after the last of the conspirators had been slain! At the same time, Octavian's own messengers arrived in Alexandria, in order to explain to the other triumvir that not he, but only Fulvia had provoked the war; he wanted only to live at peace with his allies. When they read this both Antony and Cleopatra knew that Octavian's love of peace was born of his dread of Pompey, who ruled the sea.

At once came the proof: Fulvia, with three thousand cavalry, on board five ships, had fled from Brundusium to Athens; Antony's aged mother was with her, and she was under the protection of Sextus Pompeius! And there was more still! The new civil war had encouraged the Persians to make fresh advances; already they had broken into Asia Minor; Syrian princes had made alliance with them, and they were now pressing the Roman governor hard, while fresh Persian troops were penetrating Syria from the Euphrates.

By this news Antony was abruptly sobered. He must march, and that at once! The queen had every reason to help him; why, what if Octavian, who today was still anxious for peace, were to be victorious at the close of this new conflict! What would then become of Egypt? All that she had was his; she got together two hundred ships; her treasury would supply as much money as he chose to ask for.

Cleopatra was beset by conflicting emotions. She had not long been pregnant. What would become of her and her children if this man were to vanish for ever? Did his character give her any security—did it even allow her to hope? She might indeed hope that Fulvia had played her last card; Antony would never forgive her for placing him in this situation through her jealousy. If Cleopatra was losing the man to his wife, she was winning him back in the same moment. But there were so many women in the world, and if he forgot them both a third would charm him until she too was pregnant and had ceased to please him.

Suddenly the queen realized that this cheerful adventure

was beginning to look sinister. She saw that before long she might be left in the midst of her hostile countrymen, the mother of two children by two Roman fathers; uncertain how long the shifty malice of the Alexandrians would tolerate her, whether the dangerous magnates of the Court would put up with this state of affairs when the last Roman had left, or whether they would exploit it against her. Her love for the first Roman had begun with a battle for life or death, and ended in feasting—what if her love for the second, which began with feasting, were to end in desperate battle!

Antony, she thought, has troubled himself little about Cæsarion. He has a son of his own at home in Rome, or now perhaps in Athens. If his wife and his mother put their heads together, and his son and his daughter are there, and they all weep in company . . . what will be the effect on Antony's easily moved heart? Nothing is certain; victory was more probable with Cæsar, although he seemed to be menaced on every side!

When Antony was bidding farewell to her she told him of the consequence of their love. He laughed, and wished her good fortune with the child. He was no longer attending to her; his thoughts were all given to his army; he stood surrounded by reports and orders. In spirit he was already crossing the sea, to deal with the Persians, and then with his wife.

VIII

When Cleopatra, crouching in her window-niche, saw her second Roman sail away she did not smile, as she had smiled when the first had set sail. Then the master of the world had invited her to Rome; he had waited until her labour was safely over; he had gazed into the wizened features of the child, and above this tender pledge the rainbow of the great dream had arched the heavens. Today she was seven years older, but the world seemed to have aged a century; nowhere could she see a man of exalted mind who would control chaos. All was confusion, and she herself was entangled in it.

Why? That question her cynical innocence did not ask. She did not seek to know how much was due to guilt, and how much to destiny. Self-examination and remorse were alien to her nature. Things were as they were. Now she sat in her window-niche, alone in the palace of her fathers, pregnant by a soldier who was sailing back to his wife oversea, and would perhaps never return. He had promised, of course, to return; promised with pious oaths and straining arms. Yet between his intention of today and his return there were countless other women; there was Octavian, whom one must live with or conquer; between them were the alien peoples who for want of an overlord were straining at the leash and fighting; and even if there had been none of all these there was the sea, that devoured its ships as destiny devours the hearts of men.

Soon she would have two children; perhaps a sister for

Cæsarion. He would marry her ten years later, after the custom of the Ptolemies, and the royal pair of Egypt would be half of Roman blood. But what would she herself be? A woman at the end of the thirties, who on summer evenings would send for a half-grown Syrian slave and teach him how to love? The country must be made secure, and the treasury, or one would lose the liberty to act as one elected! New alliances must be concluded, if not against Rome, then with the most powerful of the Romans. Would he be Antony?

Often enough she was thankful that he had gone. Like a storm-wind he had blown everything topsy-turvy; he had had his way with the Court and Alexandrian society, shaken the old parties, and disappointed many of the friends of Rome. For this reason the man in the street adored him; the legendary consumption of goods by the Court had kept all the traders and artisans busy, and even the masses had had their share of profit from the whims of the foreigner. Never had Antony been as popular in Rome as here, and he had sunned himself in the genial mood of the metropolis. Even the Museion, which scoffed at his culture, could not dislike him; everybody who met Antony had to like him; but no one conceived a passion for him. In her silent comparison, Cleopatra told herself that with Cæsar it had been just the other way about.

And yet she was able to value the significance of Antony as "Imperator," as general, as triumvir, and she realized that it was a shrewd and sensible policy to be the friend of the lord of the Eastern world—a better policy, in the long run, than to be his lover. When he was absent, so it seemed to her, she had but little influence over him. The only thing that bound these two superstitious people together was a soothsayer whom

she had sent away with him, who was clever at making political capital of his Egyptian mysteries. She was now listening
through her thousand ears to every sound that reached her
from the shores of Greece. And the news that presently
reached her was confused.

The encounter of husband and wife in Athens had been
terrible. She could so plainly see the pale, haggard, wild-eyed
Fulvia; knew how she liked to thrust her fingers into the beard
of the massive, sun-bitten man, and to tickle him; and perhaps she did it now, for where had he been hiding so long?
What did he look to get out of the Egyptian woman, when
the fate of the world was being decided in Rome? But then
Cleopatra heard, interrupting the shrill voice of this wild Fulvia, the great thundering bass of the Roman Hercules; who
had given her the right or the mandate to shatter the alliance
with Octavian, to take cities, to garrison fortresses, to risk
sieges, and to force a premature decision on her as yet imperfectly equipped husband?

Cleopatra could hear the two voices across the sea; she saw
these two people raving to and fro in an echoing hall, shaking
their fists as they passed each other; probably, she thought,
he actually beat her. She is satisfied; she has got her way;
but she is still suspicious; could he perhaps find a way of
divorcing her without strengthening the hands of his allies?
And if he does divorce her, will she not poison him? Fulvia
is one to dare anything; she is a mad woman when she is in a
rage.

But now a second woman made her appearance; Cleopatra
was soon to learn of Octavian's latest political device. Sextus

Pompeius, the last surviving son of the great Pompey, who had protected Antony's wife and mother with his ships, at present her born ally, might, as a dreaded pirate, bring Antony's fleet up to a dangerous strength. Forthwith Octavian, son of that Cæsar whom Pompey's family had opposed in years of warfare, sent a messenger to Sextus: he wished to take his niece Scribonia for his wife and to make his peace with him. True, Scribonia was older than he, twice widowed, and even so, just pregnant again, perhaps by her last husband; but the lord of Rome abrogated the law of the ten months' delay, quickly divorced Fulvia's daughter, and took the Pompeian woman to wife, with great midsummer wedding festivities, which set all the Romans laughing.

Octavian's perverse character was to some extent explained by the inheritance of power, without preparation, at the age of nineteen. It was as though the shy, sickly youth, a sort of twilight philosopher, had been struck by an invisible thunderbolt. Already he was having young girls, on whom his cold glance had rested in passing, dragged out of their homes; in later years he had them stripped by his agents, who examined them to make sure that they were intact.

Antony, still in a rage, all emotion, and therefore infuriated by the repudiation of Fulvia's daughter, and by Pompey's defection, stormed out of Athens like a madman, without bidding his wife farewell. He took his legions by surprise; now, he cried, they would avenge Perugia; but he saw how reluctant they were to fight their own comrades yet again. Still, he forced them to fight, and he was advancing victoriously when suddenly a messenger from Greece brought the

[195]

news that Fulvia was dead. She was barely thirty, but the will to power, which was nourished by hatred and revenge rather than the desire to shine, had worn her out.

For Fulvia's ambition was destructive and nihilistic; Cæsar's was constructive and emotional. Antony's ambition was to rule in order to enjoy; Octavian's was the unconscious longing to thaw the icy armour that enclosed him. It was Cleopatra's ambition to preserve her absolute liberty of choice.

The death of her rival did not appease Cleopatra; it alarmed her. For Fulvia's disappearance must bring the two allies closer together again; and this was what they really wished. But what would become of Cæsarion, what of herself, if the wavering Antony allowed himself to be persuaded that Egypt was at last ripe for becoming a Roman province? Friendly relations between the two triumvirs were dangerous to her; and of this she soon had a surprising proof.

The more reasonable soldiers now suddenly and emphatically demanded that their generals should do what they had been slowly and diplomatically endeavouring to do. For fifteen years Romans had been forced to fight against Romans, rushed hither and thither under famous leaders and obscure, simply to assuage the passions of the heads of parties of which each regarded itself as the protagonist of a moral programme, which was to "put an end to disorder," or "save the fatherland," or "the family," or best of all, to "protect private property," which no one had threatened.

At last, it seemed, there was to be an end of the senseless brawl. A new treaty, concluded in Brundusium, specified more precisely than the treaty of three years ago how the triumvirs were to divide Cæsar's legacy. Lepidus was restricted to Roman Africa; Antony was given the East as far as the frontier of Albania; but Italy and the West it left entirely to Octavian. How could a Roman be guilty of this insanity, unless in his heart he no longer felt himself to be a Roman? To leave Rome to his rival meant exile; it meant that he became a proconsul, even though he should unite half a dozen proconsulates and have to account to no one.

When this treaty of peace had been concluded the two found it an easy matter to persuade Sextus Pompeius, the last of great Pompey's sons, to conclude a treaty: especially as Sicily and Sardinia were ceded to him. But he was even less inclined than the others to keep his word. In the Bay of Naples, when he had invited his new friends on board, Menas, the pirate, came to him as they sat feasting, and asked him: "Shall I seize the fellows? Do you want to be the master of the Roman Empire? I have only to weigh anchor and haul in the gangway." There was a pause; Pompeius was considering. "Menas," he said at last, "you should have done it without asking! It is no longer possible: I have pledged my word."

Now at last (at the beginning of the year 39 B.C.) it seemed that the civil war was over. For the first time in fourteen years Italy believed that peace had been concluded. "When the three potentates"—writes Dio Cassius—"confirmed their alliance, before the eyes of their fleets and armies, by clasping hands and exchanging the kiss of peace, there rose an unending jubilation from the land and the ships alike. All these thousands, both soldiers and people, who had execrated the war, suddenly raised such an acclamation that the mountains re-echoed with it, until many of those that shouted fell senseless, and in the turmoil were trodden underfoot or crushed.

Those who stood upon the ships could not wait until they were put ashore, and leapt into the sea; others ran towards them from the shore and sprang into the sea to embrace them. Many there were who against all expectation found that their long-lost friends were still living; others, who caught sight of those whom they had never hoped to see again, believing them dead, stood stupefied and stricken dumb, not trusting their eyes and yet longing to trust them. And they were not convinced of the reality until they called each other by name and heard the other's voice.

"Many wept in the excess of their joy. Others, who believed that their long-dead sons and fathers were still living, ran hither and thither and questioned all they met; they were like men crazed, for they hoped to find them, and feared that they had lost them for ever. Then they plucked out their hair and rent their garments, calling upon him who was lost and lamenting as though he had only now died and lay dead before them. Those who were but onlookers were overcome by grief and joy, and so it continued for the whole of that day and the greater part of the night."

IX

Cleopatra was daily expecting the birth of her child, when —soon after the news of the reconciliation—a messenger appeared who did not dare to deliver the message entrusted to him. Only when the queen sternly ordered him to speak did he inform her that Antony had married Octavian's sister in Rome.

It had all come about quite naturally; having regard to the interests and the characters of the actors, it was really impossible that it should have been different. Since their first alliance the two men had not met, but on the other hand, there had been no exchange of hostile letters. What did they care today for the intrigues of the dead Fulvia, who was willing to plunge all Italy into war in order to drag her husband out of a love-affair? The japes which the younger Pompey permitted himself whenever there was talk of Egypt when he sat at wine had angered Antony; Octavian was more careful. He waited awhile, and then secretly confided his wishes to a few officers; they repeated them to the delegates of the army, who repeated them again as the spontaneous desire of the soldiers. Then Octavian could decently tell his friend that their soldiers hoped that they might become brothers-in-law; but that was doubtless impossible, if only because of the queen?

Antony (writes Plutarch) did not deny that she was his mistress, but he added that, after all, she was not his wife. With this explanation he endeavoured to quiet his conscience and fight against his passion.

From this to actual consent was only a step for Antony. His position, as general, was not favourable; it was time to return to Syria, but for that he needed troops from Octavian. Now that he was once more obliged to approach Egypt a new marriage seemed to him a sort of safeguard against Cleopatra. For Antony put much faith in omens, which he always interpreted in his own favour. In the mimic warfare that accompanied the endless festivities Octavian always defeated him. Perhaps he had grown too fat, too heavy, as the result of wine-bibbing; the younger, slenderer man was always victorious. And the Egyptian soothsayer, Cleopatra's confidant and her spy, came to him and told him:

"Great good fortune awaits you, O Antony, but only if you avoid the shadow of Octavian! Avoid the young man, for his genius threatens yours! When he is at a distance your genius is proud and valiant; but when he is present it is weak and unmanly!"

Since these omens threatened his interests, Antony, as weak natures will, twisted them round until they were favourable to him. Evidently Octavian's sister was the mediatrix who should reconcile their geniuses! Evidently she was his guardian spirit, who even if he went to Syria would keep him away from the Egyptian woman! Was it not really Cleopatra's fault that he had missed so many opportunities at home—her fault that he had allowed Fulvia to rule in his stead? His child would soon be born, and then he would in all respects have followed Cæsar's example; but then the circle would be completed: the spell would be broken: the adventure ended.

And was it not evidently the will of the gods that his wife and Octavia's husband should have died at the same time? Octavia was beautiful; every Roman knew that. She had never enticed him; she was too virtuous for that. But what if one taught these noble ladies things that made them blush? He had often heard that there were women who blushed. A new experience! Her character was better than her brother's; that was because she was only his step-sister, and was not descended from the money-lending grandfather. She had loved her Marcellus, whose second child she now bore in her body. At the wedding she would have to sit down as much as possible, or the people would laugh and say the triumvir was taking the child as dowry. After all, her brother would have to hand over his legions—that would be the dowry! Then he would be able to go ahead.

Octavian was married at the same time as his new brother-in-law. Since his reconciliation with Sextus Pompeius the latter's niece had become superfluous, and his eyes had fallen on a far lovelier woman; he obtained a second divorce, and struck a bargain for Livia, who was given a dowry by the husband who divorced her. She too was pregnant when she prayed for fruitfulness in the temple of the gods, and the two triumvirs may well have bandied jests about their brides on the occasion of their double wedding.

Something of all this Cleopatra heard as the messenger told her of Antony's marriage. In her self-controlled way she asked him, quite coolly, whether it was true that Antony had wept when Fulvia died; whether he drank wine the same day, and if not, when; whether he was seen in the company of singing-women immediately afterwards; what sort of funeral he had given her; and how much time had elapsed between Fulvia's death and the new betrothal.

But when she was alone again she tried in vain to take a cool survey of her new situation. Her physical condition had enfeebled her, and robbed her of the youthful combativeness which usually inspired her. Would it be tonight, or not until the morrow? was her question, and her situation was more depressing and her patience less than on the former occasion. She kept Cæsarion near her; explained that now he would no longer be alone, questioned him as to his childish thoughts, and kissed him. For a quarter of an hour she imagined that this second child also was Cæsar's, in some mystical fashion engendered by his spirit. Again, she tried to recall Antony's face and figure with the greatest exactitude, and what he was really like as a lover. There came into her mind a crude soldier's expression which he had used on one occasion when he had cried, laughing, that now he had assuredly begotten a son.

Later she was suddenly seized by a fit of savage wrath to think that she had ever surrendered herself to him, had indeed seduced him. She flung herself on the floor, tearing her shift and striking at the slave-women who took her in their arms in order to lift her up. Exhausted, she lay back, moaning; she could not rest in any position; then, very softly, she breathed the name of Antony, and suddenly even the long-forgotten name of her mother rose to her lips. She realized how alone she was; that she had had her brothers and sisters put to death in order that she might rule alone. She could not understand the audacity with which she had twice detained a foreigner at her court, with the result that she was now alone in her palace with two children of different fathers; and of these two men one had been murdered and his body burned, while the other might at this very moment be celebrating his nuptials with music and feasting.

Suddenly she recognized, among the dancers in Antony's house near the Capitol, the cold eyes of Octavian, his great enemy, and she shrieked aloud that they must bring Cæsarion, and when the child had come they were not to leave her alone. The boy was frightened; he did not recognize his mother, and ran from her; and then she sent her slave away, and was alone. She dreamed herself back in one of those nights when she had shared her couch with Antony, and had pulled the hair of his shaggy breast until he cried out and cuffed her.

On the following day Cleopatra brought twins into the world, a son and a daughter. From this moment she was haunted by no more visions; she asked the gods only what this unusual gift might signify. The priests gave her confused answers. She, however, thought that the twins might perhaps have two fathers, Cæsar and Antony; and then she laughed. The children she called "My little Sun-god" and "My little Moon-goddess." She swore to herself that she would never again give Antony a thought; but suddenly she burst into tears, for Antony was far away, asleep beside his new wife, and would never return.

In this nadir hour of her life neither Cleopatra, nor Octavian, nor anyone knew of a certain sentence which Antony had written at the time of his wedding in Rome. No one knew of it, save the two friends who had to sign the document as witnesses; for the talkative man had his rare secrets, which he confessed only to himself in his solemn moments. In such a mood he had recalled Cæsar's sudden death, and the consequences that followed from his testament. Presently he himself would be off to the Persian war, and so, in his forty-third year, at the time of this third marriage, he made his own testament, in which he remembered his children and his friends.

In the final clause he declared that it was his wish that after his death his body should be carried in solemn procession through the Roman Forum. But then his remains were to be carried by sea to Alexandria, so that he might be buried by the side of Queen Cleopatra.

This was Antony's last will and testament. He sealed the roll and gave it into the keeping of the Supreme Vestal.

res

Passion brings sorrow. Who shall give thee peace,
O heart oppressed, whose loss is all too great?
Where are the hours that had so short a lease?
Oh, what availed thy beauty, that was fate?

—GOETHE

Augustus

CHAPTER IV

Ares

I

FOR three years (by our reckoning, the years 39–36 B.C.) Cleopatra ruled alone in Alexandria, and played no part in the history of Rome. As in the days of her father, the ships went sailing to and fro, and when the wheat of the Nile valley that filled their holds had been discharged onto the quay at Ostia, they returned, perhaps, with a cargo of Spanish silver or Gaulish timber. Athletes and play-actors, traders and bankers, rhetoricians and speculators, were living links between the declining kingdom and the failing republic, but the history of each State unfolded itself independently, and a short peace allowed the two nations, and the other Mediterranean peoples, to draw a few quiet breaths. During these three years Cleopatra lived much as did any other queen on the shores of the Mediterranean in the time of the Cæsars, though indeed more fully.

And yet there was a difference. For she was a woman with three fatherless children, in the position of a deserted mistress, whom society would have attacked if the power of the Ptolemy had not held her enemies at a distance. And for all her power, there was danger to her in the circumstances. Must it not seem a natural thing to poison a queen without legitimate heirs or defenders, in order to found a new dynasty, if one happened to be one of the discontented nobles then living at the court of Alexandria? And what could have seemed easier than to come to an understanding on the point with Octavian in Rome, who hated Cæsarion, his only rival? No document records for us the intrigues of this court during these three years, but from the general situation we may deduce something as to the thoughts and feelings of the queen, who must have wavered between caution and energy, hope and renunciation.

This unaffrighted Amazon, who had eaten stale army bread in wartime and slept in a draughty tent, was at the same time the most pampered woman of her age. She did not know the numbers of the slaves and eunuchs who served her in silence. When she lay in her bath of a morning—one of the great porphyry troughs that are still in existence—half a dozen maidens waited with hot towels in order to rub and anoint her. Then, lying back on the cool linen pillows, before a great mirror that gave a greenish opalescent reflection, supporting her head on one hand as was her custom, she had her chestnut-brown hair dressed (but never dyed or bleached, although fair

hair was the fashion); not in the towering chignon with
which the Roman ladies sought to outdo one another, yet no
longer in the loose curls of her girlhood. Now, as the bust
shows, she wore it lying close to the head, in seven short
waves, so that there was no parting to continue the line of the
nose. It was caught up in a knot, rather high, at the back of
the head, and only one coquettish little curl over the left eye
broke the austerity of the Greek form. It was a queen's fashion; only the curl was Cleopatra.

She had no affection for the *mafortes*, a robe that was
really no more than a veil, and which was bound to disturb
every man who spoke with her, because he must try to divine
her breasts beneath it. If the veil was rose-pink in colour, it
seemed to flush the white of her skin as though by a longing
that did not dare to become desire. Over this one of her slave-
women drew the himation of Milesian silk, crocus-yellow or
sapphire-blue; but if she had a fancy to wear the dalmatic, a
dress with sleeves, two pairs of hands must help her, in order
to shorten the moments of robing. If a slave failed to present
the arm-hole at the right moment, Cleopatra would kick her,
for she had never soiled her hands by beating a slave. The
kick had survived as a Pharaonic gesture.

She liked to wear a robe with a girdle and clasp when she
had to receive a distinguished foreigner; for clasps and girdles
made a man's hand itch to undo them, and engrossed his
imagination, so that he became distracted, and easier to out-
wit in business. Her little leather shoes, which had a separate
housing for the big toe, were made with high heels, in order
that she might seem taller; and on certain days, if she had to

receive an important envoy, superstition led her to hide a secret love-spell in the soles, although she had not the faintest
intention of having an affair with the man.

She loved cedar-oil, because it reminded her of the dry heat
of the desert; but if the perfume-slave had failed to divine that
on this particular morning she had a fancy for myrrh, the flask
would soon lie shattered on the floor, and since now the scent
of cedar-oil was stronger than ever, the slaves were all frightened out of their wits. No one must hand her an ornament
unasked; she would have a number of necklaces displayed before her, and sink her chin in the direction of the one she had
chosen. She often gave the preference to topazes, because the
golden shimmer of their sensuous tints reminded her of honey.
On other days she would have nothing but cool, gleaming silver. This was when she thought of Cæsar.

The twins would come rushing in with a train of cats and
tame monkeys and a huddle of servants, but they had learned
that their mother was not to be touched when her toilet was
completed; so their tutors trembled, for how could they know
whether they should or dared restrain them? Cautiously Cleopatra lifted the boy Alexander. He alone of the three was like
her; he had inherited her sharp nose, and he was doing his
best to reproduce her lovely mouth; and further, he was lithe
and slender like his mother. The little Cleopatra, on the other
hand, was Antony all over; people laughed to see how comi-
cally the broad, masculine features, with their gay and lively
expression, were reproduced in miniature in the two-year-old
little girl. Their mother laughed at this amusing exchange of
roles; already she could see the little girl using the whip on her
servants and comfortably issuing her orders; whereas Alexan-

der would be a slender, studious youth. The sort of boy I should have been, she thought; but she never wished that she had been born of the opposite sex.

The moderate-sized hall in which she received her ministers had to remain empty until she entered it; she could not endure the presence of servants until she had seen her papers. Only one person was allowed to wait here: Cæsarion.

The boy of ten, almost as tall as his mother, was like his father "in form as well as voice," as Homer would say; for he was tall and kingly; he spoke warmly and thoughtfully, and one saw in him the earnestness which may still have been Cæsar's before he lived a life of fashion, and which he revealed once more in his later years, when he begot the child. In this earnestness he had inherited a legacy which increased his mother's hopes that he would inherit the throne; so that by virtue of his character, and his parentage, he felt called upon, as it were from three sides, to learn everything, and to store up knowledge, as early as possible, as his mother had done.

Cleopatra was teaching Cæsarion to rule. The complicated circumstances of the Egyptian Empire and its capital, all the ethnological and financial problems, the products of the country, and to whom they were sold, and further, all the intricacies of the ruling houses on the shores of the Mediterranean—all these he must learn to understand betimes. It was this that she had in mind when she required his presence every morning, here and in the audience-hall; also she wanted to lose no time in accustoming her officials to their future king. As a woman, too, she felt herself supported by his presence. The recollections of her early childhood, and also the immemorial history of her house, suggested the presence of a younger brother, formally her husband, and ruling jointly with her. Indeed, she even regarded him, secretly, as a sort of protector; as though in affairs of State she were assisted by Cæsar, in the person of his son.

First of all there was the Court, whose gradations the earnest boy learned to distinguish during these morning lessons. Such titles as King's Kinsman, King's First Friend, Chief Satellite assumed a bodily form in the persons of the magnates of the empire, who made their bow to the queen and to him. Then there were the scribes, in number as the sands of the Libyan desert, just as in the days of the Pharaohs; the scribes, the chief of whom ranked equally with a minister, and read the decisions of yesterday, which gradually became rules of law, from his official record, the Ephemerides. Then came the councillors, who proposed the decrees affecting Alexandria, and the prytanes, who had to execute them, for Alexandria enjoyed still the privileges of a "free city," in the Greek sense, being regarded as "outside Egypt." The boy learned to distinguish the *demi* and *phyla*, the tribes and families whose seniority and privileges led to endless legal processes; all the privileges of the Greeks and their intrigues against the Egyptians; the legal status of the Jews, of whom there were no less than a million in Egypt, and the civic rights which many of them had acquired; the arrogance of the Alexandrians, and the vengefulness of individual Egyptians when they acquired power; and the jealousy of the Greeks in respect of the Macedonians, or those who so called themselves, for even now, two and a half centuries after its foundation, the royal house insisted on the fact that the land of its origin was the birthplace

of Alexander, and everybody wanted to prove that his people
came from Macedonia.

When the great priests came with their suits and proposals
—the highest of whom, the priest of the god Alexander, was
the first man in the empire after the monarch—Cæsarion
learned to understand the admixture of rituals, the theocracy,
which the Greeks were practising in Alexandria, with a shrewd
regard for the old Egyptian cults, so that Isis was also Aphrodite, and Pluto, Serapis. He detected the factitious earnestness with which the queen inquired as to the health of the
Divine Bull, and her genuine interest when the inventories of
the temple treasuries were laid before her, down to the last
golden beaker and silver spoon. And following closely on these
sacred and traditional matters came the report of a police-
officer, which told them how yesterday the disturbance caused
by the lentil-sellers in the market had been suppressed, and
why the venders of melon-seeds ought to be given a stand
nearer the lake, as the trouble had been caused by this new
source of competition.

Then Cæsarion, always standing a little in the background,
but very erect, would hear the Gymnasiarch, one of the highest officers of the empire, in his red dress and high white
boots, reporting the victory of the Egyptian athletes in the
contests at Pergamon; and further, the arrival of a large con-
signment of the finest oil, which the wrestlers needed for mas-
sage, and which was excepted from the monopoly. Then came
the chief administrator of the Nile, explaining, by means of
maps and diagrams, which canals were silted up, which would
have to be widened, why the vegetable crops had been poor

[213]

above Thebes, and what taxes might be used to pay for a few hundred new water-wheels for irrigation purposes. After him the steward of the monopolies submitted to the queen the accounts in which the production of papyrus and wheat, oil and salt, was shown for each month. Now the heir realized that the State monopoly was the source of the famous treasure which he was one day to inherit, as the source of power, and which, so his mother declared, was also the source of liberty; he learned how the farmers of the royal bank, the royal shipyards, and the royal estates calculated their dividends, so that while all the traders were growing rich, yet all that was done in Egypt brought gold to the treasury of the Ptolemies.

But Cæsarion felt proudest when he saw the Romans enter, if on account of some great wheat contract they made their way even to the queen, or perhaps they wished to announce their runners for the following year, and were using this pretext to get a glimpse of the famous queen whose legend in Rome was still unfaded. They were always very much aware of themselves, and usually importunate; and he noted how the queen, when dealing with a Roman, would readily increase a figure or exaggerate a demand, but in the end she often conceded more than she had apparently intended. At such moments the boy felt that he came of better stock than his mother, for although he admired her, Cæsar had a higher place in his imagination: Cæsar, whose name seemed to excite more reverence than the name of Ptolemy.

It was his ambition that was aroused when the chief Court Marshal, in the great Hall of Audience, introduced ambassadors and foreigners, whom he learned to distinguish by their weapons and costumes: Thracians and Bithynians, Lydians and Persians, Troglodytes from the Red Sea, Nubians from the Upper Nile, or Galatians, and even Chinese. Then he felt a renewed respect for his mother, since he heard her address many of these people in their own language, so that foreigners and Egyptians were equally amazed.

During the heat of the day, between two o'clock and six, the boy saw nothing of his mother, and she saw no one. These were the hours when she desired to be neither queen nor mother. Then she was free to lie for hours alone on her favourite divan, between a new edition of Sappho, recently issued by the Museion, and a mirror, stroking a luxurious cat, or picking up a roll of papyrus whose obscene verses from the latest political comedy brought her a whiff of Roman air. Then she would send for the letters of her Roman agents, and read one again and again, waving it up and down in her long, slender hand as though to weigh its truth; and frowning a little, she would consider whether Sextus was perhaps powerful enough to weaken Octavian and so strengthen Antony. But again a shadow rose between them—Antony's Roman wife—and she tore the letter to fragments. Should she have the woman poisoned? For the hundredth time she repudiated the idea, and fell to stroking the cat.

Sometimes—the eunuch whispered to the palace spies—instead of the cat a young slave lay beside the queen, but not often, and not for long, and as a rule he then disappeared into a familiar cellar.

Towards sunset, if she drove abroad, Cæsarion on her left, she wore a purple robe with Laconian ribbons; she had no hat, but a little parasol; but the Macedonian guard which surrounded her carriage wore white felt hats, and carried the huge lances that were used in the days of Alexander, when throughout the Eastern world they were as dreaded as the Cretan bow. First they drove past the Museion and the library, where the trampling of the horses always lured a few bored-looking faces to the windows, and Cæsarion saw that the queen saluted them. In the distance they could see the race-course and the riding-school, and from the public baths they heard the shouts of the young men who were diving and playing pranks on one another.

When they reached the Tetrapylon, the Fourfold Gate at the cross-roads on Alexandria's main street, they drove more slowly, and as they passed through the crowd the queen, with the eyes of a huntress, looked for many things of which her councillors told her nothing. Only a yard above the level of the street, Cleopatra found it possible to endure the crowd, the filth, and the poverty, despite the smell of the butchers' stable and the sewers, for she had learned in Rome that the temper of the people is like a boiling cauldron, and her disdain did not prevent her from sniffing the ingredients of the stew.

In the city the boy, eager to learn, saw the glass-blowers and the linen-weavers, men and women, in the open colonnades. The great buildings of several stories were the factories where the sheets of papyrus were prepared, as he could see from the bales outside the doors; that morning he had heard the government's sales of the commodity discussed. Goldsmiths were humming at their blowpipes; silversmiths were wielding their hammers with short, sharp blows; fish venders bellowed on their way along the streets; but the coppersmiths made more noise than all the rest as they banged away at their trays and basins, and it seemed to the boy that they struck with redoubled vigour because the queen was passing, though he did not know whether they did so in hate or in love.

Even in the evenings Cæsarion was not free. In the great gardens of the citadel he had to respond to the greetings of fashionable people, and learn to observe the manners of the so-called tax-free philosophers, some of whom gave him lessons in the afternoon. He had to learn how much to give a singing-woman, and when it was fitting that he should withdraw; but late into the night he could hear from the window the lascivious songs which some women were singing to the guitar in the garden below; or the voices of the anatomist and the chief justice from where they sat in a corner of the garden, supping on salt beef from Byzantium, and debating whether Libyan or Syrian wine went better with Chian cheese.

Later still the queen often found him reading beside his lamp, and then they would have a good laugh over the latest gossip of the city, which they had heard that evening in the garden. When she left him, with a kiss, he saw a great amethyst on her finger, but he never told her what he had heard concerning its powers. Sometimes she would then sit long before her mirror, thinking with realistic mockery of her life.

It is comical, she told herself, turning her head a little to the left in order to judge of the effect of the new long pearl earring in her right ear. A mighty queen, reputed beautiful and a dangerous woman, living almost a widowed life, because she cannot find a man who continues to please her. The master of horse has graceful legs, but his eyes pop out of his head, and he fancies himself. Cæsarion flushed up suddenly when the dancing-girl flirted her dress at him. To whom ought

[217]

one to trust him first of all? A healthy hetaira is better than a princess. . . . If one puts up the price of salt by a half-drachma one can cover the oil deficit for this year. . . . Why is Cyprus buying less papyrus? . . . We want twice as many garland-makers. . . . The Miletus idea isn't bad, but who knows who may not seize my ships before they come to port? Sooner or later there's sure to be a crisis. Everybody is afraid of it; which is just why things are so peaceful. . . . When the boy laughs he's just like his father! . . . They'll be wanting wine next, in-stead of milk. A comical existence. . . . Tomorrow they can move the curl a little nearer the left eyebrow. . . .

II

In the meantime Antony was amusing himself in Athens. Octavia, his wife, pleased him after she had regained her slen-der figure; for a few months after the wedding she had to bring yet another daughter into the world, the child of her late husband, to whom Antony, in a generous moment, gave the name of Antonia; and after this it amused him for a time to make this puritanical lady less of a puritan. This man, whom women found it hard to withstand, seems to have swept her away, if only for hours at a time, into the vortex of his *joie de vivre*. Octavia was like a solemn governess whom a pretty boy has forced to laugh against her will, and who then feels a little embarrassed.

What did he not do in order to amuse himself and her! At the games, when as Gymnasiarch he stepped in between two wrestlers in order to stop a fight, the giant lifted one of the men into the air with one hand, and held him there struggling, while the public shrieked with delight. He dismissed the guards at his gates, and went roaming through the streets with scholars or comedians. Then he invited all Athens to a great athletic festival, for which the city had to pay. Above the theatre he built a bower of Bacchus, a sort of suspended stage, where he and his friends lay drinking on beds of bracken, to the music of flutes and tambourines.

How thankful he was to know that Octavian, the difficult brother-in-law, was far away in Italy! The very sight of him always made Antony feel cold and clammy. Now, when he heard that the young man had had himself proclaimed "the son of the Divine," he resolved to outdo him. One night, with his roistering train, drunken with wine and ringed about with torches, he stormed the Acropolis and had himself proclaimed by heralds as the resurrected Dionysos. Thereupon he celebrated his mystic nuptials with Athena, and himself represented the statue of the god in the temple, which the Athenians made the subject of malicious epigrams. At the same time he required the city to pay a wedding-gift of a million drachmas; at which a councillor cried: "Great God, Zeus took thy mother Semele without a dowry!" Antony laughed, but the Athenians had to pay.

Since the victory of his captains on the frontier of the Persian Empire had alarmed the rulers on the coast, these latter came to parley with him; and it amused him to appoint petty kings: Herod he made king of Judea, Darius king of Pontus, and a third king of Lycaonia. These kings, he said, were only men, but he was a god. And when he was drunk he believed this.

Cleopatra

Cleopatra heard everything, but it does not seem that she ever sent him a message during these three years. The ancient writers record only a single conversation, in which, having been reminded of his forsaken mistress and her twin children, he is said to have replied: "I cannot entrust my whole line to a single woman. Hercules, my forebear, like me, left his blood in many places, in order to found new dynasties." If this saying was repeated to her it could not have surprised her.

She remained a distant observer. If she ever longed to send a messenger or a letter to Antony, she rejected the notion at once, feeling, as a queen, far above this citizen who had risen to be Cæsar's favourite only because of a certain talent in the field. In moments of womanly fear her healthy mind even grasped at her contempt for Antony as a reason why she would not under any circumstances send for him. In the depth of her heart there was a confident premonition that before long he would return of his own accord.

Once the rumour of a quarrel between the new brothers-in-law filled her with hope, but the rumour passed. Sextus Pompeius, affronted by Octavian's sudden divorce from his niece, and always ready, as the son of Pompey the Great, to strike a blow at the Cæsars, had broken his promise, and inflicted a crushing defeat on Octavian—hastening to the war—in his first naval battle, off Messina. Cæsar's twenty-five-year-old heir lost his head completely; surrendering the command in the thick of the battle, he fled to the coast, and there, without a fleet, appealed to Antony for assistance.

Antony, who himself had many requests to make, sailed at the end of the winter for Brundusium, where Octavian was to meet him. But Octavian, now on his feet again, did not keep his appointment. Now, and on a second occasion, grievance was heaped upon grievance, and on each of the occasions the civil war was postponed only because both antagonists wanted to gain time.

Octavia acted as mediatrix. Antony, who, as was his habit, had immediately made her pregnant, called this second daughter also Antonia, as though in spite, and hastened to beget a second child, for he wanted yet another son. Under the circumstances his wife no longer interested him as a mistress. But so soon as he began to weary of her he was bound to remember the ecstatic delights of Alexandria. Watching his wife, he conceived, with some suddenness, a positive distaste for her virtue. He got a friend of his to lead her into temptation, and was angry when she repulsed him; for he attributed her refusal, not to her love for her husband, but to her "old Roman" moral arrogance. But that other woman, the woman whom he had deserted, and of whose doings he was constantly receiving reports! She could bring two children at once into the world, and still remain a fascinating creature! There was really nothing she could not do, but Octavia—well, she was just a mater-familias.

Divorce was impossible, for that would have meant a breach with Octavian. And why divorce her? It was enough to put the sea between them; then all would be better than well, and so long as he did not go to Alexandria she could live quietly with her daughter and the son to whom she would give birth in Rome; and from Rome the fortunate wife of Antony could exchange letters and greetings with her husband.

Cleopatra

It was doubtless not only Cleopatra that he longed for, but his old bachelor freedom. Yet when he turned his eyes toward Egypt he was impressed by the great advantages of a political alliance; for he must make the most of the next few years, if as the mightier he was to threaten Rome. Since Octavian would rather be friends even with a distant Antony, and since the two men had once more begun to exchange threats, it probably suited both that Octavia should declare that she would be the unhappiest woman in the world if her husband and her brother should go to war.

So, at Tarentum, the triumvirate was renewed for a further term of five years. Antony gave his brother-in-law a hundred and thirty ships with which to fight Pompey; in return he received two legions to help him in the Persian war, which had hitherto been waged in a fragmentary fashion, being repeatedly interrupted. To please the superstitious soldiery, the old custom of giving a pledge was followed: Octavian's daughter was betrothed to the son of Antony and Fulvia. Now, at the age of twenty-six, Octavian united his daughter to the brother of the child to whom he himself had once been betrothed.

Now Antony discarded his white shoes and transformed himself again into the general. Once more his ears were filled with the challenge of Persia, whose trumpets had too long been drowned by his Bacchic drums. In accordance with the law of the dictatorship, this general was forced to make war, since the new triumvirate, concluded without real inclination or logical necessity, could not permanently mask the rivalry of the triumvirs. He who would retain his usurped power when the institution collapsed must fight. Cæsar's papers, which Antony still carried with him, entrusting them to no one, had never lost their symbolic virtue; and indeed, during the last few years, when the unrest in the Roman Empire had incited the hereditary Persian enemy to advance upon it, they had once more become of practical value.

But in order to make war upon Persia one must have money, even for an army of moderate strength; and though the quæstors admitted more and more iron and copper into the coinage, the legions still went unpaid for months at a time. Octavian, of course, in Italy, could resort to the expedient of giving confiscated land to his soldiers; but Antony had to provide cash, for it was doubtful if there would be enough loot and booty in Syria. But where was money to be found in the Eastern world, save in Egypt? Was it for nothing that one had become the lover of the wealthiest woman in the world? Practical and political considerations mingled with those of the adventurer and the woman-hunter, and the darling of the gods—for Antony was surely that—could vary his motives as he pleased; they were always adequate. Cleopatra's wealth was the key to Persia; but Antony had the key to Cleopatra, and when the wine had gone to his head, and he imagined her lying naked, a bag of gold lay beside her.

He broke up his camp. In Corfu he parted from his wife; probably he patted her on the cheek and told her, paternally but absently, to take care of the children. Then, in obedience to an oracle, he took with him to the war a branch of the sacred olive and water from the spring which was known as Clepsydra. But first of all he must dust the coats of all the little kings between the sea and Persia, in order to expose all the intrigues which they had been hatching against Rome for the last three years and, above all, against Antony.

Octavia parted from him with maternal emotion, a loyal wife who in spite of all the follies and jealousies of her kinsmen took charge of the children, who were truly helpless; for the time being, Fulvia's children and her own daughters, but later there were to be more than she had anticipated. She was certainly not unhappy as she bade farewell to her husband; to her he must have seemed a likeable madman. Her old Roman sense of duty required her to sacrifice her personal welfare to that of her family or the State; and she was inwardly the richer for the sacrifice.

A third person watched their farewells; in silence, but cherishing a secret hope, Octavian saw Antony depart for the East. The two men never saw each other again. Octavian suffered no apprehension that his sister might finally be sacrificed in this affair; he meant her to be. If, when he had reasserted his power against the eternal Pompey, ruling alone in Italy, parted from Antony by the Mediterranean, which could not be crossed by troop-ships in winter—if he could quietly strengthen his position at home, the moment would presently come when the probable victory of his brother-in-law must injure him in public opinion. For he felt that Antony was everywhere more popular than he, and regarded as an abler general. But one day it must come to this: that of the three men of the alliance, who were already only two in actual fact, one must make himself sole master.

III

"That unruly steed, to which Plato compared certain passions, once more broke loose, and in spite of honour, interest, and prudence, Antony sent Fonteius Capito to conduct Cleopatra into Syria." So Plutarch speaks, when he wishes to explain why Antony acted thus and not otherwise.

No one would have expected him to act otherwise. It was not surprising that he sent for her, but only that nearly four years went by before he did so. Perhaps the reader would like to see the proud queen refusing to join him, and the remorseful Roman hastening to cast himself at her feet? But according to the records the story followed a much more realistic course. Antony was a general; a great army had crossed the sea with him; it was destined for the East, and could not march westwards; while Cleopatra, though a reigning queen, could move about as she wished. Everything impelled her to hasten to the side of the only person who could save her from her loneliness; and in her, too, motives of every kind, political and private—motives of the Queen of Egypt and those of the mother of three children—urged her toward the same goal.

As she sailed for the second time toward that eastern bight of the Mediterranean—for Antioch lay opposite Tarsus on the Syrian coast—her feelings had nothing in common with those of five years earlier. Then the woman who lay in the shadow of the red sail wished not only to approach the avengers of her murdered husband, but also to protect her wealthy country, that lay open to every attack, from falling into the hands of a conqueror. If she did this in her own elegant way, an unconscious longing for untasted pleasures had inspired her to a delicate cunning, a proud sensuality. A fearless woman of twenty-five had set forth on an adventure; then she was still Aphrodite.

But now Cleopatra the Seventh stood in the bows of the ship; Queen of Egypt, a ripened woman of thirty-three, from whose breasts three children had drunk, in whose lap a Hercules had sated himself. The high bosom was fuller that pressed itself against the silk of her pink chiton, and in measure as her youth departed, there seemed to radiate from her the knowledge of the gifts of life, and the desire of a queen to gather them all into her grasp. Her gaze seemed tenser, her veins were more prominent, and the knot of hair was dressed higher on her head. Only her lips, in their beauty, were like two boats upon a narrow strand. They seemed still expectant of a nameless kiss, no one would have believed that they could open to utter a curse.

Her will to power, whose first unfolding had been checked by the appearance of Cæsar, had grown during the years of danger and responsibility, years of continual friction, of conflict with subordinates. The natural timidity of the lonely woman whose youth had been supported by the greatest man of her time was long outgrown, and her reawakened self-consciousness was aware of new possibilities; but now human schemes had taken the place of divine dreams.

For the cold, cynical side of her character the Bacchic winter, which had taught her madness, and whose halcyon conclusion had left her with twin children, had soon faded to an alien episode; indeed, when Octavia had appeared on the horizon, as her lover's new wife, a wife freely chosen after his great adventure, she had been inclined, for a moment, to break with him for ever. But her common sense had soon made her change her mind; for this man was still the master of half the world, and might be a danger to Egypt. Her jealousy, therefore, was not long-lived; reason curbed her longing to revenge herself. The children whom she brought into the world just as their father was marrying his new wife absorbed her vitality for a time, and as the genuine pledges of a savage love they transmuted her resentment into a sense of superiority. Was it matter for surprise, when she had stooped to an intrigue with a Roman citizen, that he, without understanding for his kingly fate, should promptly sink to espousing another Roman citizeness? It was the sort of thing a plebeian would do!

Yet during these four years she had never lost sight of him; and as a forsaken wife, and an imperilled queen, it was inevitable that she should long for his return. Since of the two men who ruled the world one was her son's deadly enemy, her mind would have been bound to dwell upon the other, even if she had no longer loved him. Moreover, she was so much cleverer than he that there were times when she forgot all resentment, accepting his character as the gods had created it, and considered only how she could resign herself to his weaknesses. Was gold then less than beauty? Had not her forebears hoarded such wealth in the last three centuries merely in order that she, their remote descendant, might one day find that this gold would buy her freedom when all else had failed?

This time, she thought, as she stood on the deck of her ship, her eyes straining towards the eastern goal of her voyage, this time she would not appear to Antony in the bark of Aphrodite! Of course, he would want to possess her, but first he must give her some security; for three children needed a father, and the kingdom an alliance. Never against Rome! her father had taught her. She had been seduced by the great dream of founding a world-empire with Rome, but then the dagger of the self-righteous Brutus had been plunged into the body of the man who was a world in himself. Then she had followed the great Roman. If today only half Rome were accessible to her plans, the lesser Romans must follow her. Since she no longer saw anyone above her, Cleopatra's sense of royalty craved more territory—and more than ever her father had possessed.

But she knew Antony through and through; she felt that he had not, like her, after Cæsar's death, shown himself equal to envisaging new aims. She had never believed that Cæsar's genius had passed, with his papers, into the keeping of this cavalry officer; she would never have ventured to transfer the Alexander-dream to him. She knew, before she saw him again, that he was still the same, lovable and vacillating, and if henceforth she had to negotiate with him she herself would have to take the lead. Whether she would succeed in enticing him away from Persia was uncertain; her principal task would be to keep him away from Rome. If she could quite divorce his Greek nature from the Latin world, for which he seemed, as a matter of fact, to have no excessive affection, he could make her the mistress of the southern Mediterranean. Only one little step was needed: he must become King of Egypt.

While Cleopatra revolved such thoughts, at the bows of her ship, in the light sea-breeze, the witness and heir of the

man whose all but fortuitous landing in Egypt had once engendered all these plans of world-empire was standing beside
her. Cæsarion, for whom this voyage was to reveal a fragment
of a new world, was, as a travelling-companion, indispensable
to her policy and her pride. Everywhere the people must learn
to honour their future ruler in the tall, serious boy of fourteen.
To this woman, who stood high above the peoples of the
Mediterranean in her boldness of conception and imagination, it never occurred to present his own children to her returning lover; she felt that this Bacchant, who had mistresses
everywhere, would see only the ridiculous aspect of these little people; at the very sight of them he would regard the wild
season of their begetting with more sober eyes. The son whom
she would show him in their stead was Cæsar's son, and for
that reason alone must interest him.

With a definite programme, which comprised all her demands, the queen approached that fateful corner of the Mediterranean from which three paths lay open to every conqueror,
leading to three different points of the compass. She gave
orders for a great review of all her clothes, decided which
brooches and earrings were to be worn with each dress, and
how her appearance might be enhanced by the deft use of
colours and the display of precious jewels. Cæsarion stood beside her for a while, gazing with vacant eyes at all this trump-
ery, and then turned to watch the working of the ship.

IV

In the citadel of Antioch there were rare doings. Antony had wished to receive the Queen of Egypt with a nocturnal banquet such as he had never yet given, in order to show her that even a Roman knew how to hold festival. For weeks he had been getting together everything he had ever seen at her banquets, though many details were given a more masculine colour, lest their Roman quality be forgotten in a multiplicity of foreign usages. But when the queen made her entry on horseback, surrounded by guards in resplendent uniforms, with her slender son, who might have been her brother, beside her, all Antony's preparations suddenly seemed commonplace to him, and only the compliments which she paid him two days later reassured him as to the unprecedented brilliance of his banquet.

Cleopatra had held her old lover at arm's length for a couple of nights; a new experience for Antony. With his overwhelming exuberance, he had wanted to come to close quarters directly they found themselves alone, as though he were merely continuing a love-affair after a journey. But he found her a changed woman. It was not that he no longer pleased her; it was only that she did not betray the fact. No flood of reproaches followed, such as Fulvia had poured upon him in Athens. This woman merely smiled at him, and when, half pleading, half threatening, he played the Hercules, she burst out laughing in his face. She did not lift a finger, yet he drew back, and as nothing better occurred to him, he too began to laugh.

On the second day the marriage was celebrated. They were both matter-of-fact and cool in their bearing. Antony agreed that a coin should be struck in their joint names, but he wished to be described in the superscription as Autocrator, not as King, for then, although the queen's husband, he could remain a Roman proconsul. She recognized the advantage, and indeed the necessity of this precaution; if he became king, or proclaimed his divorce from Octavia, the triumvirate which had just been concluded for another five years would be broken, and the war with Octavian would be inevitable. It was too late to hold him back from the Persian war: her first sight of the enormous camp told her that. And to lead all these troops to Egypt would have been impossible. With a sense of uneasiness she saw thousands of talents from her treasury vanishing in the direction of Persia, for she had granted with a nod of the head the money which he required for the campaign. Well, he thought, when it comes to fulfilling her requirements, she is the richest woman in the world. A political treaty was laid before him.

And now, on the third evening, music rang through the halls; hundreds of officers, from Antony's staff and the queen's retinue, drank brotherhood in the sweet, heavy wines of Syria; the finest dancing-girls in camp were invited, and were embarrassed by the surplus of men. Love and friendship were affirmed so fervently in half a dozen languages that few understood the words, but all the meaning; and the Syrian nobles who had been invited did as the others did, but silently smiled; they had already sworn brotherhood to so many conquerors in their ancient city, and had fought them afterwards.

In one of the smaller rooms Cleopatra stood at a larger table on which lights were burning. Before her a great map was unrolled; four slaves held its corners. Cæsarion, in the costume of a Macedonian horseman, with high boots, holding his felt hat, stood at the narrow end of the table, his head bent over the map between the candles. Two paces from him sat Antony, not quite at ease in the heavy purple cloak which he had to wear that day as Imperator, leaning far back in a deep armchair and staring at the queen. Never had he seen her so beautiful; hitherto he had been noting the glances of all the petty kings among his guests, how they were all admiringly fixed on his famous mistress. Now they were alone; the slaves did not count; at last he could have a good look at her.

In her silver robe, with her high-heeled shoes, she looked almost tall, and as the light of the candles glittered on her jewels, and revealed, in the diadem that rested on her curls, the finest diamonds which the world then contained, she seemed to the now silent reveller an apparition more like an alien goddess than the noble Roman matrons with whom he was obliged to compare her. Above all, he was fascinated by the earnestness with which she gazed at the great map, while with a peacock-feather, as though in sport, she drew vague circles and figures over land and sea. She knew the effect she was producing, and gave him time to drink in the magic of her appearance. Then she turned her head towards him and smiled, and with a gesture of the chin she directed his gaze to the map, until he pulled himself together, and rising, stood close beside her, on her right, while the boy retained his position on her left. So the pictured world lay outspread before the Roman, the Egyptian Greek, and the heir to the Alexander-dream, which was one day to bind them together.

But Queen Cleopatra, standing before the great map, demanded, as Antony's bride, her wedding-present: the old provinces which the Pharaohs had possessed fifteen hundred years before. To win these at a stroke, to be able to offer her Egyptians, and more especially the eternally grumbling Macedonian magnates at home, an empire of which they had only dreamed for centuries past, this was the way to make her Roman marriage, despite all the anticipated opposition, the glorious climax of her power. It was this that she had continually revolved in her mind on board ship, and explained to her son, who now stood beside her, silent, with a non-committal expression, as though through him Cæsar's spirit was seeking to protect her in this hour of conquest. For what she asked, even if it was not the formal property of Rome, was yet the territory of princes who obeyed Rome as her vassals.

There she stood, very erect in her silver robe, the peacock-feather waving gently in her right hand. She lightly touched a few places on the map with it, but without naming them; saying only, quietly: "This . . . and this . . . and this . . ." And these places comprised the peninsula of Sinai, part of Arabia Petra, the principality of Chalcis, part of the Jordan valley, Jericho, parts of Samaria and Galilee, the Phœnician coasts, Lebanon, Cyprus, parts of Crete, and that portion of Cilicia that contained the tin-mines on the slope of Taurus, westward as far as the cedar forests.

Antony stood beside her; she moved until his arm brushed against her. When she had finished, he thought: An expensive wife!—and he let his arm suddenly sink upon hers, as though to indicate that otherwise he would have collapsed with dismay. But this made no impression on her; she smiled, picked up the peacock-feather, and threw it, quill forwards, across the world of which she had just conquered a few fragments. The feather struck the head of one of the four slaves, but he did not move.

Antony nodded. He granted everything, with the exception of two points. He could not take quite everything from Herod, whom he had only just made king of Judea, so he must hold Jericho on lease from her; further, King Malchos must not surrender Sinai; he must become Egypt's lessee under the warranty of Herod. However, there would be only trifling differences.

At this moment Cleopatra regretted that she had asked her son to be present; she realized his excitement. Of course, she had taught him that it is sometimes wiser to give way. But would he understand that now? A debate, even a quarrel perhaps, was impossible in the rarefied air of this high sphere. Since Antony had fallen in with her wishes *en bloc*, the event was so tremendous that it was unfitting on this royal occasion to haggle over a lease. So she too nodded, silently, as he had done. Then she suddenly twirled round on one heel and laughed. Antony stared at her, but Cæsarion wrinkled his forehead.

She seized the boy by the hair of his head and gave him a little shake; then she took her husband's arm, and together they went back to their guests.

V

Even before the huge army had marched off in the direction of Persia the news of the astonishing treaty of Antioch, and of Antony's marriage, must have startled Rome. The citizens felt a cold shudder of terror. But Antony's messengers explained in his name that Rome was great not by what she took, but by what she gave. Everywhere Antony had founded new dynasties; a dozen kings fawned upon him; and what he had given Egypt only magnified the fame of the generous city. Antony was lavish of such phrases.

Octavian refused to be won by such words. He still hesitated to accuse his ally in the Senate, for by so doing he would have admitted that this assembly, which had long been regarded as contemptible, still possessed a modicum of power. His campaigns against the last of the Pompeys had been grievous; he was not yet powerful enough to seek an excuse for a breach with Antony. And this Antony knew when he dared to provoke his brother-in-law by marrying a second wife. And had not Cæsar—so the friends of Antony's party replied to Octavian—had not Cæsar himself required the Senate to introduce a law which would have allowed him to take several wives? Egyptian law was not Roman law; of course, he would bring the Egyptian wife to Rome.

If any Roman was indignant at the notion of a triumvir who was all but king of a foreign country, someone would show him one of the new coins, on which there was no mention of an Egyptian king. This was merely the most ingenious and most peaceable way of making Egypt a Roman province without letting the Egyptians realize the fact. In order to make the situation quite plain, together with the news of his second marriage, Antony had sent a friendly letter to his Roman wife, and also to her brother Octavian, writing as though nothing had happened. The comedian in him could not resist such an impulse; moreover, he was firmly persuaded that he was playing a reasonable part, for among Romans he was a Roman, and had to find some way of justifying himself. But he had soon forgotten Rome again, and was boasting, in the deep tones of a Silenus, that he would make as many women pregnant as his procreative powers demanded.

However, he was sober for whole weeks at a time; how otherwise could he have achieved his tremendous task? Perhaps no human eye had ever seen such a review as Antony showed his second wife immediately after the wedding. There were sixty thousand Roman foot-soldiers, ten thousand cavalry, Spaniards and Gauls, and thirty thousand foot and horse furnished by his satellite kings. This was just the size of the army that Cæsar had planned in his sketches. On the maps, Antony showed his consort the route that Cæsar had intended to follow; a longer, and perhaps also a safer route from the north, so that Romans and Orientals would not have combined their forces until they had entered Asia Minor. There were an enormous baggage-train and a siege-park. They would march to Aras, and there they would probably encounter the famous Persian cavalry, whose closer acquaintance the former captain of horse was eager to make.

One evening, as Antony was pointing out Cæsar's route to her and the boy, and comparing his own with it, Cleopatra's attention wandered from what he was saying. Quietly she drew back into the shadow, behind Antony's back, until she was able to watch Cæsarion, and note how he was cautiously questioning the general. This delighted the amiable Antony; he nodded, and told the boy exactly what he wanted to know. Then, when the boy questioned him as to the mountains, and asked where the horses would get their forage if the climate was severe and the winter caught them there, Antony listened with an amused expression, pressed the boy's shoulder to make him bend his head over a special map, and pointed out the roads and the rivers by which the forage would be brought from the plains. Then he laughed, and tapped Cæsarion on the breast, as much as to say: There are the makings of a soldier in you!

Cleopatra, in her shadowy corner, was never weary of this picture. Here was Antony communing with the rejuvenated spirit of Cæsar; and she felt that these moments justified the thoughts that had passed through her mind when she came to Antioch to marry her crazy lover.

As far as the Euphrates she accompanied Antony and the army. At Zeugma they murmured their farewells. Antony, in a state of nervous tension, was glad, at first, that she was turning back. His temperament had taken its usual revenge; his wife was pregnant again; the athlete needed this sort of credential. Now she turned back with her son.

On the way home death lay in wait for her. She had crossed the Lebanon to Damascus, and then, following the Jordan, she had come to Jericho. There she was greeted by King Herod, whose elegant ambiguity had captivated Antony. Now he began to haggle with her over the scrap of Judea which she was supposed to receive. He planned to have her murdered on the way to Jerusalem. It was not difficult; even in those days the zigzag road lent itself to such an ambush; and he thought he would be obliging his friend Antony by such an action. In the end, however, he did not dare to molest her, though he put it about, according to Josephus, that the lovely lady tried to seduce him, but that he withstood her. With these two pitiful stratagems and a present of balsam-bushes Herod makes his fleeting appearance in the history of Cleopatra.

If she had perished then—of course, with her son—the history, not of Egypt, but of Rome, would have followed another course. The Bacchic Imperator might have co-operated with the frigid Cæsar for many years, and Octavia might have borne him another half-dozen children.

But in her palace Cleopatra brought her third son into the world. Such a woman can bear only sons; a daughter, if she produces one, will at most be thrown in with a son as a sort of make-weight. Again, as four years earlier, the father was far away. But now he was at least her lawful husband; the courtiers could, or should, congratulate her, and the priests offer up prayers of gratitude. Only Cæsarion was displeased.

Why, he thought, has he done this to her when he himself was going on campaign? Cæsar did not sail until I had come into the world. And why was he afraid to call himself king; why does he bear a foreign title? Is it so difficult to be King of Egypt and at the same time a Roman?

Antony's Persian campaign ran its course like a stupendous parody. Cæsar had dreamed of renewing the lustre of Alexander; Antony parodied the Macedonian. Cæsar had reckoned on a three years' campaign; Antony grew impatient after a few months. Cæsar saw a crown within reach of his hands, and thrust it from him, for he meant first of all to win it in the Persian East; but Antony, between his kisses and his draughts of wine, was gambling with another crown. Cæsar was preparing to impress men's imaginations by a great spectacle, yet he reckoned up every horse and every saddle; Antony regarded the legacy of a few papers as the talisman that guaranteed the help of the gods. And this was because in Antony's heart the flames of an easily intoxicated temperament would blaze up fiercely, and presently flicker out; while Cæsar was lit from within by a steadily increasing fire, but was never scorched by it.

Yet the Persian campaign gave Antony the opportunity to prove his manhood in the eyes of posterity. Such natures as his, subject to caprice and desire so long as they make headway, become confused and impatient in the face of the least opposition, but reveal their strength in disaster, provided this does not swallow them up. Antony had shown his mettle on two stricken fields. All Western Asia, as far as Bactria, trembled as the great Roman army pushed its way eastward. The Armenian king, a neighbour and enemy of the Persians and the Medes, whose aid was an essential part of Antony's plans, gave the Roman a brilliant reception, offered him advice, and supplied him with troops, and had neither cause nor real inclination to betray him. This Artavasdes was not only a king and a soldier: he was also a philosopher and a poet; Plutarch knew some of his tragedies. Perhaps he was disappointed by Antony's personality; for in Antony no one who knew something of men would have envisaged the born conqueror. It is merely because he was a poet that his motives interest us after this long interval.

It was not Artavasdes alone who brought about the catastrophe. We know this: that in Media Antony lost patience, and suddenly announced that he was going to return to the sea before the winter. Here, says Plutarch, he acted without lucid reflection, like a man under the compulsion of a magic power. But the desire to enjoy his fascinating wife again was apparently not the deciding factor; Antony was not hard to please, and such women as he needed were to be found everywhere during a campaign. It seems, rather, that the enormous size of these countries intimidated him, that Cæsar's spirit without Cæsar's word of command crushed him, and that he longed to escape from the depression which so suddenly and terribly took possession of the Dionysiac into the cheerfulness of his easier and more luxurious days. It became apparent that he was not of a stature to realize Cæsar's plan of world-conquest; he had been no more than Cæsar's right arm, and the mind of Cæsar could not be replaced by a few papers, nor his passion by the ambition of an heir. Antony was heading for disaster.

Instead of preparing winter quarters in Armenia, in order to take advantage of the spring, when the Persians commonly took the field, he made a dash for the capital of Media, moving his troops by forced marches, so that he had to leave behind his three hundred wagons, which could not keep the pace, with their burden of siege-engines, nor could these be replaced or repaired, since there was no hard wood to be found in Media. So the whole siege-train was cut off by the enemy and destroyed, while he himself, with the help of a few ladders, in vain beleaguered the capital. The Armenian ally had suddenly disappeared; there was no help to be got in this foreign land; the army had perforce to turn back, and on the retreat it allowed itself to be defeated by the enemy issuing from the city. Antony decimated the guilty legions and gave them barley instead of wheat, the mark of dishonour most dreaded by the Roman soldier, since he felt that he was thereby placed on a level with the beasts.

An isolated Roman, who had been living here since the last defeat of the Romans under Crassus, and was now encountered by chance, was able to guide the retreat to the river frontier of Armenia. All these thousands, who were to have recaptured the old Roman eagles—these men who in fancy had already seen and heard themselves thundering through the streets of Rome in a Roman triumph—had now to trudge homeward after a single Roman whom many of the generals, and many of the men as well, believed to be a traitor. Winter found them in the mountains; with the winter came starvation, and with starvation, sickness.

Then Antony showed his greatness. The men loved their general; "from a variety of causes," as Plutarch writes, "Antony's noble birth, his eloquence, his candour, his liberality and magnificence, and the familiar pleasantry of his conversation. These were the general cause of the affection he found in his army; and, on this particular occasion, his sympathies with the wounded, and attending to their wants," so that the sick and wounded were readier to serve him than the sound. There were poisonous plants in this country, that produced insanity in the starving men that ate them, so that they suddenly became crazed and began "to turn over and move every stone they met with." If they were given wine as an antidote they recovered; but soon there was no wine left, and they died. There were spies and trouble-makers among the allied peoples, who, though hitherto they had been peacefully inclined, now, when misfortune had overtaken them, suddenly realized the superiority of their own race, and brought accusations against the others. When at last the mutineers made their way to Antony's wagon, and his men began to steal his golden beakers, Antony had to draw his sword upon them.

At this nadir of wretchedness, when even Antony began to distrust his Roman guide, who in the desert mountains was always promising to lead them to his Araxes, where they would find not only water but the security of an allied country —in these latter days of dissolution, when the glittering army had become a horde of brigands, and all its brave young men were dead or sick, Antony made his shield-bearer swear "that he would stab him and cut off his head whenever he should command him, that he might neither fall alive into the hands of the enemy, nor be known when dead." He was to repeat this command before he died, at the time of his second defeat.

At last, on the twenty-seventh day of the retreat, they noticed a cool freshness in the air, and knew that they were near water. Thousands of men, half dead with thirst, rushed into the river. The survivors of the splendid army felt that they were saved, but almost half of them were lost. "Oh, ye Ten Thousand!" Antony is said to have cried out during the retreat. And indeed this second Anabasis needed only a new Xenophon to make it as immortal as the first.

VII

Cleopatra received the news of this defeat with mixed feelings. If she thought of her own fame she felt aggrieved; if she thought of Cæsar's fame, and of their joint victory in Alexandria, she felt disappointed in her second Roman. But if she considered her own destiny—as Queen of Egypt, and the mother of four children—she had no reason to complain. The only thing she had need to fear was a great victory in Persia; it would have made Antony once more the Roman Triumphator; he would have celebrated the victory on the Capitol, and then, for a time, he would have rediscovered the domestic virtues of his Roman wife. Further, as the most interesting man in Rome he would begin to look about him, in the salons and the taverns, for the sort of women who would please him for a day. What would the Queen of Egypt be to a victorious Antony? He had conquered and enjoyed her gold and her beauty, the heritage of the Ptolemies in treasure and erotic refinement. Why continue to weaken his position by the ambiguities in which the double life of an Alexandrian Roman must needs involve him?

As long as Cleopatra thought realistically—and her realism increased with the passing of years and the birth of children

—she was bound to hope, for her own sake, that Antony would be defeated, for then he would be ripe for Egypt! The cunning fellow would be a match for any mockery; for the Roman generals were all carefully trained in the art of turning defeats into victories with their tongues. Through her agents she had learned, not only all the details of the catastrophe, but also what the world had heard of it, which was no more than a few confused reports. But if any of her courtiers should learn too much, and should gradually become possessed of the whole truth, she would silence him by a politic display of the new map of Egypt, which the same Antony had enlarged by the gift of whole provinces.

For, like the ancient Egyptians, the new lords of Egypt had never been born soldiers. When the blazing comet of the great Alexander had burned itself out, leaving only a remote star shining in the skies of history, his successors for nearly three hundred years had shone by his borrowed light, so far did he exceed them in brilliance. In wealth and luxury, and even in learning, Cleopatra's court was the rival of the court of the ancient Pharaohs, and secretly despising the confused theogony of the Egyptians, the Alexandrians evinced only the unwarlike characteristics of their local predecessors, a peculiarity which they found as comfortable as it was discreditable to their origin.

To them, therefore, a queen who was able to increase and enrich her country without ever drawing the sword, for no other reason, really, than because she knew how to be a woman, must have been irresistible; a woman, moreover, who was able to bring her magnetic influence to bear upon a Roman, and thus, as it were, to paralyse, in the person of a triumvir, the great and much-courted power of Rome, the only power which was really to be feared. And the future seemed to be guaranteed by the serious youngster who bore the symbolic name of Cæsar Ptolemy, and whose place could be filled by his two half-Roman brothers, so well had Cleopatra secured the power of her dynasty. What discontented prince or party leader of Alexandria could hope to shake her throne merely because Antony had been defeated in far-off Persia? The only person who could blame him for that was not in Egypt, but in Rome; he was the other triumvir.

But Octavian had equally good reasons for wishing that Antony might suffer defeat, and although, during the highly popular Persian war, he offered sacrifices in the temples to ensure the victory of the Roman arms, he secretly turned down his thumbs, since for him too only a victorious Antony could be dangerous. Taking advantage of a quarrel, he had made short work of the feeble Lepidus, and had taken his share of Africa for himself; then—for he always understood how to make other men win battles for him—he had the last of the Pompeys defeated and put to flight by his friend and general, Agrippa. For six years the civil war had persisted; a lesser war than Cæsar's, yet it had made all Southern Italy and the islands permanently insecure. Was it any wonder that all should bow down to the victor, while the Senate decreed that he might confer upon himself all the honours he desired? He found himself the master of forty-three legions, thousands of cavalry, and six hundred ships; a young man of twenty-seven, who had never won a victory in person, who possessed not a drop of Cæsar's blood nor a spark of his spirit, but in all respects resembled his money-lending grandfather, for he was cruel, avaricious, and a cunning speculator.

Cleopatra learned all that there was to learn about her enemy; not merely what he was doing, but also what he was planning; as for what he was feeling, her own hatred whispered it in her ear. She laughed when the weakling was described as appearing in shining armour, surrounded by genuine warriors, himself timid and uncouth. She laughed when she saw him imitate Cæsar's bribery of the people by his amnesties to defaulting tax-payers and his prohibition of the purple. She laughed when she heard that he was planning a great temple to Apollo on the Palatine, and that he had conferred distinction upon Horace because the poet had sung his praises. But there was a gleam of savage hatred in her eyes when she learned that Octavian, who had just had Antony's triumphal car set up in front of the tribune in the Forum, and his statue erected in the Temple of Concord, had a few months earlier sent secret messengers to the Armenian king, in order to confirm him in his intention of deserting the same Antony, his ally and brother-in-law. Reared among criminals, a woman without a conscience, she was capable of having those put to death who stood in her way; but she was too queenly for such perfidy as this.

No, it was impossible to make a pact with this Roman. But since he and he alone really stood for Rome, she must modify the basis of her fifteen years' government: she must abandon the inherited principles of her father and build up a new policy. She must try, by every means, to wrest the other Roman, her husband, from his home; for only if he became king, and with him Cæsarion, would Rome in Alexandria be opposed to Rome!

The moment had come, it seemed to her, when she must subject Antony completely to herself. The appeal for help by the mournfully retreating general sounded more musically in her ears than the trumpets of victory would have done. Now he was once more on the Syrian coast, this time in the fort known as "White Hair" not far from Sidon, and he was sending her messenger after messenger, begging her to come and help him. To this third rendezvous her triremes carried no carpets, no gold plate, no girl harpers, or cymbal-clashing boys. This time they were packed with shoes and uniforms, cloaks and weapons for thousands of tattered soldiers; and after these came sacks of gold, for the treasure of the Ptolemies seemed inexhaustible, comparable only with the procreative powers of Antony.

Antony, in the meantime, sat days and nights at table, drowning his chagrin, cursing and swearing that next time he would annihilate the Persians and the Armenians too; but every now and then—so Plutarch relates—he left the table to run down to the shore, to see whether the longed-for sail was not yet in sight. Then, when at last she came, all the gratitude of the legions was hers, and their general went from tent to tent singing the praises of his wife, who had come to save them all. Yet no sooner had Antony, who always turned his back on his happiness, recovered himself a little, than he forgot how much he lacked; and his longing for revenge, at least on the perfidious Armenian, became more intense.

But now the man who had always had his way with women, even with the Queen of Egypt, encountered for the first time a harsh refusal. He wanted to march eastwards; but this woman insisted that he must return to the West. He wanted to follow fame, not his wife, but she called him back to her home. When these two passionate human beings began to fight with each other the house of love began to quake, yet it did not fall; rather their quarrel found its climax in a fierce sexual surrender, only to blaze up anew from the ashes of their amorous combat. The enemy did what more was needful in order to force Antony to end this crisis by decisive action. For in the midst of the bustle and confusion of this Syrian camp, in which the soldiers no longer knew which way they would march on the morrow, while the Staff had split into warring parties, and the general was criticized more severely every day, a messenger arrived from Athens: Niger, a noble Roman. He had been sent by Octavia. For Octavian too had his spies; he too knew the right moment for compelling Antony to make a final choice. To this end he had sent his sister, with troops, weapons, and cloth, that she might forward them to her husband, now on his way home, as the help furnished by his friend.

He added, in a consoling letter, that he had contrived to keep the people in ignorance of the actual outcome of the Persian war.

Could one strike the darling of fortune a deadlier blow than by condoling with him? Octavian knew beforehand what Antony's answer would be! It mattered nothing to him that he would see his sister dishonoured by that answer, if only, in the event of a breach, he could rouse against Antony the moral indignation of Rome!

And now, indeed, the destiny of the Bacchant was near to finding a comic denouement; now, at the same time, across the same Mediterranean, his two wives had come sailing, from two different directions, toward their unfaithful husband, in order to lure him, northwards or westwards, back to one of his homes and one of his families of children: each with a number of ships full of shoes and clothes for his defeated army, one of them, moreover, with money, and the other with two thousand newly equipped prætorians! The one offered a royal throne; the other the friendship of his powerful native country. Octavia's ship had a heavier cargo than weapons and clothing merely; beneath all these was a world with which her husband was familiar: the world of Rome; of Forum and Capitol, Arena and Senate; the cool villas of the Campagna and the frowzy taverns of the Appian Way; the roar of triumphs, and the familiar babble of the parties, all in his mother tongue, in the speech of his youth; and this in the shadow of Cæsar's temple. Seconded by that overwhelming call of youth and home, must not Octavia have hoped to conquer?

But the other wife, Cleopatra, had one advantage that could not be surpassed. It was not her money; it was not the royal crown; it was her presence. If Octavia had possessed the courage and the combativeness of her rival, she herself would have set sail for Antony's camp in Syria. The two women would at least have stood face to face, and their romance would have been enriched by an astonishing chapter. But the Roman matron was too much the great lady, too much a part of her family, to desire a contest. Such things could be risked by a queen who was also an Amazon and an artist in love, since what she did was right because she did it; but not by a patriotic citizeness whose dignity was determined by the judgment of her fellow-citizens.

How completely she was in her element, this mature, sharp-featured Cleopatra! If now the game was for a great stake, it was she who had the art to win it. She ate hardly anything, in order that she might seem thin and worn with grief. "At his approach"—so Plutarch sees her, with his incomparable poet's vision—"at his approach she taught her eye to express an agreeable surprise, and when he left her, she put on the look of languishment and dejection. Sometimes she would endeavour to weep, and then, as if she wished to hide her tears from her tender Antony, she affected to wipe them off unseen." At the same time she bestowed on Antony's officers lavish presents of money, and perhaps her smile, with its promise of bliss, so that they should tell him which of these two women truly loved him, and that this great queen would not survive his loss.

So Antony sent this answer to his Roman wife in Athens: She could send him the troops and supplies at once; apart from the circumstances, there were ships owing to him from her brother. But she herself need not trouble to continue her voyage; he was on the point of marching once more against the Persians, and he could not expose her to this unwholesome climate. She could greet her children and her brother for him; when he had returned victorious from Persia they could look forward to a happy meeting!

Niger bowed low to the general, then to the silent queen, and took his leave. But Antony gave orders that his army was

to winter here in Syria; and in the spring it would march with
him into Armenia. Then he bade them all farewell, and set
sail for Alexandria with the queen.

VIII

It was no longer the same Alexandria. The "Club of the
Inimitables" was a thing of the past, and with it all the madness of that Bacchic winter. The singular intermediate position which Antony had devised—he was not king, but he was
the queen's husband; he was an Egyptian autocrat, and he
was also a Roman proconsul—this intermediate state, in which
he hoped to balance his conflicting feelings, did not permit
of the jollity without which he could not live.

To be sure, there were banquets enough, and many lively
hours and weeks, since the queen's genius for the devising
of pleasures, whether refined or barbaric, was inexhaustible.
And there were now three young children in the palace, and
she, half-way through the thirties, was still a young mother;
but he, who was approaching the fifties, had grown heavy and
rather bloated. They had settled down to married life, and
there were times when they were both forced to realize that
they were unfitted for marriage, especially when the storm of
events gave way to a dead calm. Then, in his moody way,
Antony would withdraw completely into the small circle of
Roman officers, as though he were hardly aware of the Alexandrians; at least one could talk Latin with them! But was it
not inevitable that the conversation of this usually idle set
should constantly turn upon Rome and Octavian? Could they

forget their friends and relatives? In Rome, perhaps, they had
less money and fewer women, but at least they had the old
Roman cobblestones underfoot, which they missed most hor-
ribly as time went on, although they made for rougher walking than the Plateia here!

At the same time, they were conscious of the critical glances
of the Court, which, with its emasculate officials, must always
seem alien to them.

When Plancus, the friend and secretary of Antony, appeared on the stage in the character of Glaucus—as a dancer
and clown in blue-green tights, hung with sea-weed, with
rushes in his hair, and dragging a fish-tail after him—the Alexandrian nobles gently nudged one another: how, they wondered, could a member of the Roman nobility so disgrace
himself? As for the Romans, they wondered how much he
had squeezed out of his employer for this performance. But
Antony laughed at his clown: he knew that he was being
robbed, but he had never earned a sesterce; if people stole
from him what he had stolen, or had received as a present, he
could not complain. In compensation, the observant queen
did whatever could be done; she appointed a Roman senator to be administrator of the royal looms; and a regimental
officer was made director of the circus. As for her husband,
she found him many tasks of a military nature. In particular,
she asked him for his plan for the conquest of Armenia. This
ought to be a short and easy campaign, and a victory ought
to divert him from the Persian plans. Then she devised a
means of mystifying the treacherous king: she invited him,
through her envoys, to join Antony next year in another campaign against the Persians. Cleopatra, like a great theatrical

producer, was able to turn everything to advantage. After all, what were the twins for? In order to make the Armenian feel perfectly secure, little Alexander was proposed as the future husband of his daughter.

In the midst of these activities Cæsarion maintained his serious reserve. He was not sure that he liked Antony, and he watched him narrowly, for he wanted to be sure that he pleased Cleopatra. Since Antony had destroyed Cæsar's murderers, he must respect him; but since he was a Roman, Cæsarion wished that he had been more austere. Inasmuch as he studied and assimilated with passionate interest everything that helped to explain the character of the Romans, he had formed so exalted a conception of them that no one but Cæsar could have lived up to it. If the Romans were appointed by the gods to become joint rulers of Egypt, then they must be greater than the Ptolemies. True, he had begun to realize that even among his forefathers there had been evil and cowardly men. But his mother—was she not a great queen? How else could she have subdued the ageing Cæsar? And Cæsar— was he not the greatest man since Alexander? How else should he have chosen his mother? Here he was on firm ground, and since the Stoic philosophy had not yet affected him, since his youthful emotions were aroused by such qualities as virtue and valour, power and magnanimity, the boy of twelve was already possessed of a mature sense of a great ancestry, to which he owed the greatest achievements. In this frame of mind, how could his step-father please him? If only he had remained with all his heart a Roman! If only he had fought his mother, or even deserted her! But it seemed to him that this man had been drawn to Egypt only by the gold of the Ptolemies, and perhaps by his mother's beauty. To be sure, one could learn much from him; but if one questioned him about Cæsar he gave evasive answers, and Cæsar's son did not yet understand why Antony should be evasive. To his hero-worshipping mind, Antony had nothing of the hero.

But now, in the new year, as he saw him arming for the new war, Antony pleased him well. And the general himself was happy. The trick of betrothing the children had actually succeeded in luring the king out of hiding, despite his bad conscience. But when he came riding up to conclude the alliance he was immediately put into chains. They were silver fetters, but history does not say whether the silver was a mark of respect to the king or to the poet. The battle with those who attempted to free him was brief and victorious. The whole campaign became an unprecedented raid for loot; the legions broke up and divided among themselves a golden statue of the goddess of the country, and, as far as Roman customs went, the looting that followed was an innovation. Antony, however, was thankful to see his soldiers paying themselves.

Above all, by the reports of his victory he was able to restore his reputation in Rome, and thereby to annoy Octavian, which was really the main purpose of this campaign. He then had it given out that he was about to invade Persia. The King of the Medes, who had a quarrel with the Persians, was eager to give him assistance, and since after the Armenian episode little Alexander was free again, he was promised, a few months after his first betrothal, to the daughter of the Median king.

The whole adventure was concluded in a few months of the summer. Cleopatra saw her wish granted: Antony had won an easy victory. This man, she had concluded, needed a great deal of wine to make him drunk, but only a little victory; for he was used to the one, but not to the other. The Antony who returned to her now had proved himself a great general, and felt himself to be the peer of Cæsar; a favourite of fortune, equal to all that the gods and his wife might offer him.

That she was powerful and beautiful he knew, but he did not fully realize the extent of her ingenuity. She had been thinking the matter out for years, and ever since her marriage and the treaty of Antioch, she had been gradually leading this naïve and frivolous man farther and farther from his Roman origin. Now the moment had come to cut the last hawser. Now he, Cæsarion, must become King of Egypt.

IX

Far oversea, in Rome, Octavia cherished her children: among them four of Antony's. She had stepped out of the ranks of the women who at this time were playing a part in the history of the world by her resolve to pursue neither fame nor pleasure nor gold, but to cherish the innocent beings who might otherwise have been forgotten. And this she did without any moral display. Indeed, it seems as though the false tone adopted by her brother, and the social lies which were heard on every side, induced her to live a life of silent obscurity, unbefitting the sister of the most powerful man in Rome. Neither now nor in later years was her name ever touched by the gossip of Rome, so it seems that there were no men in her life, though she was no older than Cleopatra, and was always considered beautiful.

In her, perhaps, the frigid streak to be noted in her family was confined to the life of the senses; which was not the case with her brother. Perhaps she was religious or philosophical enough to accept with irony the part allotted to her, or to regard it as her destiny. Whatever the truth, her serious, patrician pride seemed old-fashioned to her own circle, and this was just what she desired. Yet a bright light shone on the head of Octavian's sister. Octavian was just then emerging into the Emperor Augustus, and he exploited her virtue, praising it as an attribute of his house. For this reason he was delighted when Antony sent his Roman wife home. With an austere expression he had forbidden his dishonoured sister to remain living in the house of such a man. She refused to leave it, so that Octavian received this refusal from a woman's lips almost at the same time as did his rival. People would say that the civil war had been fought on her account: that was once more Octavia's argument. She had remained in Antony's house and had continued to rear his children and receive his friends. For if he wanted to recommend or in other ways help anyone in Rome he quickly dashed off an amiable letter to his Roman wife, and he never realized that others had to pay for his generous gestures. All praised her patience and condemned her unfaithful husband.

But the Roman populace was as variable as Antony himself. Not with impunity had it learned, for the last two hundred years, to reverence victory as the gift of the gods. The sun of his fame, which Antony, after his return from Alexandria, had projected onto the tablets of Rome by the concave mirror of his eulogies, had once more made him a dazzling figure, and since his character had always been more akin to the people's than that of the ever-aloof Octavian, they were glad that it was once more permissible to love him.

Octavian, whose hostile attitude to the people made his nostrils still more sensitive to every popular mood, was quick to step in with a programme of games, which had been discontinued for a year. He also instituted a sort of lottery in the circus, and finally had a huge table covered with presents, to become the property of those who were quickest to snatch them; so that it all ended in a hand-to-hand fight, which enhanced the popularity of the princely donor. At the same time he recruited fresh troops, in order to bring up the strength of the forces in Italy to thirty legions. In the Senate he spoke of the dangerous enlargement of Egypt by new provinces and islands, but always without directly attacking Antony.

Antony laughed when he heard of this. From Alexandria he replied to the Roman Senate a few weeks later—for in the summer news travelled quickly oversea—that he had given only what belonged to others, the petty vassal kings had always been accustomed to such barter. Octavian, on the other hand—and here he went over to the attack—Octavian had deposed Lepidus and kept his provinces for himself, as well as Sicily and Sardinia, which he had taken from the last of the Pompeys. Further, he had divided half Italy among his veterans, and he had never returned the ships that he borrowed. After Antony's partisans had made this shattering attack, the supple Octavian appeared at the next session, explaining, in his vinegary tones, that he would surrender half the provinces immediately if only Antony would do the same with Armenia and Egypt. The applause was great, but no one in the hall knew that Octavian and his friends had hidden daggers under their togas, in order to be prepared for any eventuality. In the face of an approaching storm they meant to be wiser than the weaponless Cæsar.

Antony laughed at this news also, and he wanted to send an even ruder reply, but here his wife prevented him. Egypt a Roman province? Octavian's words had meant nothing else. Cleopatra summoned up all her energies, for now she must show the hated heir of Cæsar before all the world who was master in Egypt. She relied on Antony; she pointed out the breach which the cool-headed enemy was trying to mask; she spoke of her children, and how their future must be secured; she proved to him, by means of letters, that his opponents had gone to the Senate bearing arms, and made him realize, in case he imagined that he could peacefully return to Rome, that daggers were waiting for him too; she enumerated the reserves of military power which Octavian had accumulated, and which he would never again voluntarily share; she collated all the items of news, false and true, which represented the popularity of his rival; she praised the new Median alliance as a safe springboard for a future Persian war; she insisted on Egypt's ever-increasing trade, and its inexhaustible treasury; indeed, this time she even lauded Alexander, in order to send the Roman off on a false tack. All the data that the maps revealed, and all that could be expressed in symbols, she added together with an emotion which she managed to conceal, though its lure was heard in her melodious voice. The officers, who felt that they had been challenged, did their utmost, and a few days later the decisive proclamation was planned, which involved the performance, for the benefit of the people, but especially for the exuberant comedian at her side, of an unprecedented masquerade.

Antony was still applying the brake to her triumphal car, being unconsciously afraid of a swift plunge into the abyss. He still had faith in his double game of being at one and the same time a Roman and an Alexandrian, and he did not wish to be called king. Profound forebodings, such as for centuries past had made the republican dread the crown, and recollections of Cæsar's hand pushing away the crown which he, Antony, had offered him, were trying to find expression in his mind. At the same time, he realized that his wife was not pressing him in this connexion.

For Cleopatra was thinking only of her son. To see him crowned while she still lived and ruled Egypt was her passionate endeavour, for then she would be continuing the dream of her youth: Cæsarion was Cæsar. But such a plan was so new to Alexandria that it called for the powerful voice of an alien, and a world-historical setting; and since Cæsarion was half a Roman, he could not be symbolically crowned save in the presence of a Roman. In such plans, which took into account both the feelings of the people and the verdict of history, Cleopatra's statecraft excelled that of any ruler of her period. It revealed her ability to blend, with all the brilliance and lucidity of her wits and her intellect, the subtleties of Oriental tradition with an instinctive genius such as is granted only to women.

X

First came the triumphal procession; what a temptation for the Alexandrians! Ever since Rome had been Rome, no Roman had dared to hold his triumph elsewhere than in Rome. He had always dreamed of the Capitol, from which one drove to the Forum, in order to show oneself to the Senate and people of Rome. This was the reward for all adventure; for one who was Roman at heart there could be no greater day in life.

Today, for the first time, a Roman drove in the Roman quadriga through the broad streets of the new imperial city, stealing from Rome the honours of the centuries, for those who shouted applause were using Greek or still more alien words and gestures. Never had the great city beheld such things as were now accomplished by the style and guidance of the wife and the husband's delight in masquerade.

In the morning sun the procession came from the Palace, across the hill of Lochias to the Forum, through the gardens, into the main street, past Alexander's tomb and the tombs of the Ptolemies, to the Gymnasion and the Museion. The Roman legions, which led the procession with their s.p.q.r., were followed by the Armenian king, with his wife and children; but this time their fetters were of gold. Then came Antony's car, drawn by four white horses. It was followed by Armenian prisoners, then by princely vassals, wearing crowns and wreaths, and then by Egyptian troops with curved Persian swords, and finally, by more Roman legionaries.

Seated on her throne, in a wide open space, Cleopatra

awaited the victor. Now he alighted, and led the prisoners up to her. But then the Armenian king remembered that he was a poet, and refused to kneel before the queen. He addressed her only by her name, and when the husband and wife exchanged glances they realized that they would have to reward him with his life, instead of having him killed on the morrow. And so it was done. But then the people sat down to such a banquet as had never been seen, and it was as well that the coronation did not take place on the following day, for half Alexandria was sleeping off its wine.

Then, a few days later, in a great field at the edge of the city, the spectacle took on a higher significance. Six thrones were set up there: two large golden thrones and four smaller silver ones. It was afternoon. A long train of cars opened the procession; on them were men dressed as Silenus, who poured wine for the surrounding throng from their jugs and wine-skins; then came a row of half-fettered elephants. With the wine and the elephants the Alexandrians were familiar enough. Finally, when the chief actors had taken their places, Antony stood forth in his favourite role—Dionysos, in a gold-embroidered purple mantle, the ivy-wreath on his still brown curls, the thyrsus in his hand. And beside him sat Isis, the Egyptian Aphrodite—her father's double crown upon her head, the golden serpent erect upon her brow—arrayed in gold and silver, motionless as the images of the gods on the walls of the Egyptian temples, which show us how fifteen centuries earlier still the queens of the Pharaohs displayed themselves in the resplendent trappings of Isis. Cleopatra sat alone, for today she was a goddess.

Facing her, standing in front of the first of the silver

thrones, was Cæsarion: now a tall youth of thirteen, wearing a Macedonian cloak, and the crown, three centuries old, which had been worn by all the successors of Alexander; but at his side hung the short Roman sword. The six-year-old children had been given a higher place, so that the people could see them: Alexander was in Armenian costume, a tiara on his little head, a tunica with sleeves, and trousers of Persian cut; while the little Cleopatra was in white silk, with a barbaric Libyan diadem on her head. Lastly, the two-year-old Ptolemy, quite the Macedonian, with high boots, chlamys, and felt hat; but even he wore a diadem. Each of the children was surrounded by a bodyguard in national uniform.

After the fanfares Dionysos uplifted his thundering bass. He spoke of his victories; then he read out the list of all the countries which he had given the queen two years earlier in Antioch; he never spoke of Rome, but only of himself, and it seemed as though he loved to dwell on his achievements. But now he asserted his claim to a new computation of time, which they would find on all coins; "a new era, opened by Cleopatra, Queen of Egypt, Cyprus and Syria. He who stands before you, Cæsar Ptolemy, is today elevated to the rank of 'King of Kings,' as co-regent with his mother over Egypt." The boy Alexander was made King of Armenia and Media; his twin sister, Queen of Lydia; the youngest Ptolemy, King of Phœnicia and Cilicia.

And amidst the clamour of the people and the thunder of the drums, the three little children left the circle of their bodyguards and ran across to their parents, in order to greet them with the new crowns on their heads. The sun went down as though its setting had been included in the programme.

Cleopatra did not move. She was acting the goddess for her Egyptians, as she did every year, at the festival of Serapis. She heard the mob rave and shout, and thought to herself: He has no need to disguise himself in order to play Dionysos. She did not see the children as they tried to make their way to her, stumbling a little in their embarrassment. She did not see the priests and the officers, the hundreds of faces familiar since her childhood, the whole pageant of the Court. She saw only Cæsarion.

He stood before her, motionless as herself, gazing at her with his black eyes from under his furrowed brows; gazing at her across the teeming gulf of people. He alone felt that he was truly crowned, and when he was proclaimed King of Kings, and the thousands before him roared with delight, he was the only one who felt that a weight rested on his head; not an ornament, not a mask, not a plaything. He had had a long dispute with his mother in respect of the short Roman sword; at first she had ordered a Macedonian weapon. He knew that now and always he would be a Ptolemy, the heir of Alexander. But Cæsar was closer to him; Cæsar was greater than the Ptolemies; Cæsar was his father, and he felt as though his mother had never had any other lover. He would wear Cæsar's Roman sword, and one day he would draw it in defence of his mother's country.

But one read what he was thinking behind his furrowed brows. Across the teeming gulf of onlookers the golden-brown huntress's eyes were shining upon him from the face of the Egyptian Isis, because it was he, he alone for whom she had planned all these years, for whom she had prepared the crown, and provided today's pageant. Yes, she had won. The dream

[263]

of her youth had after all been fulfilled: for there stood Cæsar with the crown! The great adventure of her life had reached its climax. The audacity with which she had plotted her path, her passionate confidence in her destiny, her belief in power and beauty, all that she had held to and increased for the last twenty years, on her perilous journey, by battle and by cunning, by madness and defeat: it was all here before her, concentrated in the person of this boy who was gazing at her with Cæsar's dark eyes, while the golden crown of Alexander began to redden faintly in the failing light.

Suddenly the goddess made a movement as though something had startled her. Behind Cæsarion she had seemed to see the cold stare of Octavian.

Thanatos

He who is born to rule, he who has brought it about that every day the fate of thousands rests in his hands, steps from the throne as into the tomb.

—GOETHE

Cleopatra

CHAPTER V

Thanatos

I

WHEN the destinies of the brave begin to go awry, they seem to acquire a twofold beauty.

When the weak man collapses or is snared in the noose of self-delusion, the strong man stands up and arms himself, to confront at last, after many enemies, destiny itself. After the heat of innumerable days his warrior's heart has found refreshment in cool dreamless nights, and every new morning sees him again at work, his thoughts glittering in a hundred facets, his energies pressing on a hundred points, always encountering, always overcoming fresh difficulties. Since he is always grappling with tangible entities, always fighting at close quarters, feeling or scenting the nearness of the enemy in human or material form, he struggles forward a little farther each day, and if he is forced backwards it is only to make a new start.

But there comes an hour when he hears, behind the accustomed rumour of hostile forces, a sound that has no earthly origin. The wide skies begin to darken; faint thunder heralds alien powers; and amidst the shapes and the sounds of the familiar adversary he perceives thronging shadows and a gloom as of distant mountains. Then the brave man girds up his loins, resolved to sustain his final battle. First he is startled by an enemy he cannot grasp, and if he were to think logically he would give himself up for lost before this advance of the elemental. No stratagem will win him a moment's intermission. But he summons up all his strength, he seeks to multiply himself, to exert a superhuman force, in the secret hope that even now he may be able to avert his destiny.

Such a spectacle of dauntless courage is rarely offered by women, and even a brave woman must possess a special genius if she is to remain unshaken by power and magnificence. Warned by her innate instinct earlier than a man is warned, she may seek by twisting and turning to evade the inevitable, and by this means she may win repeated delays, and often a final period which has not the dramatic poignancy of the man's last struggle. The omens for which such suggestible natures look may allow some flashes of light to slip between their spectral forms, permitting of any interpretation which increases self-confidence. All the vacillations, all the delicacies of the feminine character, and with them the mother's instinct to protect her children more decisively than her purpose, and the hope of compromise, show them to the last ways by which the heaviest blows may be evaded.

Cleopatra, now confronted by destiny, was to wage the final battle in heroic fashion. She was to try, one by one, every trick and every evasion, and all the woman's weapons of seduction and persuasion; at the same time, she was to fight with male courage, hoping from phase to phase of the battle, yet fearlessly beholding the fast approaching tragedy, and dying, in the end, a royal death. Beset with many forebodings, which came from her belief in signs, and at the same time reinforced that belief, she must have heard the chorus of the fateful voices when it was still but faintly sounding behind the fanfares of the warrior. Her huntress's glance, her quick understanding, had long ago realized the weaknesses of her consort, and if now, in the last two years of her life, she sought to transform the half-playful methods of Antony into an integral effort, yet in her secret heart she had abandoned hope of making the half-man suddenly become a whole one. This brave woman did what few men have done: she felt the tragic end approaching, and yet she faced it.

II

Ephesus—which for centuries had been a home of Greek culture, conquered by the Romans, liberated by Alexander, and again captured by the Romans—lay in a position not unlike that of Alexandria, between the sea and a prosperous hinterland. The conquerors from the mountains of Asia Minor followed an immemorial route that led from the mountains to the Mediterranean, where today Smyrna lies, and not far from the mouth of the river. To the conqueror coming from the west the same road lay open to the mountains of Asia Minor. Ephesus was the great military port, and if one of two conquerors possessed the eastern world and fortified himself here, he lured his rival from his western base; and this was good strategy.

[269]

But never yet, since the famous Artemis, the great Diana of the Ephesians, had ruled in her glittering temple, had Ephesus beheld, sprawling between sea and mountains, an armed camp so thronged and so richly equipped as in the spring of the next year (that for us is the year 32 B.C.). For Antony, who was concentrating his forces here, was at this time the actual master of the eastern world; his power extended from the Euphrates and Armenia to the Ionian Sea and Illyria (the modern Balkans), and also from the sands of Cyrenaica to Ethiopia. So what with his hundred thousand infantry, his twelve thousand cavalry, and his five hundred ships, which included galleys with eight and ten banks of oars, he commanded such an army as neither Alexander nor Cæsar had possessed. Antony, on receiving certain news from Rome, had returned to Ephesus from a fresh Armenian campaign, concerning which the sources either tell us nothing at all or furnish conflicting reports. Here he encamped with his army, to wait for Cleopatra, who was once again to bring him herself and her gold.

This time, as she left her home, she had considered, amidst her forebodings, all that could happen, and already she knew that she might be away from Egypt for a year or longer. But where would she be, and whither were they going? No one really knew for what enemy this vast army was intended. The peoples of Asia trembled; the soldiers sang songs of revenge against the Persians, who were to be destroyed at last; their allies swore over their wine that they would march with them to the world's end; but for all that, the whole eastern world was talking of the threatening civil war against Octavian.

Both Antony and Cleopatra were well enough aware of

this. He still hoped and she still feared that they might after all be able to march against Persia. For since he constantly regarded himself as a Roman triumvir, while she always thought of him as King of Egypt, their aims were diverse, and in the end it was left to their great enemy in Rome to unloose the civil war now or whenever he chose. After a period of continual provocations, the fog of misunderstandings and mutual challenges had grown so dense that it was impossible to know for certain whether or not the enemy's fleet was already on the way.

Crossing the Mediterranean for the fourth time, Cleopatra must have recalled her earlier voyages: the first as Aphrodite to Tarsus, the second as queen to Antioch, the third as wargoddess to the "White Hair." Now she was all these in one; for now, some years after the birth of her last child, for all her power and her armed strength, she had regained the slenderness of her youth. But now she was bringing with her on two hundred ships grain and metals and cloth, and a treasure of twenty thousand talents (the equivalent of twenty million dollars), to say nothing of half her household of eunuchs and slaves; all that the ancient world possessed of lavish wealth.

When on the morrow, as her habit was, she stood in the bows of her trireme, her heart was tremulous with conflicting emotions. True, she rarely had serious apprehensions of a new Persian war; as a general thing she felt confident that she could bring Antony to the point of breaking with Octavian, and Octavian to the point of striking. Time was on his side, but now they were stronger than he; now they must provoke him, and conquer! Relations with Rome had been growing more strained with every passing year; and she, who was

[271]

wholly woman, longed to end the strain for good and all, swiftly as the tension between two persons of opposite sex is ended; for to her it had become intolerable. The laws of dictatorship, the thirst for sensation that swayed the masses of the people in the two great capitals, the restlessness and intrigue of the many princes of the Mediterranean, and the threatening expiration of the triumvirate, all made it impossible that these two men should continue at peace, each in his own half of the world.

Or could the triumvirate be renewed once again? This would have necessitated Antony's reconciliation with his Roman wife. But then, against the two men and the woman who was sister to one and wife to the other—against such a triumvirate the queen would have been defenceless. Her policy was now directed to compelling Antony to obtain his divorce from Octavia, so that she might have him all to herself. But this divorce meant war, and war meant settling the great question between Rome and Alexandria; and since it was a Greek woman who ruled in Alexandria, this was really once more the old contest between Athens and Rome, now maturing to a decision. But what would be the outcome of the hazard? And, on calm consideration, was a settlement desirable? Yet this was no time to think of what was desirable. They were no longer free to choose!

So the shrewdest and most intelligent woman of her time, although she was alive to Antony's deficiencies, although she felt that the dilettante side of his character made him finally impossible as master of the world, was now compelled, ensnared in the labyrinthine evils of her destiny, to urge him on

to a final battle: a battle to which a Cæsar would have been
equal, but not an Antony. Hence her gloomy forebodings
when she heard that Pisaurum, a colony which Antony had
founded, had been swallowed up by an earthquake; hence her
pallor when she learned "that Antony's statue in Alba was
covered with sweat for many days, which returned, though it
was frequently wiped off."

But then she thrust all these dismal moods behind her, and
on the morrow she stood again in the bows of her ship, a warrior queen, her youth renewed; summoning up all the powers
of heart and intellect, so that in the coming conflict she could
supply what her husband lacked.

But she herself lacked her son. Cæsarion was now too big
still to accompany her as a page; now he must rule in his capital, supported by experienced servants of her house. This was
a risk and a deprivation. Nevertheless, Cleopatra parted from
him, for he was the only person to whom she could confide
the power of the State for any length of time, and also because this was his opportunity to prove himself in the great
school of life. If he had left Egypt with her, how easily palace
conspirators could have murdered her three little children!
In the history of her house many such crimes were recorded.
Every reasonable motive had urged her to leave Cæsarion at
home.

And yet, in the twilight depths of her soul, she had heard
a faint whisper, a voice that told her that she must not expose
her son and heir to the danger of imprisonment if fortune
should favour Octavian. Since in this decisive denouement
she felt at moments despondent or disheartened, she was

bound to conceive of the possibility of defeat and flight, when she would wish to find her young co-regent with his forces intact, that she might fall back upon his strength. Yet this she confessed to herself but rarely, and to Antony never.

III

In a flood of propaganda, by which fear and ill-will endeavoured to conceal their weakness, Octavian tried to extinguish the popularity of his enemy, and his creatures enriched the record of the pranks by which Antony had shocked the Romans with a hundred lies concerning him and Cleopatra.

Antony's triumphal procession through the streets of Alexandria furnished Octavian with his most drastic accusation; and the fact that he had not killed the captive king of Armenia was a proof of his effeminacy. It was true that he had stolen the library of Pergamon and removed it to his new capital; and he did the same with Myron's famous statue of Zeus, a Hercules from Samos, and an Ajax, all regarded as booty for Rome, but not for Egypt. But then Octavian, always valiant against the absent, shot his poisoned arrows against the queen; some aimed by himself in person, before the assembled Senate, and others by his hundreds of agitators. For only if he could make Cleopatra impossible could he explain the approaching civil war to the citizens of Rome as a war against a hostile empire.

Yes, it was obvious: she possessed magical powers, for was she not an Egyptian, a daughter of the people that worshipped animals? With her magical love-potion she had so bewildered the senses of the noble Roman that he once got up at a great banquet in order to kiss her naked foot. In the street he accompanied her litter, walking at the head of her eunuchs.

Sitting in judgment in the Egyptian courts, he would be interrupted by the tender messages which she sent him on her tablets of onyx; and once, when he saw her passing, he suddenly left the Court in the middle of a speech. One could see that he was bewitched; how else could a Roman so degrade himself for an African wife! Her children were all bastards; for Antony's lawful wife was called Octavia, and the eldest child, whom she dared to name Cæsarion, could not be Cæsar's son, for where was the document in which Cæsar acknowledged him? One heard of nothing but the squandering of inherited wealth. Antony had a golden chamber-pot, and but recently, at a banquet, the queen had dissolved in wine a pearl worth millions, and had drained the beaker at a draught. But she herself was always sober in the midst of all this revelry; and this was due to the magical power of her amethyst ring!

The effect of such calumnies was not to be despised, but it was not enough to injure Antony, for they were hurled by the unpopular triumvir at the popular one. Since Octavian was aware that he was not liked, he compelled all citizens henceforth to swear allegiance to him: a complete innovation, which the Romans found detestable, if only because it definitely indicated the end of the Republic. And when Bologna refused to swear he turned a deaf ear and declared in the Senate that all Italy had sworn allegiance to him. The terrorism was so pervasive that both consuls and four hundred men of senatorial rank left the country in secret, in order to join

Antony before the outbreak of the civil war; for Antony, said his friends, would restore the Republic.

What a disappointment when these anxious Romans landed in Ephesus! Here was a fair of peoples and costumes, Egyptians and Arabs, Armenians and Medes, Greeks, Jews, and Syrians, all swarming from the ships to the river, and then upstream to the camp. In the temple of Artemis a hundred languages were echoing from the marble walls and the cedarwood galleries. Where was Rome in the midst of all this? The old legions, half Orientalized, half barbarized, saluted their consuls with the ironical nonchalance of soldiers who, together with their home, had long forgotten these wardens of liberty.

And then—who was this, receiving the senators of Rome on a sort of throne? Was this a play-actor? Was it really Antony? The purple cloak over the Roman jerkin, white shoes on his feet, and on his head the felt hat of the Macedonian! And beside him, in green Syrian silk, Isis, the goddess of Egypt, with the double crown! Around them, with the bearing of vassals, the kings of Thrace and Paphlagonia, of Lebanon and Galatia, all dipped in the colours of an Oriental world! But yes—here was still something of Rome! As the queen rose and took her leave she was surrounded by Roman legionaries—but they bore engraven on their shields, instead of the four great letters, s.p.q.r., the monograms c and a, gracefully entwined.

Quickly a new Roman party sprang up in the camp. Many of the officers joined it, and since the queen made her appearance even in the council of war, where her opinion was attentively considered by Antony, a few of his old friends put their heads together, got hold of him by himself, and implored him to send her home if he did not want to lose the sympathy of every Roman. It was easy for Cleopatra to discover what they had advised, and easy to dispose of their advice. Had she not ruled Egypt for fifteen years? Who could venture to attack the influence and the reputation of the person who was finding the money for all these troops? Who, after all, were these plebeians, these badly dressed consuls, who dared to come here and utter calumnies against her? It was time for a change of scene.

With a skilful touch, she was able to change the general back again into the Bacchant; a transformation for which the isle of Samos offered the best background. There was time to spare; the war had not begun; it was spring; there was peace, and sea and land were radiant with life. "And while all the world beside," says Plutarch, "was venting its anguish in groans and tears, that island alone was piping and dancing; so that it was natural to say: 'What kind of figure will these people make in their triumph, when their very preparations for war are so splendid!' "

So the satellite princes vied with one another in the magnificence of their presents and entertainments. Fleeing from the chaos to come, a few hundred people had taken refuge on the island, in order to forget, what with wine and women, the threat of the future. And first among all was the new Dionysos of Alexandria, whose motto was live and let live—play and let play. Once, when his cook furnished a banquet which delighted even this refined gourmet and toper, he gave the man a present of a house, and because the actors pleased him he gave them the city of Priene. Then he sailed with his retinue to Athens. He hardly guessed who it was that had cautiously guided him.

To be queen some day in Athens was one of the few wishes of Cleopatra which had not as yet been fulfilled. She had never yet visited the holy places of Hellenic thought. They filled her with mystical emotion; for her culture was purely Athenian in origin. Here she followed in the footsteps of Alexander and Aristotle; and every temple spoke to her more plainly than ever temple had spoken in Egypt. But her jealousy of Antony's wives was always getting the better of her more exalted feelings; for he had lived with both of them in Athens. In his unembarrassed way he even showed her the house in which he had beaten Fulvia, and that in which the noble Octavia had afterwards lived with him.

To eradicate Octavia from the thoughts of the Athenians was now Cleopatra's great desire. Nothing was simpler! Why had she been granted the most amiable of gentlemen for a husband? Antony was delighted to play a new part, and when a delegation of the most distinguished men and women in Athens decided to welcome her, Antony himself ushered them in, since he too was "an Athenian citizen," and he delivered the ceremonial address to his wife. Then he had a stupendous Bacchic festival organized in the Theatre of Dionysos, an orgy that amazed all Athens, and finally he drove up the illuminated Acropolis in the chariot of the god. The Athenians, already prepared to do homage to power, revered the queen as the successor of Alexander, and set up her statue in the Parthenon.

Strange emotions filled Cleopatra's heart. In Rome her

statue stood in the temple of Venus, and here in Athens in the temple of Athena! Was it perhaps the intention of the gods to unite in her two cults and civilizations—to show that power was above beauty and wisdom greater than power? Or was Athens today victorious over Rome in her symbolical person? But lately her bronze statue, which Cæsar had set up twelve years ago, had been dragged out of the temple and shattered into fragments, and it was quite possible that some newly-rich plebeian had had her legs melted down and recast as a wash-basin! The parable was clearer than ever; here in Athens, near Alexander, from whom her ancestors had sprung, she was at home; but in Rome she had only enemies. Rome had become her enemy, for it belonged to Cæsar's spurious son, who hated the real son. To get her husband away from Rome for good and all: that was her next task. Everything depended on her ability to persuade him to divorce his Roman wife.

IV

Unexpectedly, his first wife helped her against his second wife. Antyllus, Fulvia's son by Antony, had come to Athens. Antony took a great fancy to this boy of fourteen. True, he was smaller than Cæsarion, and in Cleopatra's judgment was not his equal in any respect. He came from Octavia's house, where she had reared him in common with Antony's other children; so that he had only pleasant things to say of his kind mother.

But what did he say? What was happening here? Geminius, an old comrade in arms, had come from Rome with the sensible intention of warning Antony against a breach with Rome. The queen at once regarded him as an enemy and gave him the lowest place at table. Then she asked him, from the head of the table, what it was that he wanted. He hesitated, and when he was once more questioned as to what his mission might be, he answered, quietly, that it would be better for Antony if she would return to Egypt; otherwise they would proclaim him in Rome as the enemy of the fatherland. At this—so Plutarch relates—Antony struck his fist upon the table; but the queen replied, very coldly: "You have done well, Geminius, to confess without being put to the torture."

On the following day Geminius had flown; he was soon followed by Plancus, Antony's secretary and court jester, and then by another of his friends; and even some of the senators hurried back to Italy. Antony heard of this, said nothing, and laughed; but Cleopatra thirsted for revenge. The accumulated wrath that was glimpsed for a moment in her public reply to Geminius was trying to break loose. What! Was Queen Cleopatra, she who had borne Antony three children, to contend with the shadows of a couple of used-up women? She had heard a good deal about this Roman in the meantime. She had learned from Antony that Octavian had sent him a letter containing accusations against herself; but only spies could have told her his answer to his brother-in-law. It hardly astonished her, but it interests posterity, for it is the only private letter of any one of these four people which has been preserved—and then only a fragment of it, which is cited by Suetonius, who found it in some archive. Antony writes to Octavian:

"What has put you out of temper with me? That I sleep with the queen? She is my wife. Is that anything new? She has been my wife for nine years now. And you? Do you still sleep with Drusilla? I wager your life and your health that by the time you read this you will have had Tertullia, or Terentilla, or Eufilia, or Salvia Titiscemmia, or all the lot of them! After all, what does it signify which woman a man satisfies his lust with?"

Here is one soldier talking to another. Is not the whole Antony in these lines—warrior, Bacchant, and plebeian?

Now Cleopatra knew enough; now she went to him and insisted upon his divorce. She was ready to overwhelm him with reasons for her request.

Did not Fulvia's son dare to rave about Octavia, and to threaten that Roman, and to warn a certain senator? Did not Antony himself strike his fist against the table? He wanted her to be dishonoured by Roman gossip, for those who had fled would describe everything they saw here! She was to be sacrificed a second time! As when he had celebrated his honeymoon with Octavia, here in Athens itself! The war was close at hand; Octavian had not yet enough money for the campaign; the new taxes had made him absolutely hated by the people; now was the moment for dealing with him, since the huge army at Ephesus was awaiting the word of command. Forward, then! Divorce from Octavia; that meant the declaration of war against her brother!

But then, as Antony still said nothing, and hesitated, what a gamut of emotion she had at her command! Pride, resentment, power—power over her ships and her money! And again, the magic of her voice, and the arguments which she

could unfold at night! A few days later Antony called together his generals and a few senators, and since each felt that
matters could not continue as they were, they all voted for
what had been approaching for years past; for the sooner it
came now the better. A few doubters had been previously
cured of their doubts by the queen's gold. Antony proclaimed
his divorce in a letter, in which he ordered his Roman wife to
leave his house forthwith—it was Pompey's palace, for which
he had never paid.

This was a great day for Octavian, when all Rome saw the
sister of a triumvir, who had borne four children to another
triumvir, leave the house to which her husband had led her,
in the sight of the people, eight years earlier! This was a blow
against Antony's good name; his adversary could not have
dreamed of a shrewder stroke! Yet even more was to follow.
People thronged round the senators who had returned from
Athens, readily forgiving them their twofold apostasy. One
declared that Antony gave his guests sour wines while he himself drank Falernian; another related that Cleopatra would
exclaim, at every opportunity: "As surely as I shall one day
deliver judgment on the Capitol!"

But Plancus, the blue-green sea-god, and his friends, in order to recommend themselves to Octavian, betrayed a still
greater pledge of their friendship for Antony. They had once
subscribed their names as witnesses to the testament which
Antony wrote in Rome when he married Octavia. Now they
revealed to their new patron both the whereabouts and the
content of that testament. There was no more sacred place in
Rome than the temple of the Vestals; and Roman history
had never before this, to our knowledge, recorded, amongst

all its many crimes, a theft of papers which had been deposited in this temple in the keeping of the gods. Octavian coolly weighed the harm which this infraction might do him against the profit which he might derive from publishing the testament. He decided to risk the harm, and sent word to the Supreme Vestal. She replied that the documents in her charge were inviolate until Antony's death; the triumvir could obtain them only by force. Octavian went to the temple, entered, and removed the testament.

Of such means as a stolen testament Octavian made even more masterly use than Fulvia had made of the papers forged in Cæsar's name. He knew that Plancus had filched money from Antony; everyone knew it; and he concluded that the man had fled because he feared discovery. Now he made him read in the Senate a sensational report on Antony's manner of life; so full of exaggerations that an elderly senator called out to him: "By Hercules, Antony must have spent a busy day!" But this was only the introduction.

Now Octavian himself ascended the tribune, and explained that Antony had been deprived of his understanding by a magic draught. His army was commanded by an Egyptian eunuch, but the real command was in the hands of Charmian, Cleopatra's tiring-woman, and Iras, her hairdresser. Rome being in such anger, for the Egyptian woman was trying to become its ruler, he had been compelled to break the sacred seal of a testament—and he read the testament in question. In it Antony acknowledged Cæsarion, and any children born to himself by Cleopatra, as his lawful heirs; and among them he divided the following provinces . . . In the event of his death his body was to be carried in solemn procession through the Forum, but was then to be sent by ship to Alexandria, in order that it might finally rest at the side of the Queen Cleopatra.

Antony, who committed so few words to writing, could have left no fairer memorial; its theft by Octavian was a rascally trick. Yet Octavian had correctly estimated its effect. How much had not the Romans already forgiven Antony! He had always been a cheerful gambler; was he not Cæsar's most loyal lieutenant, and was he not victorious in the field against Cæsar's murderers? True, since then he had celebrated his triumph, had celebrated the victory of Roman arms, in a foreign country. But now, now it was made plain that he never was a true Roman at heart; in the face of death he had scorned Rome, and he wished to rest in foreign soil! Only a man bewitched could be so disloyal! So it was true that the woman had laid a spell upon him! The consulate for the following year, already conferred upon him, was immediately abrogated, and he was deprived of all his offices; but his reputation was still so great that he was not yet proclaimed an enemy of the fatherland.

Octavian had no need of this last gesture; he simply declared war upon the Queen of Egypt. At the temple of Bellona he cast the spear over the symbolical frontier into the land of the enemy.

V

Signs and omens multiplied themselves. While Antony was in Patras, lightning struck the temple of Hercules, his ancestor. In Athens the figure of Bacchus in the frieze of the battle

[284]

of the Giants, on the southern wall of the Acropolis, directly above the Theatre of Dionysos, was carried away by a whirlwind. The same storm swept away two colossal statues on which his name was engraven. And on Cleopatra's flagship, which was called *Antonias*, strange birds destroyed the nest that swallows had built in the stern. At the report of such omens Antony laughed, but the queen was silent.

They had both returned to Ephesus, when Octavian made them a curious offer: his adversary was to let him debark in Greece and there grant him a tract of land, no larger than a horse could encircle in a day; five days later he would be ready for battle. Antony threw the letter aside. He saw through the plan: Octavian shrank from meeting him on the Macedonian battlefield, the natural meeting-place of the two armies; for there, at Pharsalus, the young Antony had once been victorious under Cæsar. For this reason Antony proposed to Octavian, by the same messenger, that their battlefield should be Pharsalus; if this did not suit him, he offered to meet the younger man—he was twenty years younger—in a duel. No one heard the shrewd Octavian quietly laughing at this offer.

Now Octavian turned to the business of manning his ships, for no one knew whether the battle would be decided at sea or on land, or on both elements. Octavian, however, assumed that his opponent would compel him to a battle in the Balkans. For this reason he offered the king of the Getæ, whose help might then be decisive, his daughter Julia as his wife; indeed, he even promised that he himself would subsequently marry the king's daughter; all this to obtain auxiliaries. His army and fleet were rather smaller than Antony's; however, he had ninety-two thousand men and two hundred and fifty

[285]

ships. His plan was to hold up the enemy in Epirus with twenty legions, as he dreaded the battlefield of Pharsalus. Antony, again, had lost a third of his ships' companies, mostly by sickness, and to make up for the loss he pressed into his service all the young men of Greece, no matter what their calling; there was talk of hundreds of ass-drivers from the mountains who had never seen an oar.

But the decision did not depend on the ass-drivers, nor the king of the Getæ, nor even Antony's testament, with all its consequences. It was the heart of Antony and the heart of Cleopatra that here, as in all the tragedies of history, decided the course of destiny.

In the months preceding the decision the wife had often observed her husband in silence: in Samos, in Athens, and now again in Ephesus. She had watched him when he had no part to play; as he crossed the street alone in the sunlight, or gazed at the stars at night from his chamber window, or turned round out of doors to gaze after some sturdy young wench, or on some quiet evening, when he sat beside her staring into his beaker; the unobserved Antony. At such times she was horrified by the decline in the bearing and expression of this man of fifty: the prominent belly, sagging over the slack knees; the pendulous cheeks; the double chin; and above all, the glassy eyes that stared, stupidly, seeming to recognize nothing, and still less to seek for anything. Many whispers that had reached her from his staff—that he came too late to consultations, that he often did not listen to what was said, and sometimes dozed for minutes at a time—had confirmed her in conclusions which his better hours had seemed to confute; but then he was fired with love and wine.

So she had come to doubt his power to win a victory; for which reason she had turned to omens and oracles, and these portended ill. Would he be strong in the hour of decision? Would Cæsar's spirit favour him simply because he stood on Cæsar's battlefield? What was she to expect from the discipline of a heterogeneous army which had now been a year in camp: from officers, many of whom shared her doubts, and therefore already had one eye on the other Roman? Could this man with the bloated face still win a battle for the mastery of the world against a cool-headed man of thirty, who had the assistance of two expert strategists?

She knew well enough what her enemies in the general's camp had been advising him for weeks past when they were alone, and no witness compelled the leader to maintain the official attitude. There was Canidius, who had hitherto served her, perhaps only for her money, and had used his great influence with Antony in the interests of her party. There were still a few senators in camp, and they one and all urged him, in respect and comradeship, to fight on land instead of on the sea. He should send the queen home with her swift galleys, and march into Macedonia, where some part of his troops were already, win the alliance of the king of the Getæ, and then, on the field of Pharsalus, or not far away, compel the weaker enemy to give battle. He, the greatest of generals on land, was then assured of victory!

And why should he not win the victory with her? Because she wanted a naval battle; and on land, with her whole court, she was a hindrance.

This was the truth, but not the whole truth. Only once did the old, aristocratic Ahenobarbus tell his friend the whole truth: With Cleopatra, whom all Italy resented, he could never, even as victor, enter Rome; but without her, popular as he had been for twenty years, he could make the people forget all the evil gossip for which he had to thank Octavian and the testament. They thought of him as the last Republican; he was the only man whom the people understood; only he, and not his opponent, had promised the legions to restore the old liberties of Rome after the victory.

The heavy man with the glassy eyes gave a little groan as he followed this last appeal of a Roman who begged that he would once more become a Roman; but he said nothing.

A few hours later she knew everything, even that he had groaned. What these Roman friends advised him, even if she gave no thought to her own part in the battle, was the very contrary of her own advice. Once more must the woman who had drawn this man into the circle of her power, offering him honours and delights incomparable, and bearing him three children—once more must Cleopatra, who had proved her greatness in the field, and had never failed in courage, prevent her friend and consort from winning a victory, just as she had dreaded his victory in the Persian campaign. But this time he must not be defeated! And because it seemed to her that in his enervated condition he might be defeated in a great battle on land, she must avoid such a battle entirely; the more so because then there could be no question of her assistance—the assistance of her fleet, which constituted nearly half his naval strength. Moreover, a war in Macedonia would be quite withdrawn from her influence, which was still decisive here on the shores of the Mediterranean. Because she had so little confidence now in the mind of Antony, with its vacillations, she must safeguard him and herself against final decisions. Defeated by Octavian, he was lost, and she with him. As victor over Octavian he would return to Rome, but not as king beside his queen, as she had once expected of Cæsar; he had none of the impetuosity which had inspired Cæsar at the same age.

In such a dilemma the inventive mind of Cleopatra devised a third way, an expedient; by a sham battle she would once more evade the decision. Such a thought can have occurred only to a mind confused by the multiplicity of omens; but to her it seemed that salvation was still possible; otherwise she would have lapsed into fatalistic silence. Antony, again, who in Athens had risked far more by the breach with Rome than was endurable to his weak character, was now thankful that he could once more elude a decision which he had been avoiding for years, ever since the treaty of Antioch. Not a magic potion, but his own character, made him follow the governor of his destiny.

But while hitherto a great woman had uplifted a man of mediocre gifts into the dry, clear atmosphere of her own lucid intellect, she was now descending into the humid mists of his Bacchic nature. Here, for the first time since she had been able to act and think, her daring began to fail, and here the history of Cleopatra begins to lose its clear-cut outlines.

VI

Agrippa, the general who usually won Octavian's victories, had learned, from many messengers, that confusion prevailed in the camp and in the heart of the enemy. In forced marches he hurried his troops to the south coast of Italy, and shipped them in swift transports to the northern coast of Greece, while another portion of his army continued its march to Macedonia, so that all his forces were converging in a south-easterly direction against the enemy. On his side all was suddenly in rapid movement, for the failing energy of the hesitating is by some magical transference conveyed as a plus quantity to the energy of the resolute.

Yet Antony also was still a man and a general. On receiving the news of Octavian's advance he suddenly got his great army into motion; like Octavian, on land and on sea, as he forwarded part of his Greek army by water to Patras, and sent another part on board the fleet, both going in a westerly direction. Since he hoped to engage the enemy afloat, but needed the whole land army as a sort of chorus in attendance, to reinforce him or cover his retreat, he thought to deliver battle on the west coast of Greece. Today, voyaging from Smyrna to Corfu, one takes ship through the Corinth canal; but since Cæsar's plan for piercing the isthmus had not been put into execution, Antony's fleet had to sail south-westwards, round the Peloponnesus, and then steer northwards for the islands that lay between Greece and Italy, just where the frontier between the two halves of the Roman world had lately been drawn by the triumvirs. Since Octavian's voyage was the shorter he met the enemy a little to the south of Corfu, near the island of Leucas.

On this coast of what is today the north of Greece, a coast abounding in bays and inlets, the force of the waves has at one point fought its way through the rocks of a promontory, and has hollowed out a bay some thirty miles in length and half as wide, whose narrow entrance is little more than half a mile in width. This Gulf of Ambracia, today known as Arta, is, as a natural harbour, of inestimable value to those who seek shelter from the wind, but it is perilous in war to those who are pursued, since it can be blockaded even more easily than the Dardanelles, whose entrance is ten times as wide. Round about it is marshy land, on which reinforcements would find it difficult to advance, and behind it rises Pindus, which then (at the beginning of August) would probably have lost the last remnant of its snow-cap. Here, by the promontory of Actium, precisely in the centre of the Roman Empire, the two armies of that Roman Empire met to decide the course of history.

Octavian had reached a position on the hills to the north of the inlet. On his right was the Ionian Sea, extending to his native shores of Brundusium, Tarentum, and Messina; and there he stood like a watchdog who does not take his eyes from the gate. For in the bight lay the whole of Antony's fleet, in touch with the greater part of his army, which reached away far inland. Since the enemy had cut off access from the sea, long supply columns, never resting day or night, brought all the army's victuals from the hinterland, on the packsaddles of mules or the shoulders of human carriers. The narrow entry was completely closed by a number of Antony's galleys; it was unassailable, but only as a defensive position. If Antony went to the point of the coast where the great statue of Apollo was standing, and from there surveyed his enemy, who lay not a mile distant on the hillside, he saw that enemy lying in wait, inactive as himself; but he also saw that beyond him, and farther than sight could reach, lay the ships that were ready to fling themselves upon his emerging fleet. He himself, when Octavian arrived, had deceived him as to the strength of his land army, by disguising his sailors as legionaries and ordering them on deck. Must not each general have remembered those two other battles which had decided the fate of Rome?—for this was the third civil war in one generation. Just so had Cæsar and Pompey faced each other; and six years later the avengers of Cæsar and the conspirators. On both occasions Antony had been victorious: at Pharsalus under Cæsar, at Philippi by himself. Octavian, on the other hand, had still been a schoolboy at the time of the first battle, and in the second he had run away.

Even the psychological atmosphere was the same; had not Cæsar himself described his war against Pompey as a war without battles? For weeks they had lain facing each other, and if neither had lost patience the battle might never have been fought. Just so lay Octavian and Brutus at Philippi: they had faced each other for weeks and neither had forced the other to fight. Always there was this hesitation of a Roman when confronted by his fellow-citizen; a hesitation born not of moral reluctance, but of uncertainty as to the parties engaged; while each side shrank from a decision which it might perhaps have been more intelligent to negotiate by treaty. Then it had been Antony who had distinguished himself in both battles, first under Cæsar, and then alone; and now he might have attacked for the third time. But now he was weaker in heart and head. Seventeen years earlier, as Cæsar's youthful general, without political responsibility, he had had nothing to do but advance, since Cæsar had so commanded him; and on the second occasion his longing to take vengeance

on Cæsar's murderers had excluded the possibility of negotiation. Now, to outward seeming, Roman was fighting Roman;
but inwardly, in Antony's heart, a Roman was contending
against an Oriental, and the Oriental was seeking to avoid the
decision.

On board ship, during the weeks of the sea passage, he had
come to understand his wife's advice, and had given it the
force of a resolve; the naval battle was the solution; yet the
objective of the battle would be, not the destruction of the
enemy's fleet, but only the saving of his own. And here he
never exposed his pessimism to the light of reason. What
would actually become of his land army, as far as it was present here, prepared for battle? He had left four legions on
board ship in Cyrenaica, four in Egypt, and four in Syria;
none of his staff could understand why the general did not
concentrate these thirty thousand men here, for they still believed there would be a battle on land. He himself was secretly counting on these troops for the future. In any event,
after the clash with the enemy he wanted to sail unmolested
southwards—he never said to himself that he wanted to escape
to Egypt. Had Cleopatra spoken of flight? She had never even
thought of it. No, it was the expedient of a man half paralysed, who no longer dared to call things by their name.

The first part of this plan, the sea-fight, could not be longer
kept secret, since one must make preparations for it. Was the
general crazy? thought his officers. The great general, with all
his cavalry and infantry, meant to hazard his destiny on the
sea? Had he forgotten how badly many of the ships were
manned? And that Agrippa's fleet had destroyed the younger
Pompey? Parties began to be formed at headquarters. Once

again, at intervals of a few days, there were deserters who doubted his success, and Antony learned, first, that two of the allied kings had fled, and then the Roman Domilius. It was so easy to desert; a few hundred strokes of the oars, and one reached the enemy lines. Then Antony laughed in his Herculean bass; he sent the Roman's possessions and his servant after him, and heard, perhaps with satisfaction, that a little later he had suddenly fallen dead, perhaps from remorse. Then it was said that Ahenobarbus had contracted fever on the hot lagoons; he wanted to go for a sail outside; the sea-breeze would cool his blood. Half an hour later he was with Octavian.

Then Antony was angry. A nobleman and a friend, a man on whom he had relied! What could not such a man betray to the enemy! And when it was suggested to him that another senator was suspect, he had him killed out of hand, and then he was horrified by his bloody deed. Perhaps on this evening, under the impression which all these desertions had made upon him, he unloaded his wrath upon another, as weak natures do; naturally, upon his wife.

In the close quarters of this camp, which had no longer a great city to depend on, with the daily sight of the enemy, and in the expectation of prompt action, Cleopatra had recovered her former energy. When the conflict was imminent, it occurred to her that since Cæsar's battle in Alexandria she had never taken part in any actual fighting; that was seventeen years ago, as long ago as Pharsalus. Once more she lay in her tent, but now a hundred differently coloured silks had transformed it into a room, which the sultry atmosphere of the enclosed bay, surrounded by marshy flats, filled with its hot, moist breath; while there, on the Egyptian frontier, the aridity of the desert had cleared one's mind. Was it surprising that a melancholy possessed her to which she was at other times a stranger?

She kept her tiring-slaves about her; the very women whom Octavian had named in the Roman Senate as the secret rulers of Egypt. She often treated them as friends; but no one knew how long she would continue to do so; she played with them as one plays with faithful animals, for neither the age nor her character made real friendship with a slave permissible. She lay in her accustomed attitude, her feet drawn up on her cushions, before her a heap of necklaces and girdles, earrings, and clasps for the hair, that glittered in the light of suspended candles; a collection of precious and half-precious stones such as a woman might worship in silence for a while. Lying there, she was wholly the Oriental; plunging her long fingers among the gems, combining colours which harmonized with her mood, always humming softly, while the two tiring-women, one crouching before her, the other behind her, lying on her stomach before the gold-bound jewel-case, picked up and handed to their mistress what she had let fall, or desired. Perhaps a quarter of an hour was passed in this wordless recreation, while she sang softly in her lovely voice, almost always in deep minor tones, as though oppressed by something.

Suddenly heavy steps were heard without, and the clank of weapons; Antony entered; the two slave-women silently vanished. He burst forth at once, in a blustering voice: His best friends were deserting him; kings and senators, Romans and foreigners; just now he had perhaps had a loyal man put to death; his officers pressed their lips together when he gave them orders, lest they should be tempted to come out with a refusal; and all because she had had this crazy notion of a naval battle! Yes, she! Because she had always been drumming it into his ears that he must avoid Macedonia, although the memory of Pharsalus and every reasonable calculation drew him thither! That was the curse of taking a foreign woman to wife! When a Roman forgot his fatherland he had to pay the penalty! Now it was too late, and all was going to ruin!

With clashing steps he swept about the tent, now crossing it, now pacing a semicircle, often stopping in his progress to stand before her and hurl his curses at her head. She had at first risen to a kneeling position on her couch, a long necklace of sapphires in her hands; but as he continued she picked up the sapphires, drawing them through her fingers, lightly swinging them to and fro, catching them from underneath with a hollowed palm, and seeming to take pleasure in the play of light. If at first she was startled, her expression, as his blind anger increased, grew colder and colder. This made him furious, and at last he came to a standstill before her, stamping and stammering in his rage. With a maternal gesture she drew the jewels toward her, in order to protect them from his feet. But he followed them with one of his gigantic boots, and crushed the last links, which were still within his reach, until they grated under the pressure, and she suddenly sprang to her feet.

Now she stood close before him, shooting her golden-brown arrows into his reddened face. She was silent. Then she went swiftly past him, and began in her turn to wander about the narrow tent, but with far quieter steps. He, in the meantime, fell heavily on the pelt that lay before her couch.

Suddenly she began to laugh. A pity that he now had one galley the less! The chain that he had just been stamping underfoot was worth at least a galley! As for his sacred Rome, he had better make his peace with Octavia on the morrow. She asked nothing more than free egress from the bay with all her sixty ships.

He laughed, and hurled an insult at her. This made her suddenly furious; she snatched a dagger from the wall of the tent, where it always hung above her couch; and holding it in her lowered hand she went close up to him, pointed with her left hand to the exit, and ordered him out of the tent.

When she seized the weapon he sprang to his feet more swiftly than one would have expected in a man of his weight, grasping his sword as he did so. But now, since she held the dagger pointing to the ground, he felt only the threat of her imperious left hand. The warrior in him was silent; the man of the world conceived the scene as a nervous outbreak such as he had sometimes experienced in women; he laughed shortly, growled out an obscene expression, and slowly left the tent with another stupid laugh, and for a few seconds, as an old and practised comedian, he continued to laugh, for her ears only, as he stood outside the entrance.

When late that night he visited the queen again, neither spoke a word as to what had happened. She only held the crushed necklace under his nose and laughed.

By the following evening all preparations had been made for battle. At such close quarters each army was able to observe the preparations of the enemy; and this was in accordance with the ancient custom of openly making ready, on both sides, for a battle to be fought on the following day. In order to persuade the enemy spies that he was certain of victory, Antony gave a banquet at sunset. He had given orders that every dish was to be offered to the queen before it was brought to him; so greatly did he distrust her in his heart of hearts, despite a laughing reconciliation. She had had the flowers which she wore poisoned before her hair was dressed, and now, as she sat beside the general, who was growing flushed with wine, surrounded by tippling officers, she suddenly took the flowers from her head and tossed them into the beaker which stood before her. Then, hailing him as Dionysos, she invited him to drink of wine and flowers with her. He grasped the beaker and raised it to his lips; but she seized his arm, crying:

"You see, Antony, you see! I was to taste your food for you, was I? You wish to protect yourself against me? Well, if I wanted to kill you, see how easily I could do so!" And before all the guests she forced a criminal, whom she had summoned for the purpose, to drink the wine into which she had dropped the poisoned flowers; and presently, after writhing on the ground, he was dead.

This scene, which Plutarch has recorded in all its antique

cruelty, would of itself suffice to prove Cleopatra's superiority; for while she proclaimed his distrust of her to the gazing officers, and through them to the whole army, she not only put her husband in the wrong before his own friends, but she also stole a march upon him in case he should think of poisoning her, and all this as she sat at table, with flowers in her hair, between one draught of wine and the next, immediately before a decision which must completely weld them together.

Next morning, when he boarded his flagship, Antony saw that it was followed by a small fish, an echeneis, the so-called "ship-stopper"; he therefore left the ship, in accordance with an ancient superstition among seamen, and went aboard another. He angrily told his people to say nothing of this, but Cleopatra heard of it, and turned pale. Antony, on perceiving this omen, took all those Romans who were of noble birth on board with him, so greatly did he distrust them. At the same hour of the morning Octavian met a man who was driving an ass, who, being asked his name, was shrewd enough to reply: "I am called the Fortunate, and my ass is called the Conqueror." And about the same time an old soldier is reported to have cried to Antony:

"Have our wounds and our oaths given you so little confidence in us that you entrust to these old wooden bottoms? Leave the Egyptians afloat, but set us ashore, where we know how to die and conquer!"

The two generals might almost have heard each other's voices, for Agrippa, the real leader of Octavian's forces, approached in three squadrons to within sixteen hundred yards of the enemy fleet. All waited for the sea-breeze, for Antony's great ships, having five to ten banks of oars, were likewise drawn up in three squadrons, and were now motionless before the entrance of the gulf. Covered by them, and practically invisible, partly in all the shadow of the great ships, and partly in that of the hills, the sixty Egyptian ships were still lying quietly in the gulf, under Cleopatra's command, as she had previously insisted that they must be. So far, neither of the Roman commanders had ventured to approach the other, and they might perhaps have come to a standstill again, had not the sea-breeze, rising in the afternoon, driven the rigid barrier of Antony's vessels asunder. It seemed as though the gods were more courageous than the human combatants; but they might well be, as they were only onlookers.

But a certain doubt had entered the minds of Antony's soldiers. For being ten legions strong, they were placed upon one hundred and fifty ships, so that each ship, with fifteen hundred men on board, was already much too heavily laden; and must they also take the heavy sails on board? Why? Strange! Further, it was rumoured that the Egyptian woman, during the last two nights, had secretly had all her treasure carried on board her vessels by her slaves. That was the truth, and it was already known to the enemy, since, the night before, two of Antony's officers had gone over to Octavian with two thousand men; whereupon Octavian, in a council of war, decided to allow Cleopatra's fleet to pass unhindered if she wished to escape. The battle between the two hesitating generals, which was finally facilitated by the god of the winds, took place before the eyes of two armies, who looked down from the hills as into an arena, roaring encouragement to their own side. "The battle was more like a battle on land than a sea-fight," writes Plutarch, "or more properly, like the storming of a

[300]

town, for there were generally three or more ships of Cæsar's round one of Antony's, assaulting it with pikes, while Antony's men, out of their wooden towers, threw missiles of various kinds from engines." "With foaming strokes of the oars," writes Dio Cassius, "the small, narrow galleys of Octavian rushed forward, always careful to protect themselves from the enemy's fire. Here and there they contrived to start a leak in one of the vessels; if they failed they hurried away before it came to grappling, and presently fell upon the same ship again, or another which was already involved in battle. Octavian's ships were like cavalry, now rushing forwards, now hurrying back, whereas Antony's were like heavily armed infantry, which tried to seek cover and hold its ground as far as possible."

For Cleopatra, this was her first battle for seventeen years. All that had then so inspired the Amazon that she had won the great heart of Cæsar—youth and love, ambition, and the fight for her throne, and indeed for her life—was silent now; and many of the conditions were reversed. With her sixty ships she was imprisoned in the narrow bight, and while the others took fire from the conflict, she only looked on and listened while foreigners decided her fate. The inactivity to which she was condemned made her restless; since the Ides of March she had never experienced such a day.

She thought of the Ides of March, and compared the situations. Then she had been in the ban of a completed destiny; she had been compelled to revise all her plans, her powers, her means of security, in order to rise to a climax of energy when the blow had fallen. Today she paced restlessly up and down the deck of her flagship, gazed out to sea, and sent out messengers, and when the shouts of the Octavians announced that yet another of Antony's ships was burning she concluded that the battle was lost. Why did she not give orders to attack in the afternoon, and support with her fresh rowers and soldiers the man who was so feverishly fighting out yonder, shouting his commands, drawing the bow, and throwing missiles with his own hands?

For the plan of the sham battle had never been made the subject of a sworn treaty between these two, nor had it been worked out like a plan of campaign; indeed, it had never been fully agreed to; and during the last few weeks, while she was coming to realize the dangers of a victory, Cleopatra, as the wife of a soldier, as a queen, and in battle as the beloved of Cæsar, must, in defiance of her ingenuity, have envisaged victory as possible; and she would have avoided it as little as any mortal will refuse the gifts of the gods in obedience to a plan. And only with this secret reservation did Antony accept her proposal, and what was inspiring him out yonder as he was fighting was nothing more or less than the antithesis of this plan: namely, the will of the warrior in the heat of battle to overcome the enemy. Whether one would then let him go and sail for Egypt was another question.

But she—imprisoned in the bay, far from the battle, yet near enough to hear it, in a position, as commander, perhaps unique in military history—must she not have imagined, from hour to hour, what would happen if this sea-fight was decided in favour of Octavian, and against Antony? Did not her destiny hang on the courage of an enemy captain who dared to approach so closely that he could fire one of the principal ships of his opponent? Was not the future of Egypt, the life of her children, dependent in this hour on the fear of a harassed vedette who would possibly desert his post in order to save himself? What would become of her if Agrippa rammed the flagship and Antony died the death of a Roman hero? To be led in the chains of Arsinoë, with the howls of the Roman mob in her ears, before the triumphal car of the conqueror, under his cold, lustful gaze, through the streets of Rome to the Capitol; and beside her Cæsarion, on whom Cæsar's other heir would at last take his revenge!

Beset by such visions, the calm considerations of the last few weeks lost their coolness in the hour of decision. She could no longer endure this paralysis. She cried for air, for liberty; Cleopatra gave the order for her fleet to put to sea.

VIII

Not an hour had passed—and the *Antonias*, accompanied by the whole Egyptian fleet, was sailing southwards into the Ionian Sea, the wind filling its hastily set sails. When Cleopatra's ships had suddenly appeared in the narrow entrance to the bay she was pursued, in accordance with Octavian's decision, by no one; and as through a lane these glistening, untouched triremes and quinqueremes passed among the smoking, roaring, fighting ships to the open sea. Antony, who perceived her, and had seen the prearranged signal—on this point all the records are agreed—did not hesitate for a moment. He immediately put off in a boat and had himself rowed over to her flagship, which he boarded, accompanied only by his son Antyllus and two friends.

Soon, however, a couple of enemy ships pursued them. Antony, who had immediately taken over the command, drove them off. Only a single man came quite close to the ship in a boat, from which he threw his lance at the general. Antony called out to him from the lower deck: "Who are you, that pursue Antony?"

"I am Eurycles," cried the voice from below. "Son of Lacharis. I am armed with Octavian's luck, to avenge my father!" That was it: Antony had had the father put to death. Someone struck at the man, but he escaped, and with the help of a few ships he contrived to take a second flagship of the Egyptians, which contained much treasure.

After this last brief engagement the general collapsed. The tension of the last few days was over; the magnitude of all that he had dared and had not dared sank like a crushing weight upon his soul. For three days, Plutarch tells us, he sat in the bows of Cleopatra's ship, silent, and neither eating nor drinking, his head often buried in his hands for hours at a time. Then at last Cleopatra's women "first brought them to speak to each other, then to dine together, and not long after, it may be supposed, to sleep together."

A few days later, as they touched the southern coast of the Peloponnesus at Tenaron, Antony was himself again. He learned what had happened; at first none of his men had observed his flight; Canidius, when he realized it, had not dared to announce it; only when the general had failed to appear all day, and the rest of the senators had gone over to the enemy, and Agrippa published the fact of his escape, did the deserted troops begin to believe the report; nevertheless, the land army did not at once surrender.

The fleet was destroyed, so much was clear, but it seemed that the land army was still holding together; so that Antony ordered Canidius to march through Macedonia into Asia Minor. According to repeated calculations, he could still rely on nineteen legions and ten thousand cavalry. He was still far from regarding himself as a lost man; he was no less extravagant than of old; to fugitive friends, who had followed him by hazardous routes, he gave one of the Egyptian ships, with its load of treasure; and also letters to his supporters in Corinth and Athens. Then he continued his voyage in the direction of Egypt.

The man who was slowest to believe in the victory was Octavian. What—with a single battle, only half won for him by Agrippa—was he suddenly called upon by fate to regard himself as the lord of the Roman world? He, who had rashly, coldly, and calculatingly wriggled onward, amidst the various movements and parties, for thirteen long years, who only a few years ago had been defeated by the younger Pompey, who yesterday was a triumvir whom every Roman disliked, who was tolerated only because Cæsar had uplifted him to be his son! And he, a thirty-two-year-old dictator, who owed his good fortune only to the wealth inherited from his father, a brilliant general, and the folly of his strongest rival—he, the grandson of the moneylender, had suddenly become the sole master of the Western world! Since Octavian lacked everything that would have fitted him for such a mission—tradition, imagination, and feeling—the only thing that occurred to him at first was that the host of new soldiers—for in the end half Antony's army had come over to him—was a most serious embarrassment, since he could not even pay his own old legions.

The only thing that pleased him in the situation was the opportunity for wreaking vengeance. Since he seldom dared to confess to himself the primitive longings of his secret heart, and always liked to play the noble Stoic, he commissioned others, as usual, to put Antony's subordinates to death. After such a victory he had time and inclination to avenge old personal grudges; such as that which he cherished for a long-defeated rival, Curio, who as Fulvia's first husband could never endure the boy Octavian. Now he had Curio's son, who had fought with Antony, put to death.

For a long while he luxuriated in the banquets and honours which a trembling Rome prepared for him. The same Vestals whom he had dishonoured but a few months earlier by the theft of Antony's testament had now to come to meet him outside the gates of the city; the beak of Antony's ship was affixed to the temple of Cæsar; a triumphal arch was set up in the Forum; all Italy vied with itself in the erection of statues; no one would confess that he had even been an Antonian. Antony's birthday was declared in the Senate to be a day of ill omen. And all Rome demanded the conquest of Egypt.

Here pressure was applied to Octavian's one sensitive point. Three months after the battle of Actium the victor proceeded to Asia Minor, in order to arm himself against Egypt. For there, at the mouth of the Nile, was still living the only person he had reason to fear: Cæsar's true son. He must at last be destroyed.

IX

Adorned with garlands and a hundred waving cloths of many colours, the Egyptian fleet neared the great lighthouse; all Alexandria was to be persuaded that it was returning home after a victory.

What did it matter if in spite of the quick summer passage, the rumour of its flight had gone before it on the lips of the people, or that tomorrow the drunken sailors would tell the truth? After all, what was the truth? Undefeated, the fleet was returning home after a year's absence, almost in its full strength; not a ship showed a wound. Was it not a victory of Cleopatra's policy that she should have steered her fleet through the civil war of two Roman generals without being made a target? If anyone in the city dared to tell another story he would have cause to regret it.

The great danger to which she had been exposed had renewed Cleopatra's youth; her ancestral soil made her strong again. With a vitality like that which had flowed in the veins of the Amazon of twenty-one who had once been driven from the throne, so that the ageing Cæsar felt himself carried away by its fiery breath, she flung herself again into the turmoil of Alexandrian life. If her power was diminished she resorted to cunning; if for the first time in fifteen years she was deprived of Roman assistance, she made use of the gold of the Ptolemies. And in the place of her husband she found a grown son.

For since Cæsarion—who was about seventeen—had now become a man ruling over Egypt alone as its king; since he was now known as Cæsar Ptolemy, so that the Alexandrians had forgotten the nickname of Cæsarion, his mother was richly repaid for her labours in rearing him. The man oversea, Octavian, still called himself simply Cæsar; but this Egyptian Cæsar had a greater right to the name. There were now two Cæsars in the world.

Yes, as her decorated flagship neared the Pharos, as her son was rowed out to meet her, tall and thin, seeking to meet her eyes with the dark gaze that was shadowed by brows that were seldom unknit, all the shadows of the last few months had taken to flight. Was she dreaming? Had she not once before sailed into the harbour of her ancestral city, to be met by Cæsar, full of new and audacious plans, eager to discuss them with her and to fight?

So it was for weeks and months. People were conscious of it. Among all the Ptolemies, brothers and sisters, had there ever been such a firmly united pair of rulers? The son's heart was filled with enthusiasm and a passion for vengeance; his, too, was the great earnestness of youth; and if twenty years of experience and moments of womanly fear moved her suddenly to excess of caution, a young knight stood beside her to give her strength.

When had she had a lover or husband or servant whom she could trust in the sultry atmosphere of this palace? Who among all her ministers had been faithful to the last? If now and again a poet or scholar had come from the Museion to advise her, it had been like a greeting from another world; she had smiled and let him go. And had not Antony, in his weakness, often lied to her, often resorted to the shifts and tricks of the drunkard, aye, and those of the Roman, which she had soon learned to see through? Cæsar was the only man she had trusted, yet Cæsar never told her quite all his plans, and in these days, if two people had been able to draw up a plan of a new world, it had been possible only because one dreamed it and the other carried it out; when he alone gave orders, and the other obeyed.

But now, in the fortieth and last year of her life, Cleopatra's womanly nature learned for the first time since Cæsar's death what the advice and support of a masculine friend can mean; and since it was her son who gave her this support and advice the new connexion was not complicated by sexual attraction or jealousy: indeed, she was able to enter into the beauty of this new sphere of life even in the midst of the turmoil which she herself had excited.

For from the very first day of her homecoming she began to apply all available means, to employ all available persons, and to exploit all available circumstances, in making preparations for every possible solution of the crisis. The winter, during which the enemy could not cross the sea, gave her time, and she made good use of it. In the capital, such persons as were suspect were imprisoned or put to death; terror, not the love of her subjects, was now the order of the day. If Octavian should come in the spring allies must be won who would help to protect Egypt. But since the battle of Actium who was there that did not tremble before the ruler of the world? The Median king, whose daughter was living here at court as the betrothed of the little Alexander, how could he be completely won over? By guaranteeing him the throne of Armenia. What was to be done? The captive Armenian king, to whom she had given his life after the triumph, as a reward for his poet's defiance, must now be put to death, and his head must be sent to the Median king, so that he need no longer fear the restoration of the poet by a possibly victorious Octavian. Herod, perhaps? Once, when she was journeying through his country, he had excelled himself in knightliness, though at the same time, as she was perfectly aware, he was conspiring against her life. Whom should one send to Herod? She chose Alexas, hitherto deeply in her confidence, for she had often made use of him in her relations with Antony. For some time there was no news. And there was no word from the other envoys to the princes of the Mediterranean, for all preferred to take the side of the victor of Actium. When troops were lacking she must take good care that there was no lack of gold! The treasury which had yielded so much to the Roman must once more be filled to overflowing! And she had wealthy citizens put to death in order that she might take their money; and had ancient temples plundered in order that the votive offerings might be melted down. But what would she do with the treasury—what would she do with herself if the Romans came? Above all, where could the children go? She thought of the north-west and the south-east. She sent envoys to Spain and Gaul, to discover whether there were no enemies of Octavian in these countries, whom she could arm and equip with her money. At the same time she sent part of her fleet from Pelusium to the isthmus of Suez, and now the ships were drawn on wheels overland to the Red Sea. Cæsar, in the floating palace on the Nile, had explained the possibility of such a manœuvre. The first ship was successfully transported, but a Roman general, Didius, who would have preferred to go over to Octavian, incited the Arabs against her, so that they plundered and burnt the ships.

She would not give in. How could she save the children? She had the two caravan routes from the Nile to the Red Sea investigated; for India, of which she had heard such wonderful things since her childhood, and in which country she had commercial connexions—India perhaps was far enough away; surely the hand of the enemy could not reach Cæsarion there! The world was wide! Why despair? Had not the mighty Octavian so many enemies that he might be murdered any day, anywhere, as Cæsar was once? Cleopatra fought on, radiant as in her youth.

X

Antony was a broken man. With two friends and a few followers he had sailed, after the return of the fleet, to Paretonium, a little port to the west of Alexandria; he had not the courage to enter the capital, to look people in the face. In this condition, he was sure, Cleopatra would gladly have divorced him. She knew his fits of depression after nights of indulgence; he had such a fit now, but a hundred times worse than usual. There he sat on the beach, with senses benumbed, still master of the greatest army on earth, still lord of half the Roman Empire: a man stupidly staring at the ground, who saw no way out of his situation; between the Greek rhetorician Aristocrates, who harangued him with historical examples of the alternation of fortune and misfortune, and his friend Lucilius, who at Philippi had given himself out to be the defeated

Brutus, and since then, being pardoned and promoted, had been constantly loyal, and his confidant, for twelve long years.

Yet one day, when news came from oversea that the rest of his army in Greece had gone over to Octavian, Antony wished to kill himself. Thereupon Lucilius went to him and spoke of Philippi: how he alone had won the battle, and how the cowardly Octavian, his ally, had crept into the rushes. By the memory of this victory, which no one could evoke better than the then friend of Brutus, he recalled the despondent man to the necessity of action.

Yet as Antony now resolved to return to Alexandria, and approached the capital with his two friends, the comedian in him won the upper hand. How ought he to appear before the Alexandrians? And above all, how should he approach his wife, who seemed to be overlooking his existence, instead of kneeling to implore his forgiveness? Had not the roles of the seduced and the seducer been reversed? By a trick, so it seemed to him, she, the guilty party, had appeared before the world as guiltless and a conqueror! He did not see that her trick consisted in taking action. He must do something more than act; he must philosophize, but in such a way that the world would learn of it, and see Alexandria in the light of his philosophy.

To the west of the small island that lay before the palace the long breakwater ran out to sea until it came to a narrow peninsula, where an ancient pleasure-house of the Ptolemies was standing. It was quickly made ready for occupancy, and the suffering general moved into it with his two friends. In memory of Timon, the Greek misanthrope, he called his house the Timoneum. There he sat, in the alternating light

and shadow of the Pharos, an object of curiosity to the Alexandrians, and presently the butt of their malicious epigrams.
He saw their boats circumnavigating his peninsula, and if a
stranger's glance fell upon him as he sat reading in the window he would wrinkle his forehead, in order to seem a little
more tragic.

Never was this most natural of men so confused as in these
few weeks, when he tried to heal his genuine despair by acting
a comedy instead of by deeds. For as Antony, for all his gorgeous costumes, had always remained a good-humoured dilettante, who was fond of playing a part out of sheer high spirits,
without these high spirits the comedy was an utter failure. So
he sat there and read Plato, whom he had not opened since
his student days in Athens. He tried to see reflections of himself in ancient legends; in the story of Timon, who begged the
people of Athens to be quick and hang themselves on his fig-
tree before he had it cut down. Or in the report that he had
never caressed anyone but Alcibiades, and that he explained
his action to his comrade Apemantus: This youth will one
day bring disaster to Athens! For by his hatred and resentment he tried to silence the voice of his suppressed love for
Rome. This, perhaps, was the reason—and perhaps it was only
boredom, and the longing for a less quiet and abstemious life
—which impelled this pseudo-Timon, a few weeks later, to ter-
minate his public isolation and return to the palace.

Cleopatra, by a tactful expedient, silenced the secret laughter of the people by holding a "feast of laughter and wine," so
that both the shaken man and the critical Alexandrians were
able to settle back into their accustomed orbits. Cæsar would
reach his majority at the age of seventeen, and if she died all

powers would be concentrated in his hands. At the same time, she had Antyllus, who was then sixteen, declared of age: Antony's son by Fulvia, whom she had kept beside her since the battle of Actium; giving him, of course, no power, but pleasing and deluding his father. In this way she contrived to regenerate State policy and stimulate public opinion, and, at the same time, to restore the spirits of her husband, whose aimless lethargy could be transformed, by a little stimulus, into activity.

These proclamations were accompanied by great banquets, which gave the Alexandrians an opportunity of applauding Antony as the father of the two youths who received the *toga virilis*, and the husband of the queen. She did what she could for his reputation, and had his birthday celebrated with great festivities, overlooking her own. She even allowed him to flirt, in his fashion, with death; for in order to renew the old festivities of his Dionysian period, and yet to symbolize the solemnity of the Fifth Act, it had occurred to Antony to revive the "Club of the Inimitables" as the "Club of the Death-Defying." So wine and revelry were reconciled for him with the solemnity prescribed by the situation.

Perhaps the queen smiled, but she let him go his way; why rob him now of his returning vitality? She loved him, of course; and if she did not think of Cæsar it seemed that she had always loved him. Were not the twins—who now, in their eleventh year, seemed half grown up—were they not proof that once their mother, without ulterior purpose, without security, without a pledge, had given herself to this man, requiring marriage of him, which lesser women would have made the condition of surrender, only years later, when the fate of her empire was involved? She had lured him away from Rome—that was true, but she was prepared to abide by this policy, the policy of her heart and her empire. Yes, she loved him, and the ancient writers, who were one and all hostile to her, have never so much as hinted that she ever took a lover during her married life.

That he hated her at certain times, as in that hour just before the battle, is no disproof of his affection for her. Wholly the prisoner of the physical, and in this sphere consistently enchanted with her, and now, a corpulent man in the early fifties, completely accustomed to an experienced partner, Antony, as a realist, in his present position, clung more than ever to his indefatigable consort, once he had abandoned his excursions into Platonism; for there was evidently little to be got out of philosophy.

Both these people had before long to give proof to themselves of their mutual love.

For Herod came to Alexandria, full of ominous news, apparently in order to negotiate an alliance. From him they learned what strength of troops and munitions Octavian was bringing with him; and that he was having his ships dragged across the isthmus of Corinth on wagons, just when Cleopatra was attempting to send hers across the isthmus of Suez.

But later, when he was alone with Antony, Herod gave him his private advice: At one stroke he could make Egypt a Roman province, thereby recapturing the heart of every Roman. He could then force Octavian to agree to a new triumvirate. He had only to kill the queen.

This was the same man who had refrained from murdering her in the valley of the Jordan only because he was afraid.

Perhaps even Cleopatra's sleuths failed on this occasion to overhear the whispered words. Antony, of course, repulsed the man. So complete was his devotion to his wife that Herod had to take a hasty departure, for he felt that he was now the guest of an enemy. He went straight to Rhodes, where Octavian had landed, did homage to him, gave him presents of gold, told him whatever he had heard while with Antony, and was allowed, as his reward, to retain his kingdom.

But Antony, stimulated to defiance by the traitor, now suddenly threw himself into the labours of active preparation, once more working together with the queen and her son. Eleven legions, only half officered, were still immobilized in Syria and Asia Minor. They belonged to whosoever could pay them. Perhaps he could pay more than Octavian? Antony set forth to win these troops, even against the will of their subordinate officers; first of all, it seems, he had to fight his own general, Gallus. But when Antony approached his old legions, and could thunder at them in his great bass voice, Gallus had the trumpets sounded in order to drown his words —and so the ageing Antony experienced the same set-back that he had once encountered at the hands of Lepidus.

Then he bethought him of a few thousand gladiators whom he had welded into a legion and had left in Syria; he had trained them with a view to celebrating his triumph. These soldiers, whom he summoned by messenger, immediately set out for Egypt. But another general intercepted them—the same Didius who had delivered the queen's ships to the Arabs —and all was lost, for already Octavian was approaching with his army. Antony returned to the capital: it must be prepared for defence.

There was then a terrible scene; Cleopatra, in order to save him, commanded her son to leave the country. Her eyes commanded him, her voice tempted him; she exerted all her authority as queen and mother; but the youth to whom she issued her commands had grown accustomed, in the last two years, to rule as king, both with her and without her. Only when she represented that all would be lost if he remained, and that he would sooner or later come to help her or avenge her, did she succeed in subduing his youthful spirit. In a few ships, laden with weapons, but above all with gold, she sent after him all that he needed to make his way to India. His old tutor was to accompany him; first through the desert to Coptos on the Nile, and then to the port of Berenice; from which point he could make the great voyage to India with the ships trading to that country. In India, among the peoples whose acquaintance the Egyptians had made through their trade with them, he could raise soldiers, and return with them to dismay the Romans.

Cleopatra could not long have entertained a plan so fantastic; it was only a pretext to get the boy away and save his life. This, of course, he understood, and he countered it with his own secret plan. If all was lost in Alexandria what would there be to save? But if he was still living, the day would come when he could lead a Roman party against Octavian, for was he not Cæsar's son? The adventure to which he now went forward was greater than a desperate final struggle. He would see it through.

The king's flight must be kept secret. On the night when the little company of horsemen, among them the disguised Cæsar, vanished into the desert immediately behind the city,

Cleopatra knew that she would not see her son again. If only the gods would save this witness to her great dream! Her own history, she felt, was ended. She could only die, in pride and beauty, as she had lived.

XI

Almost unopposed, Octavian entered Egypt by its eastern gate. He captured Pelusium. Cleopatra, in her palace, bethought herself of her youth. It was the same palace; once more the city was prepared to defend itself against an army that was approaching through the Nile Delta; and now again she had a Roman at her side; only he was not Cæsar. To fight! Not to remember! To do the thing that lay at hand! To gain time! Was it true that a messenger from Octavian was on the way? Let him come!

And Thyrsus, a noble Roman, was shown in to her. Octavian sent her his greeting. He had long loved her from a distance! He would willingly leave her the land of Egypt, the crown, and her children. She had only to get rid of Antony, and all would be peace and happiness!

How stupid he is! thought Cleopatra. How crude! And then he will march into the city to avenge the death of Roman Antony, and destroy us! What a pitiful plebeian, a disgrace to Cæsar's name!

But she did not say all this to the messenger; nor did she even say "no"; she kept the Roman at court, since on the long evenings she was able to get out of him a good many things as to which he should have been silent. But then they were surprised together: Antony became jealous, whether of the messenger or his master. Was he thinking of the poisoned flowers in Cleopatra's hair? Suddenly he entered the room and thrashed the Roman; then he drove him out, giving him a letter to Octavian: Thyrsus had been insolent; but if Octavian felt that he was affronted, he had Antony's Hipparchus as hostage, and he was very welcome to hang him!

But the queen, now that there was no longer any question of eavesdropping or suborning, suddenly changed her tactics and bade the startled Roman to tell his master: if he wanted Antony's head he had only to come, and capture the city, and take it! By this fierce outcry Antony learned of the unsuccessful plot, and he may well have told his wife, in his laughing bass, of the same demand which Herod had lately made in respect of herself.

It was time to make ready. All that she possessed in gold and jewels, and also in ivory, silks, and foreign spices, she now had removed to her Egyptian tomb, which she had built long ago in the style and according to the image of her ancestors. It was quite near the palace, to the east of the promontory, at Lochias, close to the sea, and it was part of the temple of Isis, which was also called the temple of Aphrodite; for when she had built it there, in her years of happiness, she had felt that she was playing this twofold part. Day after day she had now to divert some part of her energies, which ought to have been devoted to the problems of defence, to the bestowal, in this sepulchral chamber, of the treasures which she and her fathers had accumulated. For if the enemy came she meant to burn herself, together with all the treasures which he sought, in this tomb.

It was July, but in the windowless domed chamber, which

had only a small opening at the summit of the dome, it was cool enough. Really there were two chambers, but the door was arranged to sink into its socket; anyone left in the tomb would remain a prisoner. Who then would ignite the whole? Would they not prevent her slaves from doing so? Her faithful women had agreed to die with her, but were too weak to do the deed themselves. In this dilemma she questioned her physician, Olympus—his report has come down to us through Plutarch—and he advised her as to the surest means of dying: by the venom of serpents.

But what serpent? That was the question. The three properties which Cleopatra required of its venom were these: it must not be very painful; it must act quickly; and it must not disfigure her. A criminal was brought to the palace; she lay on her cushions while the fettered man knelt in the middle of the chamber; a slave applied the venomous serpent to him; he writhed in agony and died. That would not do. Tomorrow they must try another. The scene was repeated, with a different kind of snake. This time she edged herself closer to the dying man; she was greedy to know what he felt. His death seemed to be painless, but he lived an hour. At last they found the right species; for this time the man seemed to fall asleep soon after he was bitten; there was no struggle, his features had a cheerful expression, and when she called him by name, her lips close to his ear, the dying man made a faint gesture of defence, as though unwilling to be waked out of his quiet sleep. This was what she wanted, and she made her arrangements.

If she surveyed the history of her period, she found many examples of suicide. The Romans were addicted to suicide in the extremity of danger; and they believed that only a Roman could slay himself. Of the men who murdered Cæsar, four or five had fallen upon their swords. Of Cato she had heard that, being conquered by Cæsar, he lay in bed all one evening, reading Plato's *Phædo*, quite alone; then he plunged the dagger into his breast. Everyone had heard of the noble words of Arria, who, when her husband was condemned to die, stabbed herself and grasped his hand, saying with a smile: "*Pæte, non dolet.*" But she was even more deeply moved by her childish memory of her uncle, who had killed himself to avoid disgrace.

Cleopatra was ready to show that one need not be a Roman in order to die; at the same time, she was resolved to fight as long as there was hope. Antony too was prepared, and it would be seen that he would seek death in battle. For now Octavian had appeared before the gates of the city. Antony had recovered his youth; today he was once more the captain of horse; and just as he had once won the battle for Octavian, so now, by the Hippodrome, he put his cavalry to flight. Now his old, true character shone out; when he entered the queen's chamber he spoke like a man intoxicated. He found her, says Plutarch, fully armed; he kissed her and presented an officer who had fought most brilliantly. He beamed at him, and gave him a golden breast-plate. That same night the officer deserted to the enemy.

In such alternating moods, what with the thundering blows of the enemy rams on the walls, and the turmoil of the citizens, some fighting, some begging for mercy, in the scorching heat of July, constantly betrayed and as constantly the recipients of ominous news, they both felt that on the morrow the city would fall. Now Antony once more challenged his adversary to a duel. Octavian sent the cynical reply, that Antony would find some other way of dying. At night he sat feasting amidst his officers, and as he drank, he said that on the morrow he would seek not victory, but death. On the morrow they would all have a new ruler over them.

That same night many of the townsfolk thought they could hear the sound of voices and musical instruments, as though Bacchantes were dancing, an invisible train, out of the city and into the enemy camp.

Antony wished to fight on land and at sea. But the following day he felt that he had been betrayed in both directions. Watching from a little hill, he saw that the ships which he sent out of the harbour to engage the enemy were saluting that enemy with their oars. The enemy responded, and they all fraternized: Romans with Romans. And now, when he led his cavalry out through the eastern gate, in order to engage Octavian's horse once more, he saw his whole command ride over to the enemy. He roared like a wounded bull, rode back to the palace through a thousand fleeing townsfolk, and broke in the door, followed by only two or three soldiers. "Treachery!" he roared. "She has betrayed me! The queen is in league with the enemy!"

But just then a messenger approached him: it was said that the queen was dead.

XII

She was not dead, but she believed that no further message could ever reach her in the tomb. In the hour of surrender she hastened to her mausoleum with her two women slaves. There the three women lowered the heavy door by means of ropes, and they were alone with her treasure. At least she could now depend on a dagger. No one could enter, and she must have been there an hour when her message was delivered to Antony.

He, alone in the palace, for all the servants had gone over to the victor, had no dagger, but only his sword, and it is difficult, without help, to throw oneself upon a long sword, as many a Roman has learned in dying. But Antony still had his shield-bearer with him, and as on the retreat to the Araxes he had conjured the boy to kill him if he gave him the order, so he now made the same demand of another shield-bearer, whose name was Eros. It would well have befitted Antony to die at the hand of Eros; but Eros did not dare to strike; he turned away and killed himself with the great sword. This hardened Antony's resolution, and he threw himself upon his sword. He fell, but he was not dead. He cried out for someone to kill him.

In the meantime a few slaves had arrived. They found him there, and told him where the queen had gone, and that she was still alive; in a feeble voice he bade them carry him to her. They did so, and knocked, and gave certain passwords. Cleopatra, who never despaired, found an expedient even now, and told her people to run ladders up to the aperture in the roof—her words being almost drowned by the echoes of the enclosed chamber—whereupon they tied cords to the stretcher, and the three women drew the dying man into the tomb.

These reports of the ancient writers can hardly be inventions, for the physician Olympus, the last person to whom she had spoken, gives an account of them all, and finds that nothing could be truer. What was the wish expressed by the dying Antony? While the queen kept on lamenting, he asked for wine! And so, recovering his strength a little for a moment, he advised her as to what she should do: of all those about Octavian she must trust only Proculeius. And it was the old buoyant Antony whom Plutarch describes as saying, at the last:

"As to himself, she ought rather to rejoice in the remembrance of his past happiness than to bewail his present misfortunes; since in life he had been illustrious, and was not inglorious in his death. He had conquered as a Roman, and it was only by a Roman that he was conquered."

He was hardly dead when the head of this same Proculeius appeared at the top of the ladder. Octavian sent his respects and greetings to the queen! She need not fear; no harm would befall her!

She would open—she replied—only if Octavian promised her son Cæsar the crown of Egypt. An incomparable scene, this, verging on the comic, for the negotiations were carried on in the most neck-breaking of postures. But the Romans did not prolong the situation; they let themselves down into the vault by means of ropes; they raised the sunken door; the tomb had once more become a temple which anyone could enter.

This had all happened much more rapidly than Cleopatra had expected. Who would bring her the serpents now? But she still had her dagger. She felt for it; the Roman seized her arm. In the struggle the Amazon lost her weapon. A second and a third man entered the chamber with fresh orders; she was to surrender. In their midst the queen stood weaponless and unprotected, between her dead husband and the two women weeping on the floor. Now the officer ordered his men to search her for hidden weapons. A frightful moment! Six plebeian hands fumbled about her body, taking who knows what liberties. She stood with her hands held forcibly above her head. This was the only humiliation in Cleopatra's life.

XIII

When Cæsar received the bloody head of Pompey he is said to have wept in silence. Octavian, in the same case, sent for his friends and officers, opened a packet of documents which he always carried about him, and read them a few of Antony's arrogant letters, with copies of his moderate replies. So he showed the world which was the better man of the two. Then he shed "a few tears," and promptly sent Proculeius to take the queen alive. "For he was extremely solicitous," says Plutarch, "to save the treasures in the monument, which would so greatly add to the glory of his triumph."

In the afternoon he made his entry into Alexandria. Thousands prostrated themselves before the general, thousands who in their youth, eighteen years earlier, had seen Cæsar and Cleopatra make their entry. And there were hundreds of thousands who two years ago had stood in the open place where Antony, as Dionysos, had appeared beside the goddess Isis. Now they lay in her tomb: he dead, she a prisoner and dishonoured. But the cold-hearted man was cleverer than their fiery spirits had been; he bade the citizens rise; no one would be injured, for this was the city of the great Alexander, and beside him stood a great philosopher. This was the Stoic Arios, who had written the Greek speech for him. Then the procession, still following Cæsar's example, proceeded to Alexander's tomb. Octavian had it opened, but instead of doing homage to the dead, Octavian felt the body, so that a piece of the conqueror's nose came away in his hand. Horrified, he renounced the project of visiting the dead Ptolemies.

For a moment—or perhaps it was really for three days—Cleopatra seems to have wavered. If it were only possible to save Egypt for her children she would endure anything—anything, save only one thing! But if she learned for certain what she only guessed—that Octavian was deceiving her, that he would merely drag her to Rome, to show her to the people in his triumph—then she knew what to do. Messenger followed messenger. If she would only come forth she would be received as queen. She remained where she was, for she distrusted Octavian. Another messenger arrived: Octavian warned her not to kill herself, for then he would kill the twins. Grief, hunger, fear, and the heat combined threw her into a fever; no one knows to what she would have agreed in this state of weakness, in order to save her children, or how far she believed the man she hated. But at last, before her death, her beauty came once more to the rescue; that beauty by whose charm she had lived.

Dolabella, a young officer, had learned to worship the lovely Cleopatra from afar, and although he had never seen her, he resolved to take her part, since no one else had done so. As he was always in Octavian's entourage he knew what the latter intended: in three days' time to put to sea, taking the queen and her three children to Rome with him. At the peril of his life he contrived to visit her in the mausoleum, to interview her in the absence of any watcher, and to whisper what he knew. He was Cleopatra's last adorer.

Now she knew all that she needed to know. Now, in her imagination, she beheld Arsinoë, walking in clanking fetters, her eyes on the ground, before the four horses of the conqueror's car; so she had dragged her way to the Capitol, and she, Cleopatra, had drunk deep of the delights of revenge. Even so a hundred thousand Romans would see her in the triumphal procession, all hateful, all plebeians, like those who had recently fumbled at her body—but none more hated than he who would stand upon the car, enjoying his great revenge! Her resolve was taken. Her mind was clear again. All depended on her ability to deceive Octavian as to her intention to go on living!

She sent him a letter, begging that he would allow her to give Antony a kingly burial. He granted her request; and the woman who would naturally have been silent beside his grave acted a part for the benefit of the observers. "O my Antony!"

she cried, in the style of tragedy, for those who would describe the scene to Octavian. "Oh, that my hands were still free as they were of late! Now they are the hands of a captive! Death divides us! Thou as a Roman dost repose in Egyptian soil! I go to seek my end in thy country! If the gods of the underworld have power, then plead thou to them, since me the higher gods have forsaken: implore them, that I may not to thy shame be forced to walk in the triumph!"

On the following day the conqueror's intention was made known to her in the mausoleum.

She had neither strength nor inclination to rise; she remained in bed, her hair undressed, in a long shift, disfigured by grief and tears. Octavian entered with the courteous bow of a man of the world. But then he stared at her with the cold, piercing eyes of an enemy. Cæsar, the enemy of Cæsar! Her eyes could perceive only the enemy of her son; he sought in vain for the charm of the famous Cleopatra.

Now she must play her part cleverly to the end. The will to live, and the joy of life; he must believe that these were hers if she was to gain time, win a confidant, and secure the serpents. What had they done, through all these decades, who had begged her, the mighty queen, for mercy? They had flung themselves down before her. Cleopatra rose from her bed of sickness and flung herself down in her shift at the feet of the Roman; the only time in her life she had ever done so. He advised her, courteously, to trust herself to his clemency. Since she knew what he really wanted here she sent for an inventory of her treasure. Octavian, more absorbed in the treasure than in her, took the list with an air of interest, and when her steward suddenly exclaimed that it was not complete he laughed. She, however, to give proof of her vitality, fell upon the steward and pulled his hair, until she sank back exhausted on her bed.

"Scandalous!" she cried. "A servant accuses me of hiding a few bits of jewellery! They were meant for your sister Octavia, and for Livia, your consort, so that these ladies should be graciously inclined towards me!"

He assured her of his perfect esteem, bowed, and left her. Now he felt secure of his triumph, for she meant, at any cost, to live!

But she had won a little freedom. If the two women did not help her, then the physician must have done so. A peasant—or so the guards took him to be—appeared on the following day with a basket of figs for the sick queen; and when they examined the basket he showed them the figs on the top, not the snake below.

At the sight of the basket of fruit, Cleopatra made up her mind. She had a bath prepared; then her two women decked her out with all the jewels that she was wont to wear at the State banquets; and the great double crown of Egypt was fastened in her hair. A luxurious meal was served, including sweet wine. Then she wrote to Octavian, asking him to bury her beside Antony.

Her last thoughts must have been for Cæsarion. She knew him to be in safety, concealed in his harbour, soon to be on the way to India. Since in him the spirit of Cæsar and her own were mingled, what ill could befall him? With his image in her heart, she reached for the serpent.

When Octavian had read her letter he wanted to hurry off to the mausoleum, but he bethought himself of his dignity and sent an officer. The latter found that the guards had no knowledge of anything amiss. As he entered, he saw the dead queen lying in all her splendour, the crown of the Ptolemies on her head. One of the tiring-women was dead; to the other, who was dying, he cried:

"This is a fine thing you have done!" The girl replied: "Something fine indeed, for it was of the queen's devising."

Octavian allowed the city to give her a royal burial by the side of Antony, but he himself was not present.

He had only one thought: he had the treasure of the Ptolemies hastily brought out of the vaults, and sent all the gold and jewels on board his ship. His grandfather the usurer should have lived to see this day! Now he could pay all his legions.

Egypt became a Roman province, the greatest conquest since the fall of Carthage, one hundred and seventy-two years earlier. The three children Octavian took to Rome. There his sister reared them with the rest; in all, seven children of Antony, by three wives, grew up in Octavia's gentle care.

But where was Cæsarion? Octavian could endure to think that the queen had escaped from his triumph. But the boy, the only person still living who could dispute the power with him, the boy must go. Where was he? Since the day of his entry into Alexandria his emissaries had gone flocking forth in all directions, stimulated by the most tempting promises, seeking the precious booty. Was it surprising that they found him at length? He was still at Berenice. A courteous officer assured him that Octavian would receive him most kindly. He wanted only to acknowledge Cæsarion as king of Egypt before he sailed for Rome; that was all. Cæsarion's tutor, the philosopher—was he credulous, or was he taking a hand in the game?—persuaded him to obey. He did so, and was greeted with royal honours by the fleet as it lay before Alexandria.

In the palace Octavian, who always wanted to fix responsibility on someone else, asked the philosopher Arios whether he had a right to kill Cæsarion. Arios knew what was due to his new master, and replied with a parody of Homer: "Too many Cæsars are not good!"

Octavian gave a sign, and the youth, even before he had set foot in his kingdom, was strangled by hired murderers. Thus he perished: the pledge of the great dream which once a royal pair had dreamed upon this shore, in memory of the noblest of all human beings; thus perished the last representative of Alexander, whom the ageing Cæsar had begotten in the womb of the young queen, in order that he might gain the world for him.

Now all was in order; on the morrow Octavian would leave the country. There was still the order to be given: all the statues of Antony and Cleopatra were to be overthrown.

Then a wealthy patrician had himself announced, Archibius by name; he begged that the statues of the queen might be left standing. As he caught the Roman's angry glance, he beckoned to his slaves; ten sacks, containing a thousand talents in gold, were set down before Octavian. This was a language that the lord of the world understood; he nodded, and the order was revised; only Antony's statues were to be overthrown.

On the following day, as Octavian, sailing homeward, looked

back at the shores of that Egypt which had yielded him so much gold, the bronze statue of the last of the Ptolemies glittered at him from the promontory of Lochias. He stared at her, but she saw him not.

Cleopatra was gazing oversea, in the direction of Rome.

Appendix

Chronology

[335]

Chronology

43   Cleopatra threatened by Cassius. Second triumvirate: Antony, Octavian, Lepidus.

42   Battle at Philippi. Cæsar's murderers defeated.

41   Cleopatra visits Antony in Tarsus. Antony spends the winter in Alexandria.

40   Antony recalled to Italy. His wife Fulvia dies. He marries Octavia. Treaty of Brundusium (between the triumvirs).

36   Antony reunited with Cleopatra. Persian campaign.

35   Antony, defeated, meets Cleopatra on his retreat, goes with her to Alexandria.

34   Antony victorious in Armenia. Triumphal procession in Alexandria. Cleopatra, Great Queen of the East. Her four children invested with crowns.

33   Antony arms against Octavian. Concludes an alliance with Media.

32   Cleopatra and Antony in Ephesus and Athens. Antony divorced from Octavia. Rome declares war against Cleopatra.

31   Battle of Actium.

30   Cleopatra and Antony die by their own hand. Cæsarion murdered.

A.D.

14   Death of the Emperor Augustus.

Index

Index

Index

Index

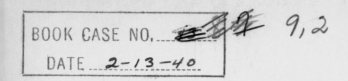